Class and Contemporary British Culture

Class and Contemporary British Culture

Anita Biressi

Professor of Media and Society, University of Roehampton, UK

and

Heather Nunn

Professor of Culture and Politics, University of Roehampton, UK

First published 2013
First published in paperback 2016 by
PALGRAVE MACMILLAN

Palgrave Macmillan in the UK is an imprint of Macmillan Publishers Limited, registered in England, company number 785998, of Houndmills, Basingstoke, Hampshire RG21 6XS.

Palgrave Macmillan in the US is a division of St Martin's Press LLC, 175 Fifth Avenue, New York, NY 10010.

Palgrave Macmillan is the global academic imprint of the above companies and has companies and representatives throughout the world.

Palgrave® and Macmillan® are registered trademarks in the United States, the United Kingdom, Europe and other countries.

ISBN 978–0–230–24056–8 hardback
ISBN 978–1–137–57702–3 paperback

This book is printed on paper suitable for recycling and made from fully managed and sustained forest sources. Logging, pulping and manufacturing processes are expected to conform to the environmental regulations of the country of origin.

A catalogue record for this book is available from the British Library.

A catalog record for this book is available from the Library of Congress.

For our parents
Ruth Lena Biressi and Alfredo Carlo Biressi
Sylvia Irene Winifred Nunn and Herbert Richard Hanslip Nunn

Contents

List of Figures   viii

Preface to the Paperback Edition   ix

Acknowledgements   xi

1   Introduction: Beginning the Work of Class and Culture   1

2   Essex: Class, Aspiration and Social Mobility   23

3   The Revolting Underclass: 'You Know Them When You See Them'   44

4   Top of the Class: Education, Capital and Choice   69

5   The Ones Who Got Away: Celebrity Life Stories of Upward Social Mobility   94

6   The Upper Classes: Visibility, Adaptability and Change   118

7   'Are You Thinking What We're Thinking?': Class, Immigration and Belonging   142

8   Austerity Britain: Back to the Future   170

Afterword: 'We Are All in This Together'   197

Notes   200

References   208

Author Index   231

Subject Index   236

Figures

2.1   Essex Man as illustrated by Collet in the *Sunday Telegraph*,
7 October 1990   31

Preface to the Paperback Edition

Most of the scholarly material for this book was gathered over the course of about ten years ending in early 2013. However, the book's conception, scope and critical approach to social class and British culture originated much further back in time when both authors were writing PhDs situated in the context of Thatcherism and its aftermath. It's fair to say that we were both interested in researching and exposing the dominant ideology of class distinction and conservative politics rather than the very important counter-cultural and oppositional movements and identities emergent at that time. In our very different ways, perhaps, we were attentive to the radicalism at the heart of conservative aspiration and wanted to expose the development of a defensive individualism which warded off internal dissent, external threats and alternative political models and ideals. Hence Heather Nunn's (2002) first book focused on Margaret Thatcher, her political persona and how the media tied her image into the imagined communities and individual subjects she was said to represent. Meanwhile Anita Biressi's (2001) first book on true crime entertainment explored law and order discourses in the context of privatisation, responsible citizenship and increasingly socially conservative attitudes. Looking back on these and subsequent publications it's evident that questions of class distinction, social mobility, class injury and the material and immaterial inequalities which underpin these have always directed and held our attention.

For at least a decade or more before the publication of *Class and Contemporary British Culture* we had been experimenting with rudimentary drafts of a book manuscript on class and culture, none of which appealed to reviewers whose view was that scholarship on social class, especially in British cultural studies, was somewhat passé. Palgrave's encouraging response to a new book proposal in 2007–8 coincided with the arrival of the global financial downturn triggered by what seemed to be a busted free market economy. The ensuing economic turbulence, insecurity and implementation of an austerity regime by the Conservative/Liberal Democrat administration brought the contours of class difference back into stark relief. This helped to reanimate debates about what was at stake for those who felt that they were either vulnerable or ill-equipped to navigate the choppy waters of fiscal 'corrections' to house-prices, public services, pay, pensions and the welfare bill . The book suddenly came together and found its final form and urgency as an analysis of the increasingly uneven terrain in which neoliberal subjects were expected to either thrive, survive or fall by the wayside during hard times. As such it bears the hallmarks, strengths and weaknesses of a project which was a long time in the making but was finally executed in response to dramatically changing political and social conditions.

This Preface is being composed only a few weeks after the 7th May 2015 General Election which resulted in a majority Conservative Government. At best this outcome has been deciphered as an endorsement of the Coalition's handling of the economy and at worst as evidence of Britons' general fearfulness, fatigue and insecurity in the face of seemingly constant change. Significantly, it also produced a picture of Britain divided by electoral preference and voting distribution with, for example, the Scottish National Party enjoying a landslide victory in Scotland. This electoral picture, together with other factors too complex to review here, naturally tests the value and pertinence of a study addressing class labelling, affiliations and media stereotypes in the context of 'British' culture. Happily, this study was well received on its own terms as an attempt to stake out the terrain, to log landmarks and to chart some of the shifts and changes which have taken place in the symbolic topography of class in national terms. Since 2013 many others have risen to the challenge of addressing the coordinates of social class, the menace of class labelling and the potential for social change from the perspective of particular British nations, regions, cultures and identities. We hope this book will continue to be read alongside these and will work in dialogue with them to produce new and productive ways of thinking about both the lived experience of class and the class stories we choose to produce, circulate and consume.

AB and HN
June 2015

Acknowledgements

This book could not have been written without the support of colleagues, former colleagues and friends at the University of Roehampton and at many other institutions. We extend special thanks to Roehampton for the award of a research sabbatical to each of the authors. We are also grateful for the friendly and painstaking assistance of Suzy Hyde and her colleagues at Roehampton Media Services in tracking down many of the broadcast resources referred to here. Staff at the British Newspaper Library at Colindale, North London, the *Sunday Telegraph* and the Advertising Standards Authority also provided information and advice.

During the past few years we have been fortunate enough to have been given many opportunities to present work-in-progress at conferences, symposia and research centres and have appreciated fellow participants' informed and insightful feedback. Special mentions should go to Jane Arthurs, Helen Wood, Beverley Skeggs, Patricia Holland, Diane Negra, Deborah Philips, Jonathan Rutherford, Milly Williamson, Gareth Palmer, Yvonne Tasker, Candida Yates, Caroline Bainbridge, Julie Doyle, Irmi Karl, Bronwen Thomas, Elke Weissmann, Vicky Ball, Barry Richards, Nancy Thumim, Christine Berberich, Nick Couldry, Jeremy Gilbert, Imogen Tyler and Jo Littler for extending invitations to present research papers, accepting conference submissions and offering feedback on research applications, personal encouragement and other kinds of invaluable support. Sally Munt, in particular, has been unfailingly enthusiastic and encouraging about the value of this project over more years than we care to recall.

We also wish to thank early mentors and former colleagues Alan O'Shea, Bill Schwarz, Angela McRobbie, Susannah Radstone, Andrew Blake and Sally Alexander; their own research, scholarly values and ethical commitment to cultural studies have been an inspiration and continue to inform our work.

Our thanks also go to Palgrave's former Commissioning Editor Christabel Scaife and to its present Senior Commissioning Editor, Felicity Plester, who have both warmly supported this project.

We are also grateful to Kathryn White, Berni O'Dea and Miri Foster for their friendship and care.

Some of the discussion of the underclass which appears in Chapter 3 has previously appeared in a different form in H. Nunn and A. Biressi (2010b). Some aspects of our discussion of class theory and cultural studies which feature in the Introduction appeared in briefer form in H. Nunn and A. Biressi (2009).

1
Introduction: Beginning the Work of Class and Culture

This book is about class and contemporary British culture, so perhaps we should begin by explaining what we take social class to be, for, as David Harvey (2005:31) has observed, it is a shadowy and dubious concept at the best of times. Here we understand social class as being formed through material conditions and economic (in)securities and as being shaped by early disadvantage or natal privilege and the uneven distribution of life chances and opportunities which these conditions create. But we also choose to recognise class as an ongoing social process experienced across our lifetime trajectories. For example, throughout our lives as classed subjects many of us are buffeted by a variety of changing socio-economic circumstances, which might be precipitated by family breakdown, redundancy, financial windfalls, exceptional professional success, and so on. All of these are also experienced in the wider context of economic eddies of boom, affluence and bust which impact on how we understand our current and future social roles. In addition, we will argue that classed subjects are shaped by the classed judgements of others and by prevailing political and popular discourses which often work to privilege, protect or normalise particular lifestyles, conducts and values. Bearing these various processes of class formation in mind, this book considers how *culture* works to classify, label and formulate class judgements. It aims to confront the ways in which culture articulates, frames, organises and produces stories about social class, class difference and its various attachments. These attachments include those explicitly connected to economic conditions and the material life (consumption, social mobility, social exclusions, work and leisure) and those linked to the interior life (hope, pride, shame, aspiration, fear and resentment), although it will be immediately obvious that these necessarily overlap. This is not a study of

1

British politics or economics, but it does locate cultural analysis within political and socio-economic contexts. We examine the ways in which culture intersects with the political in terms of its articulation of prevailing political philosophies and economic conditions such as the free market, meritocracy, neoliberalism, affluence, recession and austerity. This is not a work of sociology, but it does aim to take into account the continuing (if fiercely debated) significance of class labels and class stratification and the conviction that British social relations continue to include relations of class.

The adjective 'contemporary' clearly points to an inquiry into culture which is current, to its status as recent history and to its association with living memory. While this book considers the cultural landscape mostly from the perspective of the past decade or so, overall it situates this within a historical and political context bounded on one side by the arrival of Thatcherism and the political and social changes which followed in its wake. We make this move for a number of reasons. In social terms, the 1980s has been heavily cited as the decade in which already-foundering traditional class structures and class-based affiliations finally broke down, giving way to the more fluid and individualised social formations fostered by the processes of neoliberalism. In scholarly terms, within sociology, cultural studies and cognate fields, this was also the period in which the utility of class-based cultural analysis was being increasingly questioned and challenged. Finally, in personal terms, the 1980s were also the decade when both authors came to adulthood, so that our early working lives and political educations were lived and formed under Thatcherism, and our understanding of the processes of class formation was refracted through the experiences of this period. In sum, the 1980s were important for political, scholarly and personal reasons and we found, upon reflection, that these were deeply and perhaps inextricably entangled.

The personal starting point and backdrop to this deliberation of culture and social class arise from the two authors' divergent and common experiences and memories of young adulthood, work and political education during the decade of Thatcherism from late 1979 to 1990. In some ways it's difficult for us as authors of a book on class and culture *not* to read our early working lives, in particular, as anything other than emblematic of the 1980s, a decade which has been lived, and increasingly mythologised, as a paradoxical time of individual opportunity and deepening disadvantage, of meritocratic 'classless' social mobility and increasingly embittered class politics. Both authors were born into the very tail-end of the 'baby boomer' generation (1946–65), growing up in families whose parents' elementary education and manual or 'unskilled' jobs would help categorise them as socio-economically working-class. For many working-class people of our parents' generation, whose lives were interrupted by world war and whose career paths were stymied by their own and other people's social expectations, significant social advancement would have seemed fairly implausible, whereas by the 1980s a more fluid, more meritocratic society appeared to be emergent.

By the mid-1980s, under a second term of Conservative government whose return to office was borne up by victory in the Falklands War (1982), we would both be safely employed, even without university degrees, in jobs earning good money and with solid prospects. These middle years have been recorded in history as a boom time characterised by growing prosperity and increased social mobility. For many the deep and divisive financial recession of the early 1980s and the urban 'race riots' of 1981 were fading from view, although unemployment remained historically and injuriously high. In the mid-1980s Heather Nunn joined many other working-class people from the London Essex borders in the daily commute to the City of London to work in the Stock Exchange. As we go on to describe in greater detail in Chapter 1, this was a period in which the City and self-employed traders (many of whom were East End and 'Essex boys' along with South Londoners and those from the 'regions') began to enjoy excellent salaries and raised status. Many of these young men (and far fewer women) arrived following the City's 1986 deregulation of the Stock Exchange; a process dubbed the 'Big Bang' because it generated a dramatic spike in market activity through the introduction of electronic trading and the removal of distinctions between different trading operations. As Linda McDowell (1997:14–15) explained in her analysis of the City and social change, 'new forms of work based on the ownership, control, movement of and access to money led to the rise of new types of well-paid middle class occupations...'. She also noted that there was a widespread belief in the mid-1980s that expanded financial services would fuel a new economically secure future for Britain; a perception underpinned by the accelerated economic growth then taking place in the South East of England in particular.

City deregulation marked a significant redrawing of the cartography of social class, both within financial institutions and far beyond them into British society. As Ann Barr and Peter York (1982) explained in their best-selling lifestyle guide to upper-class culture and *mores* called *The Official Sloane Ranger Handbook*, for the established upper classes the City had traditionally been a place of discreet money-making. They noted (1982:11): 'The City is magic money...Brass without muck...There's something about the way the City works – the oldness, the public-schoolness, the merchant bank "word is my bond" code of honour – that makes it all seem like an ancient profession.' This was a predominantly male, white, upper-class and reportedly breathtakingly sexist environment where power and authority were exercised without diffidence or any degree of self-consciousness. But following the Big Bang, electronic trading and a more global orientation and accompanying importation of American business values helped to refashion City recruitment practices in more open ways, even though old attitudes were dying hard. After the mid-1980s, established 'gentlemen' financiers, whose families had worked in the City for generations, were forced to rub shoulders with *declassé* interlopers in the joint enterprise of making London the dominant financial centre of the global marketplace. But younger traders also continued to count among their numbers the usual type of highly privileged Oxbridge graduates. As David Harvey (2005:62) remarked: 'Class power had not so much been restored to any traditional sector but rather had gathered expansively around one of the key global centres of financial operations.' As McDowell's (1997:68 and 147) early 1990s fieldwork demonstrated, this collision of social groups did little to ameliorate its masculinist and elitist culture, in which dress codes and everyday conversation referenced public school, military or sporting codes; in her words, everyday talk was all 'bats, balls and bullets'.

The City became increasingly emblematic of a wider world of opportunism, conspicuous consumption and social aspiration as its operations helped to produce a new class of *nouveau riche* whose earning power was boosted by bonuses and who were less discreet than the old school when it came to spending them. Popular culture and the arts parodied or critiqued the new visibility of money and the acceptability of greed as a driver of national prosperity, although the intended irony was often missed or knowingly over-ridden by its targets. So, the Pet Shop Boys' 1985 pop song called 'Opportunities (let's make lots of money)' was embraced as an anthem of the 1980s' golden prospects to get and spend: 'Oh, there's a lot of opportunities/If you know when to take them, you know?/There's a lot of opportunities/If there aren't, you can make them.' Likewise, in 1987 Caryl Churchill's (2002) bitingly satirical play *Serious Money* was attended by cheering City financiers in droves. So too the later comic character Loadsamoney, who lampooned working-class greed and flashy hyper-consumption, was promoted as a hero by the tabloid press whose readers he explicitly mocked, and he was also championed by City traders who appreciated his barefaced greed.

At around the same time as Heather Nunn was working in the City, Anita Biressi began work as a Local Officer in a South London branch of the Department of Health and Social Security (DHSS). As a public sector employer at the lower levels of the Civil Service, it included a far greater number of women and ethnic minorities than did the City, including the descendants of first and second-generation immigrants from Kenya, Uganda, Jamaica, and so on. Their task was to process and assess claims for Supplementary Benefit. This was a means-tested benefit paid to people on low incomes, including the elderly, the sick, single parents and the young and/or long-term unemployed. At the DHSS and in the Unemployment Benefit Offices (UBOs) welfare systems were struggling to cope with the damage wrought in the first-wave recession of the early 1980s, in which unemployment had reached 3 million and inner-city youth unemployment had reached 50 per cent (see Taylor-Gooby 1988). So, too, the 1980s were a time of increasing turbulence in patterns of employment, which 'finally buried the belief in the permanency of work' (McDowell 1997:14). At this time the Thatcher government was working hard, in the face of considerable opposition from both within and without, to cut back on state obligations in areas such as the universities, health care and social security (see Harvey 2005:61). The Conservative government's commitment to reforming welfare systems and ending the 'dependency culture' was implemented through legislation which broke the links between benefit rates and inflation and between pensions and earnings and which cut certain other entitlements, restricted benefits to strikers and their families, and so on (see Giddens and Griffiths 2006:370, but also Reitan 2003:99). Many of these initiatives actually increased the numbers of people reliant on means-tested benefits. Pressures on both claimants and staff also increased as staff numbers failed to rise in line with the growing numbers of claimants and much-needed resources were redirected to investigate benefit fraud and abuse (see McGlone 1990:161).

As Beatrix Campbell (1984:212ff) observed in her book *Wigan Pier Revisited*, claiming the 'dole' was often a demoralising, sometimes shameful, experience which sapped energy and optimism. The desperation of the unemployed and the bureaucracy of job centres and UBOs during the first recession was memorably highlighted in Alan Bleasdale's TV drama *The Boys from the Blackstuff* (BBC2 1982). Other TV dramatists such as Phil Redmond chronicled the struggle to secure waged work over longer story-lines. His series *Tucker's Luck* (BBC2 1983–85) followed the coming of age of a group of young people under Thatcherism, and his Liverpool-based soap opera *Brookside* (C4 1982–2003) consistently included stories focused on union activism, redundancy, unemployment and debt. Campbell noted that this was also a time when many DHSS officers were badly disheartened by the process of claims administration and were often radically politicised in the workplace and beyond. It was not uncommon, for example, for union representatives to bring collection boxes into the workplace in support of the UK miners' strike of 1984–85, a lengthy and bitter dispute which still looms large in public memory.

Contemporary accounts of political activism, such as those written by Campbell, together with feminist memoires signalled the rebarbative tone of the public political arena. The socialist agenda seemed somewhat impervious to feminism, women's interests and women's active participation, let alone to the growing appeal of Thatcherite values to working-class constituencies. Campbell (1984:2–3) remarked in the midst of the shifting and fraught political landscape of the 1980s that 'the eighties remained an enigma', observing that 'already we know more about the rise of the radical new Right than we do about the demise of the old Left.' It seemed to Campbell (p. 230) then that it was those *outside* the political institutions who, for better or worse, were 'changing themselves and changing their class' rather than those for whom politics was a public duty or a profession. Some perceived that the class politics of the 1980s was an increasingly esoteric or combative or exclusionary practice; it did not always speak effectively to its more 'natural' constituencies, which included, for example, working-class women and black and ethnic minorities (see Bryan *et al.* 1986:146ff, Cockburn 1991, Smith 1994). Urban DHSS claims offices could be highly politicised places. But the class politics enacted there was often either macho and militant or overly intellectual, mobilised through an intimidating combative rhetoric of 'class war' or sanctioned political tracts with which female and minority colleagues struggled to engage. Writer Clare Ramsaran (1990:174) recalled that even the media images of the period were predominantly of confrontations between men, with women placed on the sidelines. In her view, the media deployed 'various aspects of British manhood: the rioter, our "brave boys" sailing off to the Falklands, and the stroppy striking miners being put in their place by the boys in blue'. For Ramsaran (p. 175) and many others the arrival of Margaret Thatcher did the very opposite of inspiring a united opposition; instead, her appearance created 'a whole new excuse for men on the left to stop feeling guilty about sexism ... Thatcher jokes were so much more acceptable than plain old misogynist ones. And if you didn't laugh you weren't just a humourless feminist, but... a TORY' (see also Brunt 1987:22–4).

In various ways, then, in the City, in the public sector and in left political activism, the public scene was complicated not only by class, but by gender and race. Moreover, left politics, in particular, seemed to have misjudged the investments that women and their families were willing to make in the transformative potential of new Thatcherite times and the 'compromise with capital' which was taking place (Campbell 1984:229). For example, cultural historian Carolyn Steedman (1986:6–9) explored through her own family history how her mother's 'proper envy', desire for worldly things and an ongoing sense of the 'unfairness of things' became articulated with her working-class Labour background to produce a working-class Conservative. Her mother was very far from being an isolated case. The decade of the 1980s was marked by rising inequalities of income and status, but these were cross-hatched by a political rhetoric of choice, entrepreneurialism and individual aspiration towards social mobility which seemed to make sense for many people (see O'Shea 1984). Women, as ever, were signalled out in relation to certain politically authorised forms of social aspiration. As an individual, Thatcher's prominence appeared to 'normalise' female success, at least from the perspective of mainstream media representation, which increasingly showcased ambitious working women, 'power dressing' and conspicuous consumption in lifestyle magazines and imported American soap operas. However, as Heather Nunn argued (2002:105) in her earlier analysis of Thatcherism, throughout the 1980s Thatcher's own speeches and interviews frequently referenced 'the idealized scene of family life' as the home replete with material comforts and the unwaged mother at its harmonious centre. 'What's right for the family is right for Britain' declared Thatcher from the very start of her leadership (*Sunday Express* 29 June 1975:17) and for her the family was both the driving force of the good society and the motor of material aspiration and individual responsibility.

Thatcher rejected utterly the language of class; it was *individuals*, regardless of social background and regardless of earlier social (dis)advantage, who made their own success on their own merits. As pioneering cultural studies critic Stuart Hall (1988) explained in his well-known analysis of the new right, Thatcherism appealed, at different points, to various social identities such as the 'mother', 'working woman', 'tax payer', 'individual', 'proud Britisher', 'entrepreneur', and so on, and these were ideally united across class lines and set against undesirable 'outsiders' such as Marxists, trades unionists and 'trendy teachers'. The ethos here was that those who would thrive best were the self-starters, individuals motivated to improve their own lives. In other words, this was not about equality of outcome or resources but of individual drive and resourcefulness. As Thatcher (1975:16) famously declared, 'Let our children grow tall and some grow taller than others, if they have it in them to do so.'[1] Work hard to earn more to make a better life for one's family on one's own terms; nothing could be simpler or more appealing as a political philosophy for those who were well-equipped or who were determined enough to take it on board or who felt that they deserved a larger slice of the cake.

So the success of the project of economic liberalism which Thatcherism helped to set in motion depended, in part, on the dissemination of certain *values* as well as practices, including those of self-improvement, individual responsibility and personal investment, as exemplified in the practice of home-ownership and the privatisation of national industries. The Conservative imperative to be dependent on no-one but one's self and one's family served as an outright rejection of the earlier failed 'social contract' model of 1970s Labour administrations which had tried to negotiate a 'social wage' with workers in return for universal benefits.

If the home and family were at the heart of individual motivation to self-improvement and material comfort, then property and housing became its lifeblood. The introduction in 1980 of the right for tenants to buy their council houses and flats, and at favourable rates, elaborated on the older Conservative conception of the 'property-owning democracy'. By 1987 1 million dwellings had been moved from public into private ownership (Clarke 1996:383) and by 1990 around 70 per cent of all households had bought or were buying their own property (Savage *et al.* 1992:80). If the financial risks of moving from secure tenancy to owner-occupier status were not always clear, then the rewards were. Many working-class people whose traditional political affiliations, by virtue of historical loyalties and labour-based interests, would have been with the Labour Party embraced opportunities to buy their own home. In the words of Lynsey Hanley (2007:134), who wrote an 'intimate history' of working-class life from the perspective of social housing tenants: 'people decided that they didn't just want freedom *from* [poverty, ignorance, and so on], they wanted freedom *to*. They wanted the freedom to move at will, to paint their doors bright colours .... To improve, I guess.' In other words, the *promise* of Thatcherism, its rhetoric and presentation of the *possibilities* of social change, was as important as its actual policies.

As Stuart Hall (1988:262) explained in his analysis of the re-election of the Conservatives to that second term, the sense that prosperity is the key measurement of individual success and that anyone who opted in could achieve prosperity helped form an 'imaginary community' of people who, even if struggling at the time, might well benefit in future.

The accumulation of money went hand-in-hand with social success as well as with individual and familial security. Memoirist Mandy Nichol recalled the growing imperative for her and many of her family and friends to live 'the good life' and keep up with others and how it proved to be irresistible. She ruefully recalled: 'There I was, I had become a product of Thatcher's Britain. I had the good husband, the house, the 25 year mortgage and all the trappings of what it took to be acceptable and respected' (Nichol 1990:48). Historically, upper-class, and then later middle-class, Britons have always counted on property for investment, to accumulate value or, if sold on, to release capital for reinvestment and to leave as an inheritance (Savage *et al.* 1992:83ff). At the very least, as Hanley and Nichol have indicated, property has always been equated with security, self-respect, autonomy and financial independence. Indeed, the early 'baby boomers', born in the late 1940s and early 1950s and now heading for retirement, have become subject to criticism since the 'credit crunch' specifically for their success in building individual resources via the housing market, concentrating wealth among their own generation and then taking advantage of state pensions and other welfare support (Willetts 2010). Nichol's brief memoir of the Thatcher years highlighted the narrowing intersection between property, credit and social aspiration which apparently made this option more widely available. She recalled, with some regret, that it was not long before the family felt encouraged by low interest rates to borrow for a new car and then to make a move to an even better house – actions which left them working all hours to fix up the house, repay loans and generally fund the life they had elected to lead but which they now had no time to enjoy.

The consequence for those who could not or would not participate in the home-owning democracy was often damaging social disenfranchisement. As Hanley explained, during the 1980s, the council estates where the majority of tenants were renting rather than buying had become ever more neglected and unloved places, housing mainly those who had no escape route out to somewhere more desirable. The residents there became increasingly segregated, becoming 'ciphers for a malingering society' and frequently blamed for the poor conditions in which they lived (Hanley 2007:146). A longer-term by-product, then, of the reorganisation of the City, the sell-off of the better-quality, more desirable council housing stock and the extension of affordable credit to even more mortgagees was the geographical and social polarisation of the haves and the have-nots. As will be discussed in Chapter 3, the latter became increasingly disparaged through a moralistic language which labelled them as an unproductive, financially draining and socially corrosive underclass.

Economics journalist Will Hutton (1996:205) argued in his well-received treatise *The State We're In* that the burgeoning new class of home-buyers were also in fact quite vulnerable, becoming initially one of the engines of growth and then later of 'economic instability and personal insecurity'. The 1980s witnessed the exponential growth of lending and an upwards surge in house prices. But over time a housing market which had seemed both rewarding and buoyant became dangerously volatile, thanks to the unique structures of British housing finance and their relationship to schemes devised by the deregulated City (Hutton 1996:205–9). Hutton (p. 207) observed that by the early 1990s around 90 per cent of new mortgages were based on repayment plans linked to stock-market schemes. In other words, the repayments of many home-purchase loans were planned to be delivered through new speculative investments. As these failed and the property bubble burst at the end of the decade, home-owners, especially those from the lower-income groups, found themselves in dire straits and battling to keep their homes. So it turned out that the mid-1980s, the years in which we worked in the London Stock Exchange and in the Civil Service, formed the boom between two busts. Only months after Margaret Thatcher was re-elected to a third term in 1987 there was a stock market crash. By the early 1990s a second recession had taken hold alongside new outbursts of public disorder.[2] These included the 1991 summer of riots in the municipal suburbs of Cardiff, Tyneside and Oxford, which, in Campbell's (1993:xi) view, became symbolic of an era in which the new economic order of Thatcherism had left struggling subjects to their fate.

In the mid-1980s, then, as a City worker and a State worker respectively, and as subjects inevitably and uniquely marked by our own formations of class and gender, we encountered a diversity of experiences of work and of worklessness, of affluence and subsistence, of lived class relations and of the more formal politics of social class. These were the best of times and the worst of times, but what they were *not* was a tale of two separate cities or socio-economic realms – the City of London and the rest. In fact, financial deregulation and welfare state reform, money-making, credit and poverty, aspiration and struggle, entrepreneurial success and social exclusion were intricately tied up together in the material, cultural and even psychic lives of individuals and communities experiencing the turbulent birth of neoliberalism (see Harvey 2005). Scenarios of struggle, ambition, opportunity, resistance and failure were played out across the piece, and no one was untouched by the impact of Thatcherism and its underlying ideological drivers. The deregulation of the City worked hand-in-hand with the wider neoliberal project and the Thatcherite 'experiment in enterprise' (Engelen *et al.* 2011) to effect a transformation of class and culture whose impact is ongoing. As already indicated, these were economically unstable years. New patterns of waged work were established which were based on flexibility, impermanence, outsourcing, casualisation (in short 'feminisation'), all leading to the emergence of what has been described by Guy Standing as a new 'precariat' class. Standing (2011a) argues that, while this is not a class in the Marxian sense, it is 'a class in the making':

> approaching a consciousness of common vulnerability. It consists not just of everybody in insecure jobs.... The precariat consists of those who feel their lives and identities are made up of disjointed bits, in which they cannot construct a desirable narrative or build a career, combining forms of work and labour, play and leisure in a sustainable way.

So, too, the 1980s saw the emergence of other new class formations or fractions such as the 'new service class' or 'cultural classes', which might include people in the finance sector, the creative industries and the 'caring professions': a broadening middle class who would be regarded as being of 'key significance in the socio-economic changes' which took place at the time (see McDowell 1997:14–15). These workers, too, would often occupy positions which were precarious and always under threat of erasure.

With the benefit of hindsight, we can see that the implosion of financial systems in 2007 and the deep recessions which followed had many of their roots in that moment of City deregulation and in the wider project of neoliberalism in which Thatcherism played its significant part. So Engelen *et al.* (2011:212) contended that, 'while the mainstream political imaginary cannot conceive that Thatcherism inaugurated an unsustainable business model', it is clear that the national background to the financial crisis of 2007–08 was indeed a 'thirty year experiment in enterprise' launched in the 1980s and perpetuated by subsequent administrations. We suggest that the experiment is now in a new phase, rather than a final phase, as governments, finance and business attempt to hold on to, or even extend, neoliberal values and practices in the light of massive debt, limited resources, and deepening and entrenched inequalities. As will be seen in our concluding chapter, part of the promotion and extension of these values takes place in the cultural arena, where austerity discourses are deployed to marshal, harness and legitimise certain kinds of conduct and attitudes and to marginalise others – all in the service of sustaining the neoliberal project and with the effect of restoring or reconstituting class power (Harvey 2005; see also Couldry 2010:4–5).

Class-work: social change and class critique after the 1980s

For some thinkers the changes in culture, economics and politics which were inaugurated in the 1980s have more or less invalidated the usefulness of class as an analytic concept and class stratification as an analytic model of how society works and how culture might be understood and interpreted as an expression of social change. And, while we have focused so far on social and political shifts which took place in 1980s Britain, there were, of course, also wider Western or global developments which intersected with these and which contributed to the disruption of established social patterns and ways of thinking about class and social distinction. Writing in the mid-1990s, social historian Patrick Joyce (1995:3–6) presented a useful overview of the key macro changes in Western society which suggested to many that class-based concepts were increasingly unequal to the task of illuminating social, economic and cultural conditions. First, there were economic changes, shifts in employment practices, the move from industry to the service economy, changes in patterns of consumption, and so on, as briefly signalled in our discussion of the City of London and of the British housing market. So, too, Joyce (p. 3) observed the impact of unemployment and under-employment, the result of which has been not only the decline in number of manual workers but also a decline 'in the significance of manual work, and … certainly of work as a stable, uniform, lifelong experience'. This was concomitant with the rise of neoliberalism and the new right, whose 'rhetoric of privacy, choice, freedom and the individual' forced into retreat class-based solidarities and sentiment (Joyce 1995:4; see Harvey 2005:31ff).

Joyce (1995:4) also makes the case that of 'equal weight' with neoliberalism in weakening class as a concept was the rise of identity politics and movements around issues such as gender and race equality, consumerism and environmentalism; noting that 'the identity that has not been registered in this "identity" politics is class.' In the introduction to their edited collection on the working class and representation, Sheila Rowbotham and Hugh Beynon (2001:3–5) also noted that since the mid-1980s any discussion of class, and especially working-class, experience had become 'peculiarly unmentionable, politically and theoretically'. They had good grounds for the belief that in social sciences, in history and (perhaps above all) in cultural studies class had come to be regarded as an unhelpful and outmoded analytic category. It seemed to them, and to many others at the time of writing, that class was increasingly superseded by other kinds of identity politics. By the 1990s, therefore, analytic practices and theoretical inquiries into culture were ever more disconnected from an interest in the economic and material conditions of everyday life or in the ways that class labels worked to ascribe social position or to form moral judgements. As Stuart Hall remarked in an interview far later, 'Cultural studies ceased to be troubled by the grubby worldliness... in which culture has always to exist' (McCabe 2007:28).

By the early 1990s it was certainly the case that cultural studies (our own disciplinary background) was experiencing a 'crisis' marked not only by its own institutionalisation but by the lessening value of class as an organising principle of cultural critique (O'Kane 2001). This principle was partially lost through a post-Marxist 'turn' which rejected economic determinism and its materialist explanations of ideology and culture in favour of a new emphasis on how discourses construct the social field and identities within that field (Smith 1998:55–62, Savage 2000:13). These were important ground-breaking initiatives, which offered fresh and sharply attuned insights into a radically changing political terrain populated by new social movements formed across national borders (see especially Laclau and Mouffe 1985). In addition, as we also briefly indicated, during the 1980s class politics *on the ground* failed to speak meaningfully to subjects whose identities were experienced and politicised primarily in or equally with gender, race, sexuality, and so on. Much of the battleground of resistance to new right discourses and practices was occupied by left-oriented political activists and cultural critics working against racism and homophobia or for nuclear disarmament rather than for class struggle alone. Sociologists Pakulski and Waters (1996:1) went so far as to suggest in their mid-1990s book

The Death of Class that for cultural critics themselves class politics was increasingly rejected because it was intellectually unfashionable: 'Like beads and Che Guevara berets, class is *passé*, especially among advocates of the postmodernist avant-garde and practitioners of the new gender-, eco- and ethno-centred politics.'

In addition to these factors, Joyce (1995:3) also foregrounded the declining significance of the nation state as the centre of power within the context of an increasingly globalised economy and culture and the ways in which consumption has usurped production 'as the new basis of structural divisions and unities in society'. In tandem, there were massive changes in communications, digitisation and new technologies which allowed and even fostered dispersed surveillance and self-surveillance rather than the more top-down operations of power which had come to be associated with the apparatuses of historical nation states. These developments inspired critical work on governmentality, technologies and power which revealed how a more capillary process of self-monitoring and self-fashioning had come into play. New critical assessments proposed that, where power is decentralised, elusive and dispersed, the onus rests on the *individual* to become the author of their own lives (Beck 1992, Giddens 1991, 1994, Beck *et al.* 1994). In advanced liberal capitalism the self became both the subject and the object of rule, and thus the modern subject was now 'fated to be free' with all of the burdens or obligations that this entails (Joyce 1995:4). From this viewpoint older philosophical paradigms of power and social control which attended to ideology, hegemony, class formations and collectivities and the manufacture of consent no longer seemed to be tenable.

Finally, the late 1980s also witnessed the collapse of world communism, which helped smother the Marxian critiques of class already being radically overhauled by post-Marxian philosophy (Joyce:ibid.). At this time Frances Fukuyama's 1989 landmark essay 'The end of history' and follow-up book (Fukuyama 1992) helped shape a consensus that Western liberal democracy had trumped communism for good and finally seen off a utopian grand narrative of popular political revolution mobilised through class struggle. Indeed, Pakulski and Waters (1996:vii), writing in the wake of communism's collapse and what they described as processes of 'postmodernization', declared one 'obvious truth': that 'class can no longer give us purchase on the big social, political and cultural issues of our age'. For some time after this the expansion of the intellectual project of cultural studies in particular, its new adventures in identity politics, theory and philosophy, could only be weighed down by an attachment to class politics, attendance to the experience of classed living and the apparently inflexible or overly structural models that had once supported its enquiries.

Class-work after 'the death of class'

So in many ways the changes wrought in the 1980s appeared to represent the beginning of the end of the usefulness of class as an analytic or explanatory concept and/or as the organising principle for enquiries about power relations, culture and society. They certainly marked its near evaporation from the British scene of cultural studies and cognate disciplines. Nonetheless, despite the conviction by some that the 'season and purpose' of class analysis had come to an end by the 1990s (Pakulski and Waters 1996:vii), there were new and established British scholars working in sociology (and the sociology of education, politics, geography and crime in particular) who remained committed to modelling class stratification and to classed readings of current social conditions and/or who wished to remain alert to the moral valences of class-based language and labels (see, for example, Goldthorpe 1987, Saunders 1990, Goldthorpe and Marshall 1992, Devine 1997, Mahoney and Zmroczek 1997, Skeggs 1997, Reay 1998 and Young 1999). Much of this work insisted on the use-value of continuing to scrutinise society, communities, groups and sub-cultures in terms of material inequalities, impaired or uneven life chances, the social and geographical polarisation of social groups, the demonisation of certain classed subjects and their (non-)participation in formal politics or civic life. These works frequently advanced class analysis by taking into account both identity and economics and by articulating social class to discussions of gender, race and ethnicity, social aspiration and material resources. In these and other ways they worked to reformulate class-work around different theoretical and methodological axes; re-energising and re-equipping it to account for the significance of culture, consumerism, individualism and neoliberalism and the ongoing restructuring of class relations (see Savage 2000).

The importance of culture, in particular, to new class-work was evident in the widening British engagement with newly encountered research on the sociology of taste and class fractions initiated by Pierre Bourdieu, whose study *Distinction* (1979) first appeared in English in 1984. Class-based research such as Beverley Skeggs's (1997) landmark book *Formations of Class and Gender* illustrated the contribution of Bourdieu's work to the 'reinstatement of class' as a legitimate object of study. As Skeggs (1997:9) explained, his work helped provide an entry point for 'understanding how access, resources and legitimation contribute to class formation'. So, for example, Bourdieu demonstrated through his fieldwork undertaken in the 1960s how taste is deployed by class fractions as a kind of 'cultural capital' which serves to distinguish and differentiate social groups one from another and which works to exclude some lower-class groups from social advancement. Bourdieu's work allowed scholars interested in class or identity to articulate class difference specifically to the changing landscape of consumerism, lifestyle discourses, the domestic and the private spheres as well as to public culture. Thinking about social distinction through a consideration of consumerism, taste and cultural capital also helped reveal how exclusionary or punitive discourses and practices work to elevate and consolidate middle-class preferences, status and above all power (e.g. Wynne 1998, Adkins and Skeggs 2004, Devine *et al.* 2005, Lawler 2005, Bennett *et al.* 2009, McRobbie 2009).

Work (often inflected by feminism and an interest in gender and sexuality) in a variety of academic fields by scholars and writers such as Beatrix Campbell (1984), Carolyn Steedman (1986), Beverley Skeggs (1997), Sally Munt (2007) and Angela McRobbie (2009) also highlighted the emotional and experiential dimensions of contemporary classed lives – attending to the importance of self-respect, community esteem and/or private and public processes of social judgement. So, too, the theoretical 'turn' to emotion in cultural analysis (e.g. Ahmed 2004, Ngai 2005) and its invitation to theorise affect, shame, envy and other mostly 'ugly feelings' added a new dimension to these considerations of class feeling and increasingly became articulated with analyses of social class and its *moral* ascriptions. Recent work by scholars in media and cultural studies has, for example, underlined the ways in which popular culture, and especially reality TV, has worked to shame or discipline (lower-)classed subjects for their perceived inadequacies or to judge them in moral terms; judgements rooted in emotion and the perpetuation of classed hierarchies.[3] As social theorist Andrew Sayer (2005) suggests in his own thesis on the moral significance of class, class is very much experienced in emotional terms and framed through processes of judgement. He suggested, therefore, that the confrontational phrase 'Think you're better than us, do you?' is an indication of the ongoing challenge 'real or imagined [that] gets to the heart of the moral significance of class in everyday life' (Sayer 2005:vii).

Thus, in these and other ways, scholarly interrogations of class continue to be strategically and fruitfully harnessed to other theories of social distinctions, identity and selfhood rather than dispensed with altogether. Many of these threads of scholarship, especially those allowing for the embodied experiences and feelings of class, understand that class is not fixed but subject to process, that it is a site of cultural struggle and shaped by the operations of cultural, symbolic and social capital as well as by economic capital. They also call to mind the critical analysis of 'structures of feeling' developed by cultural historian Raymond Williams (1958, 1961, 1977) to describe the workings of society, class and culture (see Higgins 1999: 38ff). This highly influential critical innovation characterised the ways in which the social is embodied *through* subjects and marked by memory, place and experience for each generation in a particular moment. Williams described the structure of feeling as the shared values and perceptions which are articulated in culture and materialise in cultural forms such as the novel, journalism, art and what used to be called mass culture. As Sally Munt (2007:16, her emphasis) explains, 'implicit in this theory is the notion that the structural organisation of class *produces* structurally organised experience, and hence, feeling or emotion.' Hence Williams described 'a kind of sensibility negotiated between ideology and practice' and in this way his work (and also that of his near-contemporary Bourdieu) served to connect the superstructural (the world of culture, ideas, institutions and rituals) with the individual and their personal experience of social class (Munt 2007:ibid.).

The persistence of class

We should observe that, in spite of the scepticism on the part of some scholars about the continuing value of reading culture in class terms, in British culture, media and political discourse and in everyday parlance class and class labels continue to exert their hold (Conley 2008). As already noted, these are often deployed as evaluative descriptors, helping to form moral judgements and distinctions, to include some and to exclude others, to defend entitlements and to establish and maintain what is 'normal', socially acceptable and desirable. To gloss Zygmunt Bauman (1982:193), the concept of class has an astonishing capacity to defer its demise despite a general consensus in many fields that the social reality it once connoted has disappeared. In his view, the persistence of class occurs for several reasons, including because ideas of class are deeply embedded in common sense and consequently referred to as though they continued to have real explanatory force (see also Pascale 2007). He suggests that, because common sense is knitted in with social practices, the applicability of class categories seems obvious and therefore self-affirming. In other words, the relevance of class becomes a self-fulfilling prophecy. Bauman also notes how social ascriptions of class and class-positioning (such as that of the underclass) still happen and that these have real as well as symbolic effects. Class categories therefore continue to be commonly used and ideologically loaded in popular discourses; used as shorthand to dispense judgement, criticism or praise, to evoke pride, fearfulness, nostalgia, disgust or shame. Many sociologists have also observed that 'class' is one of the very few sociological concepts that ordinary people recognise, understand and employ themselves. The language of social class continues to be drawn on to label and judge others. Its hierarchies and structures of differentiation (albeit hugely complicated and nuanced in ways we have already signalled) can act as a spur to aspiration and as a measure to calibrate degrees of struggle, failure, progress and achievement. Overall, class in Britain has become part of the architecture of self-evaluation and social judgement since at least the nineteenth century and shows little promise of entirely crumbling away. Indeed, if anything, the last few years, and especially those following the global financial crisis, have seen social class, in all of its guises, return to the centre of cultural, political and media agendas.

From our perspective it makes little sense to insist that we have moved entirely beyond class when people are still subjected to it and by it and when class continues to be deployed as an 'obvious' explanatory framework by many ordinary Britons. Our own area of interest and research, as pursued in this volume, lies in factual media and non-fiction formats, and we will explore how class is played out in political comment, lifestyle genres, current affairs, documentary, popular factual television, autobiography and everyday popular culture. As this book will illustrate, in the 2000s the media resurrected and reinvigorated debates about social class and social distinction. If we were to take 2008 (the clear start of the global financial downturn) as our opening point, this would be evident on TV and radio and especially via public service broadcasting. Explicitly class-based material has included the BBC's *White Season* (2008) focusing on the white working class, documentaries and one-off programmes such as *Prescott: The Class System and Me* (BBC2 2008), *Whatever Happened to the Working Class* (BBC R4 2009), *Portraying the Poor* (BBC R4 2010), *Class Dismissed* (BBC 2 2011), *The Class Ceiling* (BBC R4 2011), *Melvin Bragg on Class and Culture* (BBC 2 2012) and *All in the Best Possible Taste* (C4 2012). So, too, at the time of writing, the BBC's Great British Class Survey is still under way, canvassing public opinion on the relevance of class to social identity in today's Britain.

Thoughtful and illuminating memoirs of classed experience have also emerged in the last decade, with some of them attracting sustained critical attention. Among them are Michael Collins's (2004) *The Likes of Us: A Biography of the White Working Class*, Lynsey Hanley's (2007) *Estates* and Sathnam Sanghera's (2008) entertaining autobiography *If You Don't Know Me by Now*, which recalled his Punjabi family's early years in Wolverhampton in the context of cultural difference and economic hardships. Alongside these were best-selling celebrity autobiographies which narrativised classed journeys of social mobility by entertainers such as Paul O'Grady (2008) and Roy 'Chubby' Brown (Vasey 2006), a number of which we discuss in Chapter 5.

New interventions into public political debate also appeared which explored inequality, the fair society, class labels or the polarisation of social classes from the perspective of social policy, social comment, personal experience and media representation; some of which triggered significant media coverage. These included the Fabian Society's *Grown Up Guide to the Politics of Class* (Fabian Review 2008), two Rowntree Foundation reports (2007 and 2008), *Estates* (as cited above, which is a housing policy analysis as well as a memoir), *The Spirit Level* (Wilkinson and Pickett 2009) and *Chavs: the Demonization of the Working Class* (Jones 2011). The recession inevitably deepened inequalities and helped polarise public deliberations around state finances, social mobility, merit and equality of opportunity. This was reflected in publications which focused on the competition for resources among and between social classes, between secure and insecure workers and between generations, including *The Pinch* (Willetts 2010), *Jilted Generation* (Howker and Malik 2010), *Injustice* (Dorling 2010) and *Them and Us* (Hutton 2011). As we will go on to demonstrate, class-based phrases and labels were also revived or newly minted to categorise the insiders and outsiders of the new 'age of austerity', which seemed to be partly characterised by an increasingly damaging competition for resources. 'Middle England', the 'squeezed middle', 'downsizers', the 'sharp-elbowed middle class', the 'feral underclass', 'chavs', 'plebs', the 'white working class', the 'undeserving poor', 'union bullies', 'selfish baby boomers' and others have helped populate the new landscape of class.

Class and Contemporary British Culture: outline

This introduction has set the scene for a cultural analysis of class in contemporary Britain by charting the ways in which established notions of class have been problematised since the 1980s in terms of both social and political change and the scholarship which has sought to make sense of these changes. It highlighted the ways in which Thatcherism and the broader project of neoliberalism inaugurated a turbulent reorganisation of economics, work and culture, and how this impacted on formations of social class and the cultivation of new and modified social identities. It has also signalled the ways in which some academic research began to contest the relevance and utility of class as an explanatory framework for new times while others worked to take class into account from new theoretical perspectives and/or via a continuing political commitment. Finally, it indicated the ways in which debates about social class continue to find a place in everyday language and in British media culture. Overall, our introduction has argued that social class, although complicated and highly contested, remains a valid and fruitful route into understanding how contemporary British culture articulates social distinction and social difference and the costs and investments at stake for all involved.

In the following chapter, Chapter 2, we begin again with the time of Thatcherism in order to critically engage with the symbolic importance of Essex, Essex Man and Essex Girl as emblems of white working-class politics, culture and consumption. Here we consider the ways in which popular fascination and anxiety about shifting patterns of class allegiance, working-class social mobility and spectacular consumption became attached to people from Essex from the 1980s to the current day. We argue that the public disparagement of these social types was symptomatic of a wider unease about the social consequences of the rolling out of Thatcherism. Chapter 3 pursues further the ways in which social classes, class fractions and social types are labelled through a consideration of how media and political discourses tag, frame and characterise the so-called underclass. The chapter outlines the development and changing usage of underclass discourses in scholarship, politics and journalism from the 1980s to the 2000s and harnesses this to a more specific consideration of how certain social groups are styled as 'dangerous' and criminogenic. We have chosen to focus this discussion via a comparative analysis of the media coverage of various public disorder events and social unrest, including the English summer riots of 2011.

Chapter 4 explores how the values which are embedded in current discourses around education and social mobility are reinforced, tested and sometimes challenged in lifestyle journalism, reality television and social observation documentary. The focus is on the media articulation of education as the key driver of social mobility, responsible citizenship and equality of opportunity. Paying special attention to political debates around educational achievement in the context of meritocracy and personal responsibility, we consider the ways in which educational choice is presented, taken up or passed by. We consider how this presentation of choice as available to all critically impacts on the class status, social mobility and futures of children and their families. Chapter 5 picks up on the themes of meritocracy and social mobility from a different viewpoint. It explores publicly related life stories as a resource for understanding the politics of class and aspiration and its attachment to the language of ambition, merit, chance and opportunity, and work. These are unpacked via autobiography in particular, and specifically the self-told stories of British entertainers and reality TV stars.

Whereas celebrities and other elites such as business entrepreneurs are highly conspicuous in the media (and also in cultural studies' critiques of power, consumption and social mobility), British aristocrats and the upper classes remain oddly under-scrutinised despite their presence in the celebrity press and during state occasions. Chapter 6 seeks to remedy this oversight by addressing the media representation of the British upper classes, their social practices and values. Through a consideration of the changing depiction of the royal family in particular, it seeks to explore the ways in which the hereditary upper classes are accommodated and condoned within an unequal society despite the often-repeated conviction that success should be achieved through merit both within and across generations. The next chapter, Chapter 7, touches on some of the topics raised in relation to the monarchy through a much more detailed consideration of nation, class and belonging. This focuses on 2005–10 as one period in which the public discussion of race, ethnicity and especially immigration became noticeably yoked to debates about social class, and especially the white working-class. Here, through an analysis of media debates arising from local and general elections, we draw on concepts of voice, home, belonging and hospitality to explore how the white working-class Briton became the object of various deleterious projected views and assumptions.

Our final chapter continues the discussion of nation and identity. It draws the book to a conclusion with an analysis of the distinctive turn in public discourse towards historical resources, analogies and stories to help citizens make sense of the current era of austerity. Here we argue that in straitened times citizens are being asked to make do, to accept the rolling back of state provision and to modify their expectations of a civil society on the basis of historical myths as well as current realities. During this process already fragile and fracturing class alliances become further weakened as certain political constituencies, counter-discourses and counter-politics become labelled as outmoded, retrograde or damaging. Having said this, we end on a more optimistic note by speculating on how British history and culture might be drawn on to help generate a more progressive outlook and politics in the light of growing inequalities and the ongoing competition for resources.

2
Essex: Class, Aspiration and Social Mobility

Essex is a Southern English county that has become associated in the popular imagination with a train of largely negative, intensely classed associations. From the mid to late 1980s onwards, as Thatcherism increasingly 'took hold' of working-class votes and of the political imaginary, the citizens of Essex in particular were often rhetorically linked to both new right political values and new kinds of social aspiration. This chapter explores, then, how Essex has become known as the home of unthinking new right working-class Conservatism and of the worst excesses of consumerism. We begin with a consideration of how Essex people, and especially the people of Basildon, have been regarded as being in the vanguard of Thatcherism, and how they were also looked to by politicians and pundits as a reliable barometer of its popular appeal. Basildon has been described as the ideal measure of the 'mood of the nation' (Hayes and Hudson 2001a) and as being at the heart of the 'new sociology of aspirations' (Hall 1992). In other words, the town of Basildon became the touchstone of new times. Our argument will be that the media's fiercely territorial or judgemental depiction of its inhabitants – Basildon Man and Woman – betrayed a profound unease about the disruption of once-secure borders between social classes and the social effects of Thatcherite policies and values.

This unease was also apparent in the media depictions of the figure of so-called Essex Man, who was a political and popular character embodying working-class aspiration. We take Essex Man as the starting point for our discussion of the ways in which an often humorous or comical disgust is publicly expressed for the working class, and especially for those who seem to be rising above their social station. Here we track the changing associations made between money, taste and class opportunity when, for example, Essex Man arrived in the

City of London during the late 1980s and became the crude marker of both the shiny success and the darker underside of finance capitalism. As we shall see, this figure represented an explosive mixture of working-class 'laddish' behaviour and a cult of toughness fuelled by the institutionalised risk-taking of Thatcherism's enterprise culture. In contrast to older versions of the middle-class city broker or the company manager, which were shaped by pre- and post-war legacies of finance and corporate culture, Essex Man became an emblem of new money and represented an instinctual rather than educated approach to business. As such, he attracted both praise and abuse. We would argue that these responses revealed a distinct nervousness about the 'don't care' aggressive entrepreneurialism with which he was associated and the ways in which this was linked to shifts in class belonging. In this context we also consider the subversively loud figure of Loadsamoney created by the comic Harry Enfield in the very late 1980s. We explore how Enfield deployed a class-based humour in this caricature, which became an emblem, at the height of Thatcherism, for working-class self-aggrandisement. We then consider the ways in which the Loadsamoney character both lampooned working-class Conservatism and Thatcherite values and was also championed by those who felt liberated by the new spirit of enterprise which he articulated.

We will also suggest that, if Essex Man and Loadsamoney are monstrous figures of entrepreneurial money-making and boom economics, then the Essex Girl is the monstrous figure of consumption. We shall see that jokes about Essex Girls are frequently aggressive and misogynistic, but they also rely on the audience's assumed commonly shared assumptions about class, consumerism and bad taste. As research on class and gender (e.g. Skeggs 1997, 2004) has already highlighted, working-class women have always had to negotiate historically embedded and tricky notions of respectability and proper conduct. Essex Girls appear to disrupt these altogether (see Skeggs 2005) by adopting a tough polished exterior and generating economic and social worth through overt investment in their grooming, dress and personal appearance. As such, the Essex Girl is also disparaged as a female 'chav' (although she pre-dates this label): a process by which the abjection of white working-class femininity is linked to broader social anxieties about work, welfare entitlement and sexuality (Tyler 2008). Overall the chapter argues that the media treatment of the cultural types and locations discussed here demonstrates the ways in which the Essex of the cultural and political imagination has become a key motif for a far larger story of social transformation with attendant classed anxieties about politics, place, taste and social mobility.

Essex, Conservatism and the 'new sociology of aspirations'

Political historians and psephologists have recorded that during the 1980s the Labour Party increasingly lost its attraction as the natural home of working-class popular political aspiration. The decline in its electoral appeal came on the back of the 1970s 'decade of dealignment', in which class-based voting had already weakened as political affiliations fluctuated and became more volatile (Särlvik and Crewe 1983, Evans 2002:218). It seemed evident that the Conservative Party benefited most from this changing political and classed landscape, going on to enjoy 18 consecutive years in office under the leadership of Margaret Thatcher and then John Major from 1979 to 1997. Both contemporary and current politicians, pundits and scholars have read the 1980s and early 1990s as thereby emblematic of 'popular Conservatism'; an era in which the Tories were able to capitalise on those loosening ties between Labour and what were once regarded as the 'labouring classes'. As noted in Chapter 1, during this period the Tories astutely tapped into burgeoning ambitions to own one's home, to buy shares from privatised national assets and to more generally participate in a meritocratic culture of opportunity (see Harvey 2005:60).

It was during the later 1980s that the county of Essex became the mythical touchstone of this 'new', strategic and apparently durable working-class Conservatism. It is clear that at that time a resettlement took place in which many (but not all) of Essex's skilled workers moved away from their traditional political affiliation with the Labour Party and towards the Conservatives (more conventionally associated with middle-class political convictions and aspiration). In spite of the fact that alliances between particular social classes and political parties became less fixed across the country, it was the Essex resettlement that attracted consistent media commentary. Somehow Essex was taken to exemplify that broader consolidation of the British dealignment of social class with the core values and cross-generation loyalties of party politics. Consequently, Essex and the adjacent suburbs of East London, from which many Essex citizens had migrated as their earnings increased, became the focus of extensive political and cultural commentary as the region was increasingly regarded as the locus of a changing culture of working-class or even 'classless' social ambition.

From the 1980s onwards, the citizens of Essex towns, including Billericay, Chelmsford, Harlow, Chingford and Southend-on Sea, were rhetorically attached to the stereotypes of tastelessness, unreconstructable Thatcherism and rampant materialism epitomised by characters such as Essex Man and Loadsamoney, whom we go on to address later in this chapter. Perhaps most prominent among these was the town of Basildon. Situated on the Essex side of the M25 London orbital motorway, Basildon had always been regarded as a frontier town, a suburban new-build on the 'edge' whose inhabitants were keen to embrace progress (Barker 2009:41). As a new town built to accommodate London's East Enders in the early 1950s, it promised for its inhabitants a sanctuary from the poor, shabby and inadequate living conditions of the post-war condition. It was also built on the cleared 'plotlands' where previous generations of entrepreneurial citizens had from the turn of the twentieth century engaged in a land rush; paying £5.00 for the privilege of building shacks and sheds on their own plot of ground without recourse to planning regulations, proper services or utilities (Beaven 2001). Consequently its residents had already been styled as a 'cockney diaspora' (Parsons 2001); as people keen to make a better life for themselves.

So Basildon seemed like the natural territory for ordinary working and middle-class people who would embrace the Thatcherite values of home ownership, individual responsibility and self-reliance; a position which rendered the Basildon voter the subject of endless political debate. Indeed, Basildon had become one of the key imaginary provinces of 'middle England', which was less a location and more a shorthand designation for a group of people who were joining the expanding middle classes (Moran 2005:14–15). Moreover, Basildon in particular had become a reliable barometer of national political trends in terms of General Election results. As social researchers and Basildon specialists Dennis Hayes and Alan Hudson (2001a:9) recall, 'Throughout the 1980s, Basildon's reputation hardened as a laboratory of the Thatcher revolution.' Consequently, the more narrowly defined figures of Basildon Man and Woman became ideal–typical figures whose political support was apparently needed by whoever aimed to win nationally. As such, they became rhetorically attached to and mobilised by the two major British political parties. Indeed, in Hayes and Hudson's (2001b) view, Essex Man and Woman became 'pioneers' of the 'First Way' (Thatcherism), 'emblems' of the Second Way (John Major's classless society), and by the late 1990s even a testing ground for the appeal of New Labour's 'Third Way' philosophy.

In 1992 Stuart Hall, the cultural theorist who first coined the phrase 'authoritarian populism' to capture Thatcherism's contrary but powerful mobilisation of populist and authoritarian discourses together, turned his attention to the town of Basildon.[1] Writing in the wake of the 1990–91 recession and just after the Conservatives had won a fourth term in power, this time with John Major at the helm, Hall observed that Basildon was the heartland of the 'new sociology of aspirations'; a science in which the Conservatives were well practised (but see also Norris 1993). He (1992) argued in this analysis of Labour's defeat that, while the party had offered a realistic model of taxation (reckoning what people could actually afford to pay), the Conservatives offered a model based on aspiration, recognising that in post-Thatcher Britain people would calculate their tax obligations not on what they earn but on what 'they hope, desire or aspire to earn'. Basildon was regarded as both the testing ground and the evidence of the truth of this conviction and for the changes in class identity and class relations that this attitude exemplified. So in the1992 election, news reports turned to the people of Basildon for explanations of why Labour had failed, yet again, to win, even during a period of sustained economic downturn when it might have been expected to attract back its core support. For example, Channel 4 Evening News (10 April 1992) featured vox pops with people in Basildon market, whose opinions seemed to suggest that, regardless of whether individuals were unemployed or earning good money, the Labour Party was not for them. Public opinion as expressed here seemed to be of the view that Labour was not only ill equipped to solve the unemployment problem but would also over-tax those who were still earning a reasonable wage. The news package failed to include any views at all from Labour supporters: we will never know why, but perhaps they couldn't find any. In any case, it was capped by an interview with Tory David Amess, who was clearly triumphant following his re-election as MP for Basildon. He explained his election success in these terms: 'the organised working class, this is disappearing as people have more individualistic aims, more privatised aims. They buy their houses, they purchase their shares and changes of that kind.'

So Basildonians seemed to be at the forefront of a new conception of 'progress' which had been rolled out under Thatcherism and which no campaigning party could afford lightly to dismiss. In 1989 Charles Leadbeater (1989:398–9), then industrial editor for the *Financial Times* and later an advisor to Tony Blair, made a perceptive assessment of the major shift in notions of progress that Thatcherism had pioneered and the near-impossibility of rewinding them in future years. He argued that, before the advent of Thatcherism, the trajectory of progress had been clear, even if its mechanics were fiercely struggled over and disputed. Until then progress had been achieved through industry, order and planning, and much of it was collective in orientation, whether it was through the production of mass market consumer durables or the provision of mass welfare. The generative power of this idea of progress was evidenced also in the investment in industry and development, for example, through the installation of the Ford's car manufacturing plant in Dagenham, Essex, in 1931 and the new estates which were built to support it and to house its workers. Modern town planning resulted not only in these new estates but also in the establishment of entirely new towns (such, indeed, as Basildon). In contrast, the 1980s experienced a growing attachment to hospitality, financial and information services rather than to making and building things as the route to advancement. The emphasis was increasingly on global rather than national markets, with a concomitant growth in risk-taking, insecurity and individual responsibility for making one's way in the world. These shifts, as reported in our introduction, required people to step up and subscribe to this new notion of progress based on flexibility, adaptability and an individual freedom to strive and thrive.

Understandably, perhaps, it was also the case that, during a period of flux, globalisation and economic upheaval, which might best be understood as a form of 'creative destruction' (Schumpeter 2012), enduring 'British' values of nationalism, hearth and home were also increasingly revalorised. Leadbeater (1989:404) observed: 'Thus Thatcherism is open and closed. It forces people out into the market, but as a compensation offers them a retreat into a secure, private world.' This new, privatised world and the aspirations it exemplified, as identified by commentators as various as Hall, Amess and Leadbeater, was a long way from the social housing, estate life and shared employment in industry which had characterised the experiences of many working-class people before Thatcherism. It also seemed to encapsulate some core truth about the shifting formations of classed identity and social progress which were taking place during the period. But it would be a mistake to assume that these transitions were smooth, that these new values were always fully welcomed and embraced or that Essex people in particular were consistently and 'breathtakingly right wing', vulgar and individualist. Hayes and Hudson (2001a:14) demonstrate, for instance, that the media image of Basildon Man, as an exemplar of an emergent social and political formation, was unreliable with regard to both issues of taste and image and also political affiliation. They point out that, whereas the media image of Loadsamoney was dominant, in reality in 1992 64 per cent of people earned less than £15,000 per annum, and by 1997 this was still 60 per cent; figures which made Basildonians 'relatively poor by the standards of the South East'. So, too, the notion of Basildon Man as a fully sub-scribed 'classless' subject was erroneous, with 75 per cent of people describing themselves as 'working-class' in 1992 and 73 per cent in 1997 (Hayes and Hudson:ibid., see also Evans 1993). For Hayes and Hudson the political trajectory of Basildon Man and Woman was towards an increasing *disengagement* with politics rather than an enduring affilia-tion to Conservative policies and ideology. By 1997 Basildon turned to New Labour as their party of choice, and 39 per cent rejected all Conservative policies.

The discovery of Essex Man

In the late 1970s, on the cusp of the Thatcher era, the rock/punk singer Ian Dury introduced his comic-strip character Billericay Dickie (1977). In what became his trademark spiv, cockney-punk style he recounted the first-person tale of Dickie, whose bawdy sexual con-quests with a variety of Essex women took him from Billericay to the Isle of Thanet and Shoeburyness. Dickie declared: 'so you ask Joyce and Vicki/who's their favourite brickie/I'm not a common thicky/I'm Billericay Dickie/and I'm doing very well...' Dury used the voice of Billericay Dickie to satirise a working-class machismo buoyed up by a sense of 'doing very well', which no doubt aided his ability to land a range of adoring women. As such, Dickie delivered a vaudeville wink at both female sexual availability and middle-class pretentions, as well as bonding with other Essex working lads. But, while Dury played with class stereotypes in his own persona and also sent them up in his cockney-geezer characters, in 'Billericay Dickie' he also walked the risky line between cheeky in-joke and the reproduction of crude stereotypes. As such, he anticipated the crudely drawn but nonetheless culturally rich figures of Essex Man, Loadsamoney and Essex Girl.

As signalled in our introduction, in the media the inhabitants of Essex were equally lauded for their entrepreneurial grasp of the Thatcherite dream and mocked for their new-money aspirations and flashy working-class consumerism. Indeed, late 1980s Essex was commonly associated with a host of comic, satirical and mocked popular figures who have come to personify the changing coordinates of social class, the disso-lution of class consciousness and the rise of consumer culture. The key figure here is Essex Man, a vulgar, loutish, socio-economic group C2, tabloid-reading, lager-drinking Tory voter (Engel 1996). It was not until 7 October 1990 that *Sunday Telegraph* columnist Simon Heffer actually popularised the phrase, which was already in circulation (see *Spitting Image* below). Essex-based Heffer (1990:23), writing without a by-line in the Sunday Comment section edited by Peregrine Worsthorne, produced a piece called 'Maggie's Mauler' in which he observed Essex Man's unfortunate and wholly unconscious predicament: 'his badly fitting sharp and shiny suit and his lager-belly show he is a slave to fashion, yet his politics are dictated by his desire to be treated as an individual.' Here Heffer memorably offered a pen portrait which blended the cultural with the political: Essex Man was 'breathtakingly right wing' and 'young, industrious, mildly brutish and culturally barren', disliking foreigners and books. His leisure activities mark him out in class terms. The text was accompanied by a line drawing of a heavy-shouldered, 'aboriginal' young man wearing a sharp, boxy suit standing outside a former council house complete with satellite dish. He is holding a can of lager, a copy of the *Daily Express* lies by his feet and a shiny car is parked behind him (see Figure 2.1). Here the figure of Essex Man is both aspirational and pushy, making incursions into social and professional territory which was formerly out of bounds. Heffer wrote:

When one walks through the City most evenings the pools of vomit into which one may step have usually been put there by Essex Man, whose greatly enhanced wealth has exceeded his breeding in terms of alcoholic capacity. The late-night trains from Liverpool Street are not lacking drunks, though Essex Man's sense of decency means he is usually sick before boarding.

In a move which is wholly typical of class-based snobbery, the piece connects working-class male identity with the body and with bodily fluids. It is clear that Essex Man's rising career success and ingress into the City Stock Exchange, while admirable in some respects, constitutes matter out of place, and the abject signs of his presence are all too visible.

Having said this, Essex Man is also a political animal whose social progress is based instinctively on free market economics underpinned by his own personal ambition. Heffer observes that Essex Man doesn't read books – but if he did they would be written by Milton Friedman and Ayn Rand, the darlings of the new right. Luckily he was left 'largely undamaged by his comprehensive school education' thanks to the strength

ller

Figure 2.1 Essex Man as illustrated by Collet in the *Sunday Telegraph*, 7 October 1990

of family values: 'ownership, independence, a regard for strength and a contempt for weakness underpin his inarticulate faith in markets' (Heffer 1990).

The piece is credited for inspiring an extraordinary volume of Essex Man newspaper coverage as well as a proliferation of Essex jokes, a cartoon series in the now defunct daily newspaper *Today* and an entry in the Oxford English Dictionary (May 2010). According to Essex blogger Pete May, this expressed a genuine cultural phenomenon which was both recognisable and at the same time distorting. Looking back in 2010 on the astonishing media impact of that short newspaper piece, Heffer himself emphasised that his sketch was not snobbish but written in admiration. He recalled that it was inspired by seeing a young man on a train travelling into London, ostentatiously barking into his mobile phone, clearly going into the City to make his fortune. In an interview with Tory blogger Iain Dale, he recalled:

> People who had left school no longer had to go and work as farm labourers or in industrial nurseries, or even as office boys; they could get jobs on trading floors and could use their great natural intelligence and enterprise to make money. I said to my wife: 'You know that is what's happened. That bloke is absolutely synonymous with this change'... what it was celebrating was that ethos that we don't want the state to look after us, we are capable of doing it ourselves.[2]

Subsequent commentators soon developed elaborations of what proved to be an enduring stereotype that seemed somehow to help make sense of new times. For example, Bill Frost (1991), writing in the *Times*, set the scene for his visit to the Essex town of Billericay:

> Midday at the Constitutional Club in Billericay, 'dinner-time' as the hour is known in the Essex flatlands.... More pints are pulled for the men (lager, of course) and the ladies relent: 'Oh, all right then, just a small gin and slimline.' Billericay is the spiritual Barratt home of Essex Man and his equally formidable mate, Essex Woman: unreconstructable right-wing grassroots Thatcherites. He is the East End barrow boy turned City broker who came to represent the heart and mind of the party in the Eighties, still advocating the rope, the birch, and a tougher line on immigration. She looks up briefly from the latest Jackie Collins blockbuster and agrees wholeheartedly.

Pen sketches such as these reinforced the notion that Essex Man and Woman had developed a close and *lasting* affinity with Thatcherism and Thatcherite free market capitalism; that the neoliberal economics which characterised those years was wholly in line with their worldview. As it turned out, in the post-Thatcher decades no political party could rely on consistent support from the majority of the electorate, whatever their earlier shared history. The relationship between working-class people and Conservatism was not especially sustained or consistent, and 'instability' became 'normal politics' (Evans 2002:220). But, at the time, social commentaries such as this one by Bill Frost asserted that the skilled, working-class, ambitious City traders and entrepreneurs who originated from Essex were evidentially unreconstructed and 'unreconstructable' Thatcherites. Indeed, they could be identified all too easily by their social profile, non-'U' manners and vulgar tastes, including their tendency to shout into their then-bulky mobile phones in public, to mistake lunch time for dinner time and to prefer Barratt new-build houses over Victorian villas, a choice valorised by Thatcher herself when she purchased one in a gated development in leafy South London in 1985.[3]

The satirical puppet sketch show *Spitting Image* (ITV 1984–96) encapsulated the depiction of everything Essex as tawdry, greedy, shallow and unthinkingly Thatcherite in its charmless musical set piece called 'Essex is crap' (1986).[4] Opening scenes switch from idyllic images of other counties (with an approving voiceover speaking in Received Pronunciation) to the interior of an Essex pub in which a sing-along is taking place. Here white men in sportswear and white women wearing white stiletto shoes list the defining characteristics of Essex and Essex folk, a fragment of which we reproduce below:

Essex, where there's mobile phones galore and in every dream home a rottweiler, where you find the likes of Norman Tebbit [prominent Thatcherite and an Essex MP] go, where page three girls [tabloid models] buy their mum a bungalow. If you think it's posh to drink Malibu, if you need a calculator to count to two, if you think the stories in the *Sunday Sport* are true, then you're an Essex Man.

The sketch concludes with a list of classed and ideological indicators of Essex values, including shell suits, blood sports, Union Jack boxer shorts, Lucozade, the *Daily Star*, camcorders, satellite dishes and World of Leather sofas. Here, as elsewhere, Essex people became aligned with Thatcherism, conspicuous consumption and a tabloid culture which is embossed with negative class inferences.

I've got loadsamoney!

The offensive ostentation of the 'new money' classes was also later lampooned through the comic figure of the prosperous plasterer whose catchphrase was 'Loadsamoney', as played by Labour supporter Harry Enfield and who, for many, epitomised the 'gross embodiment of Essex Man' (Rojek 2001:23).[5] The inference was that, as painters and decorators, Loadsamoney and his mates had capitalised on the boom in home improvements, refurbishments and the fast turnover of the property market to charge a huge premium for their probably quite shoddy work. As Pete May (2010) observed, 'When Loadsamoney drove into the countryside and shouted, "Oi! Get this place developed up!" it could only have been in Essex.' In sketches and music videos Loadsamoney presented himself as a white working-class young man dressed in designer leisure wear and 'box fresh' white trainers, driving a flashy car and spending his time deriding a variety of other social types. The 1988 musical parody 'Loadsamoney: Doin' Up The House' became a hit single and featured in a successful live tour. In the video Loadsamoney is seen mocking the hapless poor, middle-class people in suits, opera-goers, politicians and the old-style, outmoded 'pay packet' flat-cap working class (who were represented in black and white film to signal their obsolescence).[6]

It should be observed that, while the character was clearly intended as a send-up of new working-class, consumerist lifestyles and attitudes (one of his catch-phrases was 'oi you, shut yer mouth and look at my wad'), he was increasingly regarded, when taken out of context, as a kind of anti-hero and as a tribute to wealth-driven bravado. As a member of the comic pantheon of British working-class characters which also includes Steptoe and his son, Alf Garnett, Vicky Pollard and the characters in *Viz* magazine, Loadsamoney also arguably reinforced prejudices about working-class psychology, aspiration and work ethic while simultaneously mocking the pretensions of his middle-class critics (see Lockyer 2010:130–1). The *Sun* newspaper lionised the character and chided Enfield himself for his left-wing, anti-Thatcher values. This advocacy of Loadsamoney probably contributed to the growing perception that what had emerged from the 1983 and1987 General Elections was a 'politically distinctive social segment' of the working class whose profile overlapped with the readership of the *Sun* newspaper in particular. In the public imagination this profile was synonymous with a culture of easy credit, satellite TV and video, and 'right to buy' housing (Webber 1993:205).

But the appeal of Enfield's character spanned a far wider range of constituencies than is conventionally associated with that tabloid newspaper. While he was conceived of and accepted by some as a lampoon of Thatcherite ethics, he was actually embraced by City and self-employed traders who were enjoying their new-found earning capacity and elevated status. As noted in Chapter 1, these men (and a very few women) had arrived in the City following its 1986 deregulation, which was dubbed the 'Big Bang' because of the increase in market activity generated by an aggregation of measures including electronic trading and the removal of distinctions between different trading jobs. These new workers were regarded by some as the 'shock troops of the Thatcher revolution', whose 'class, politics and styles of consumption' offended both tastemakers and social commentators (Zaloom 2006:77). As Caitlin Zaloom (2006:78) observed, they trashed the virtue of thrift: 'barrow boy traders spread the wealth they acquired, tilting the balance between saving and spending that creates a productive tension in a working capitalist economy.'[7] Looking back on those times, businessman and investor Alan Moore recalled:

> It was April 1987 and I was having a drink in a wine bar in the City of London with some stock market cronies. 'You could float a brick in a cardboard box and someone would buy it,' someone said. We all laughed. Margaret Thatcher's shareholder revolution was in full swing...there was a new ethos: barrow boy chic epitomized by Harry Enfield's 'Loadsamoney' character. For the first time in generations, it was good to be greedy in Britain.
>
> (Moore and Moore 2004:4)

Class melded with gender to produce crude ciphers of the disruption of both mannered social values and the destruction of older forms of market capitalism. Robert Smith (2010) has argued, for example, in his analysis of the entrepreneurial 'cityboy' that economic differences between classes clearly dictated the *versions* of masculinity available to men. Drawing on a range of theorists of masculinity, Smith (2010:13) argued that to be a working-class man meant living out and inhabiting a 'very different set of practices and narratives about what it is to be a real man' from those of other (professional, academic) social classes. In the case of the new City worker, these dictates of masculinity merged with an entrepreneurial ideology in the expectation that virility, a strongly projected personality and lack of fear could be marketable commodities.

Importantly, Smith (2010:10) refers to research on the ways in which 'character' became the marker of the 'self-made man' for whom 'striving for riches became a mark of their masculinity'. These character traits became skewed in entrepreneurial ideology towards 'images of deviancy, criminality and notions of the "bad boy entrepreneur"' (Smith:ibid.). Certain clothing and consumer goods in working-class culture were also used to construct and project an entrepreneurial identity, such as 'cigars, top of the range cars, tailored suits worn in conjunction with open necked shirts and accessories such as jewellery (bling)' (Smith:ibid.). However, as these items have also been used in different combinations to culturally signal a *criminal* lifestyle, Smith suggests that the signs can become confused. In the case of the Essex Man, we could argue that he is figured as an almost *criminally* tasteless 'bad boy'. We maintain, then, that the Essex Man serves as a repository for anxieties about decorum and an excessive performance of the same drivers which arguably inform other, more 'respectable', forms of masculinity within a capitalist society: ambition, virility, consumerist desire for goods, and so on. But because that desire and its embodiment are felt to be performed openly and *without restraint* it lays bare a more general unease about the working through of free market economies and the neoliberal experiment.

Overall, the Essex of the cultural and political imagination played its significant part in the far larger story of British social transformation. Looking back on Thatcher's legacy, Simon Jenkins (2007:164) recalled,

> Her rebuttal of 'bourgeois guilt' was real. In the 1980s rich lists were greeted with unashamed glee. The City was transformed from a place of aristocratic decorum to one of greed-is-good. From the repositioning of Essex as a place of tasteless wealth to the vulgarization of the Cotswold gentry, from the dramatic upturn in London cuisine to the boom in weekend breaks, Thatcher's Britain flaunted money.

In his analysis of Thatcherism, Eric Evans (1997:145) has also argued that Loadsamoney became one of the three dominant symbols of materialist Britain during the late 1980s (alongside those City 'yuppies' and the privatisation of public assets).[8] His character quickly embedded itself in the national consciousness. Labour party opposition leader Neil Kinnock was the first reported politician to use the term as a critique of late Thatcherite economics on 20 May 1988. His speech to a meeting of the party in Wales attacked the strategy of Thatcher and her Chancellor Nigel Lawson for what he described as the creation of a 'Loadsamoney economy'.[9] The following day an editorial in *The Daily Express* commented that a loadsamoney economy was, in fact, evidence of Mrs Thatcher's success rather than failure. The *Sun* observed: 'Better a loadsamoney economy than a loadsadebt economy.' Despite this support, such was its resonance as a term of abuse that Thatcher felt obliged to dissociate Britain and her party from the term. 'We are not a Loadsamoney economy,' she maintained. At the Conservative Party Conference of 14 October 1988, she insisted:

> We are told that all we care about is 'Loadsamoney'. Because we give people the chance to better themselves, they accuse us of encouraging selfishness and greed. What nonsense. Does someone's natural desire to do well for himself, to build a better life for his family and provide

opportunities for his children, does all this make him a materialist? Of course it doesn't.[10]

Even now 'loadsamoney' continues to be wielded pejoratively in Parliament by members across the political spectrum and is used, as recorded in Hansard, in conjunction with words and phrases such as 'budget', 'economy', 'culture', 'society' and even 'lager louts'. The spectre of Loadsamoney as a social type also persists; his enthusiasm for designer gear, his social crassness and his determination to display his wealth have helped locate him as both a 'proto-chav' and as a forerunner of current 'bling' Essex lifestyles such as those epitomised in the structured reality soap *The Only Way Is Essex* (ITV 2010–). The enduring fascination of such characters clearly embodies the worst features of both right-wing and left-liberal middle-class nightmares.

Class, taste and the Essex Girl

Although Basildon researchers Hayes and Hudson (2001a: above) were mainly concerned with the voting patterns and political opinions of their subjects, they devoted some space to contesting the depiction of Basildonians as 'tasteless' dressers (shell-suited men or mini-skirted women wearing large hoop earrings). They took the trouble to point out that, even if there were some truth in this description of these sartorial 'choices', these would have been based on relatively low earnings and that 'ordinary' or 'smart dressing' was also favoured. This commentary is indicative of the continuing importance of understanding the cultural dimensions of class politics and the ways in which the denigration or approbation of classed subjects takes place. As Beverley Skeggs has demonstrated across a substantial corpus of research, ascriptions of taste and tastelessness are attached to moral frameworks within which, for example, the working class are evaluated and often found wanting. For instance, Skeggs (2004) examines a *Daily Mirror* Mori Poll from 1997 which purports to explore whether Britain is a classless society via light-hearted questions about leisure activities, attitudes to the monarchy, holiday choices, home ownership and sexual practices. As she explains, implicit values had been attached to the cultural practices which form the basis of the questions, many of which were dependent on economic power, for example, the 'choice' to holiday in England or Tuscany. In her words, 'the significance of this example is in making obvious in popular culture the shift from class as an economic category to one based on cultural practices' (Skeggs 2004:50). This is also evident in the examples we have already seen, particularly with regard to the *Spitting Image* sketch 'Essex is crap' in which a long list of 'dubious' cultural practices and consumer goods were ascribed to Essex and Essex people.

Referencing those very shell suits, big earrings and mini-skirted women, Steph Lawler (2005:432) observes that 'the act of description itself seems enough to confer blame' and points to the ways in which these descriptions intersect with a mapping of spaces, of 'folk knowledge' about geographical areas inhabited by so-called Scousers or Essex Girls. Here classed stereotypes are figured not primarily by a lack of resources (perhaps too redolent of outmoded debates about inequality and social class) but by lack of taste, poise or even of 'class' itself. The Essex Girl stereotype, then, is burdened with multiple labels rooted in British social difference, including that she is working-class, that she is class-less (i.e. post-working-class) and that she has no class (i.e. she lacks good taste). The public criticism of this cultural type is also shot through with often unspoken attributions regarding not only gender but also race and ethnicity. So, as noted, working-class people (in every region) were satirised for wearing the shell suit (a shiny, often brightly coloured development from the tracksuit) and large gold jewellery (sovereign rings and heavy chains): fashions disseminated during the 1980s by mainly black popular culture. Hence Loadsamoney's music video, which, as noted above, was part of an attempted critique of a Thatcherite working class, featured white performers with a Hip Hop soundtrack and a performance of 'street' bravado. Two things happen here in relation to the working class and to Essex people in particular. First, as Lawler (2005:430) argues in her analysis of middle-class taste and disgust, the working class is rendered *emblematically white* even if this is contrary to its lived complexity. This is evident in the fact that Essex has been depicted as a predominantly white county, making the concept of a black Essex Girl virtually inconceivable even now in the 2010s. Celebrity Essex Girls (either born or moving to the area) such as Denise van Outen, Jodie Marsh, Jessie Wallace and Jade Goody are invariably coded as 'white' and reinforce the folklore of Essex as a white region.[11] Where an Essex Girl such as Goody (who relocated from Bermondsey in South London to Essex as part of her journey through upwards social mobility) has a mixed heritage, this has often been downplayed. Second, working-class taste and values are condemned due to a perception that they are formed via an adoption of black working-class fashion and culture. Our suspicion here is that certain negative cultural values are being attributed to black working-class cultural identity and these are then rolled over to apply to sections of the white working class who become equally disparaged (see also our discussion of the Summer 2011 riots in the next chapter).

The whiteness and crassness of Essex Girls in representation have also been consolidated through the many jokes which circulated about their intellectual limitations. This is evident in the way in which the many insulting jokes that had been levelled against 'dumb blondes' (who are implicitly white) during the 1990s (see Oring 2003:59) were quickly and easily transposed onto Essex Girls, underlining their white ethnicity alongside their vacuous venality and sexual incontinence. Indeed, the ubiquity of the Essex Girl joke was phenomenal. Essex-born journalist Sarah Ivens (2004) observed wryly: 'I am a much-maligned Essex Girl who has had the all-time classic jokes ("How does an Essex Girl turn on the light after sex? She opens the car door") retold in such far-flung places as Salvador, Reykjavik and Miami. It gets me every time.'

In his analysis of jokes and their targets, Christie Davies (2011:263) makes a connection between Essex Girls, aristocrats and peasants, arguing that these form the butt of stupidity jokes because they can be regarded as 'static classes in a modern world'.[12] While some images do present the Essex Girl as static (see Greer 2006 below), others present her as socially mobile within specific domains (e.g. the beauty and entertainment industries). These groups do, however, have something else in common – they tend to be badly underestimated in terms of their intellectual abilities, labour power and/or economic power. Ivens picked up on this, perhaps, when she recalled what she regarded as the increasingly damaging template for the Essex Girl forged during the 1980s and 1990s. She concluded that the condemnation of Essex, City boys and Essex Girls was rooted in a fear of meritocratic and economic success that owed nothing to inherited privilege or material advantage. From this perspective this disparagement did not derive from an easy mockery of a static or dying social class but from fear of a newly mobile class. In her piece reflecting back on the contribution of Thatcherism to women's lives, Ivens (2004) argued that Thatcher was indeed 'the mother of all Essex Girls:

> For the women of Essex, Margaret Thatcher was a beacon of independence. No, you don't have to rely on a man for wealth and success. No, you don't have to live in a council house forever – buy it!...Meanwhile...The boys from Basildon and Billericay cruised into the Stock Exchange with a manic drive that scared the aristos back to Mummy in Surrey.... The *nouveau riche* were at home in Essex.

Glamour could have been the name of a Romford suburb. Footballers and Page Three girls provided the Beverly Hills excitement we craved.

In popular culture, affluent Essex Girls with dubious sources of income and middle-class lifestyles (as in the situation comedy *Birds of a Feather* BBC1 1989–98), the 'wide boy' City workers themselves and a host of footballers' wives and girlfriends (sometimes referred to in the media as 'WAGS') seemed to signal a brash and rather shameless social mobility. Essex citizens have even embraced, with good humour, these connotations of celebrity ambition: while Ivens observed that 'Glamour' could have been the name of a Romford suburb, in 2010 Basildon actually rebranded itself as the hub for international business with a welcome sign resembling the LA Hollywood icon. The press seized the opportunity for more class-based banter (e.g. Levy 2010), while Essex celebrities explained why they preferred Basildon to LA. Entertainer Denise Van Outen (2010) declared in the *Sun*:

> all the Essex Girl jokes and white stiletto associations meant it [Basildon] lost a lot of its edge. But the people who live there know it still has a lot to offer. They've moved from that image and now the girls are all into the WAG look. They take pride in their appearance and the best place to get kitted out is Lakeside [out of town shopping centre].

Essex Girls also included the lower-class duo 'Sharon and Tracey', mythical figures whose slutty ways, common estuary vowels, fake designer clothes and stupidity featured in countless class-based sexist jokes. Since the 1990s the blended legacy of Essex Girls and WAGS remains evident in popular factual programming such as *Family Confidential: Basildon Boobs* (C5 1999), *Essex Wives* (ITV 2002) and *The Only Way Is Essex* (ITV 2010–) as well as in celebrity personas already cited. The persistent stereotyping of Essex Girls as promiscuous produced some convoluted journalism which fashioned itself on the notion that women from Essex were 'asking for it', a phrase used by Mathew Engel (1996) in his piece exploring why Basildon *asks* to be derided. Engel observed:

> The town's centrepiece is a statue of Mother and Child, which for a long while was converted into the council's logo. However, the reduction in size had an unfortunate effect: the baby merely looked like an

elaborate hairstyle, and the whole thing seemed like a clichéd representation of an Essex Girl with her legs open. The town's most famous nightclub Raquel's – was there ever a more Essex name? – closed down in 1995 ... It reopened last week with the name of Club Uropa Essex – Uropa as in urea.

This association of Essex with a particular kind of woman (a keen sexual partner rather than a loving mother) and the association of this woman with lower body waste (urea) together with the implication that Essex people are illiterate (Uropa not Europa) is common enough. It is also rarely a cause for public concern, aside, perhaps, for Essex people themselves. Perhaps the best-known journalistic pieces on the Essex Girl are by feminist Germaine Greer, who, in an apparently defensive move (she lives in Essex herself), figures the Essex Girl as rebellious and taboo-breaking, and urges us to revel in the stereotypes. In a piece for the *Guardian* called 'Long live the Essex Girl', Greer (2001) sets the Essex Girl up as a British soap opera working-class stereotype, suggesting that she 'sees herself as belonging to the real world of family loyalty, sexual unpredictability, underemployment and petty crime'. With regard to her promiscuous image, it's one she simply embraces:

> Nobody makes her wear her ankle chain; she likes the message it sends. Nobody laughs harder at an Essex Girl joke than she does: she is not ashamed to admit what she puts behind her ears to make her more attractive is her ankles. She is anarchy on stilts; when she and her mates descend upon Southend for a rave, even the bouncers grow pale.

With reference to this passage by Greer, in particular, Beverley Skeggs (2005:967) observes that what takes place here, as well as in political discourse, is the repetition of the 'historical-representational moralizing, pathologizing, disgust-producing register attached to working class women'. Greer's paean to the Essex Girl is little consolation when it is embedded in and barely reformulates an age-old lexicon of young working-class women as unruly and unclean. Five years later it seemed that the Essex Girl was still topical. Writing after the successful appearance of Essex-born Chantelle Houghton on *Celebrity Big Brother* (C4 2006: the only non-celebrity in the house, an impostor, who trumps the real celebrities), Greer (2006) writes in defence of the Essex Girl:

The Essex Girl is a working-class heroine surviving in a post-proletarian world. She is descended from the mill girls who terrorised their neighbourhoods, raucous, defiant, pleasure-seeking....
No matter how much cash might be sloshing through her household, she is working-class and means to stay that way. She is not only not interested in social climbing, she doesn't know there's anywhere to climb to.

Here Greer's proposal of a historical lineage underlines the hearty working-class core of the Essex Girl who is happy with her lot in life. She suggests that the best of them abjure aspiration and class mobility. Sarah Ivens's (above) praise of the Essex Girl is premised on the fact that she embraces opportunities for social advancement with gusto and that she is a threat to the social order. Greer's own defence is premised on the notion that not only is she uninterested in social advancement but that she isn't even aware that this is an option.

To conclude, we have tracked the ways in which the denigration of particular Essex figures is cloaked in humour and the aggression of gendered, sexualised and classed mockery. We make the case here that these figures, and the enduring political mythology within which they have been embedded, demonstrate the potency and resonance of the classed stereotype during periods of intense political, cultural and social change. Essex Man, Loadsamoney and Essex Girl are, as we understand them here, figures in a classed landscape. Their portraits bear the traces of the originating moment when consumerism, entrepreneurialism and aspiration were fuelled by and woven into the political discourses and fantasies of Thatcherism and its aftermath. And, as such, they were bound to be unsettling. They represented an ostentatious desire for the good life and for personal respect, together with a refusal to quietly and carefully brand themselves with markers of mannered, discreet good taste and decorum. They are emblematic figures who also expressed, for those who understood them more empathetically, a classed longing and a defiant belief in their own self-worth.

Finally, we propose that Essex Man, Essex Girl and Loadsamoney, like all political types and popular caricatures perhaps, also contained within them some kernel of truth, some sharp twist of the real. We think, perhaps, that part of the discomfort they inspired, the all too easy way in which they were mocked by the many but also celebrated by some, was due to the fact that they scandalously unveiled the undertow of finance capitalism for what it is: the lifeblood of going-somewhere individuals who could only succeed by leaving their slower, less successful, less fortunate peers behind. There is a brutish, bold 'get out of my way because I'm worth it' bravado attached to these figures which appears to disconnect them from their classed, collective moorings in the service of individual success. Britons may not like it, but surely this attitude and its social consequences are also part and parcel of the neoliberal culture that Thatcherism ushered in for everyone – whether they are from Essex or not.

3

The Revolting Underclass: 'You Know Them When You See Them'

The 2011 English riots and the 'feral underclass'

> From time to time the outcasts of the consumer society assume
> the role of its Luddites – going on the rampage...; committing
> acts which are immediately represented as riots and thus supply
> a further proof, if a further proof was needed, that the question
> of the underclass is – first and foremost, perhaps even solely –
> the problem of law and order.
>
> (Bauman 1997:221)

During four warm summer days in August 2011 several London
boroughs and various city and town districts across England experienced rioting, looting and arson. The first night of rioting took place
on 6 August 2011. The violence flared up following a peaceful protest in
Tottenham, North London, which had marked the death of a local man
called Mark Duggan who had been shot dead by police 48 hours earlier.
The ensuing days saw similar scenes of social unrest in other parts of
the capital, including in the 'shopping Mecca' of Oxford Circus, and
subsequently in other cities, including Bristol, Manchester, Birmingham
and Liverpool. The riots were characterised by flagrant looting of shops,
damage to cars and fire-starting (see Bridges 2012). News reports made
much of the looters' particular interest in branded sportswear and 'big
ticket' consumer goods such as televisions and mobile phones, and these
actions were read by some as 'shopping with violence'. As a result of
these events, all police leave was cancelled and Parliament was recalled
on 11 August to debate the situation. The outcome of the troubles
included five deaths, various injuries and substantial property damage
as well as significant harm to retail trading during a period of ongoing

economic hardship. At the time it seemed to be clear enough what kind of people the perpetrators were, with news reports either proposing or amplifying prevalent proposals that the underclass was to blame.[1] For example, on 6 August the *Sun* and the *Telegraph* both followed political cues with 'Feral underclass to blame for riots', on 8 August the *Telegraph* declared 'the underclass lashes out' (Ridell 2011) and on 11 August *BBC online* headlined 'England riots: the return of the underclass' (Easton 2011). As the BBC Home Editor Mark Easton (2011) observed, in one of the more considered pieces to follow these incidents, 'the word underclass with its connotations of fecklessness and criminality...is back, a headline-writer's shorthand for the undeserving and dangerous poor who are burning and robbing their own communities.'

Both at the time and in early retrospect politicians, policy advisors and commentators from across the political spectrum seemed to agree that an underclass existed, even if they disagreed on its origins, dimensions and perpetuation. So Justice Secretary Kenneth Clarke pointed to August's riots as clear evidence that the UK's 'feral underclass' was growing and that it needed to be 'diminished' (*BBC News* 6 September 2011 and ITN News 4 October 2011). So, too, Secretary of State for Education Michael Gove exposed the inner life of the underclass to reveal its essential inhumanity.

> It is from that underclass that gangs draw their recruits, young offenders institutions find their inmates and prisons replenish their cells. These are young people who, whatever the material circumstances which surround them, grow up in the direst poverty – with a poverty of ambition, a poverty of discipline, a poverty of soul.
>
> (Michael Gove in Porter 2011)

Speaking with the summer riots as a painful recent memory, Gove drew on a common reading of the underclass; one which explicitly divorced the young offenders or assumed 'gang members' from any causal 'material circumstances' or socio-economic conditions and linked them instead to an individual and internal spiritual and moral worthlessness. If ever the underclass could be read as a genuine class fraction or their trouble-making actions understood as symptomatic of a class struggle, then those times, according to many politicians and cultural commentators, were now long gone. It was mainly young people who appeared in image after image on television screens. They were seen erupting out of smashed shop fronts, arms laden with goods, or huddled in high streets contemplating the destruction, debris and scattered consumer goods. News reports generally presented the riots as a sign of contemporary urban anomie in which getting-without-paying and shopping with violence seemed to be the order of the day. The term underclass was reinvigorated as a sign of spiritual rather than material impoverishment, in which a paucity of individual ambition and a collapse of self-discipline resulted in a newly dangerous violent cycle of expectation on the part of those excluded (or self-excluded) from gainful employment, family and civic responsibility.

A few weeks later Work and Pensions Secretary Iain Duncan Smith predictably outlined the source of the getting-without-paying attitude; that is, a corrosive welfare system which provided the 'familiar context to the riots in the shape of a rising underclass characterised by chaos and dysfunctionality... and governed by a perverse set of values' (in Mulholland 2011). Later that month the *Sun* newspaper declared in a typically incendiary piece entitled 'I predict a rioter: hundreds on benefits or dole, fear at black youth numbers' that 'THUGS held in the August riots were part of a feckless criminal underclass – with one in eight on DISABILITY benefits, figures reveal' (Wilson 2011). The more informed comments of black community figures were also included, calling for the recognition of the condition of the 'workless poor' with futures they wished to reject. These were relegated to the end of the piece and accorded little reflection. Defenders of young people such as Camila Batmanghelidjh, the founder of a children's charity, Kids Company, which helps vulnerable young people, also referred to the underclass in interview. She made the case that the underclass had been damaged (and were damaging others) through civic disregard and neglect rather than through wilful antisocial behaviour, inflated resentment or media glorification (BBC Radio 5 Live 8 August 2011). In her article for the *Independent* she also contended that the 'community has selected who is worthy of help and who is not. In this false moral economy where the poor are described as dysfunctional, the community fails' (Batmanghelidjh 2011). So, too, Canadian cultural critic Naomi Klein (2011:12) observed that, while the looting was not overtly political, it still signalled a locked-out 'ballooning underclass' whose few routes to social mobility were being rapidly sealed off thanks to the wider avariciousness of the elite classes.

Others who accorded with Klein's views avoided underclass terminology but still pursued the argument that the riots were actually a symptom of a greedy society. They made the case that bankers, MPs and other elites had exploited systems to their financial betterment and the rest had embraced 'get now, pay later' values in which the acquisition of consumer goods had become an end in itself. Zoe Williams (2011), writing in the *Guardian*, was one of those who offered this 'pragmatic explanation': 'this is what happens when people don't have anything, when they have their noses constantly rubbed in stuff they can't afford, and they have no reason ever to believe that they will be able to afford it.' We will return to this configuration of anger, longing and resentment at the end of this chapter when we discuss the identification of the 'precariat' as the so-called new dangerous class (Standing 2011b). But here it is worth signalling already the way that envy sits alongside anger and resentment: feelings attributed to those perpetrating the damage to properties and commercial sites in August 2011.

In her discussion of 'ugly emotions' Sianne Ngai (2005) highlights the importance of antagonism in the affective network of social relations into which envy fits. She suggests (2005:128) that 'envy lacks cultural recognition as a valid mode of publicly recognizing or responding to social disparities, even though it remains the *only* agonistic emotion defined as having a perceived inequality as its object.' She signals the way that envy was invalidated historically as a *classed* emotion. It was informed by nineteenth-century ideologies of *ressentiment* which denigrated those who use envy as a way of expressing a sense of inferiority against an *other* by insisting that such envy is a psychological/individual flaw. Relevantly for many of the sweeping criticisms of underclass rioters, Ngai (p. 129) argues that dominant cultural representations of envy strip it of any polemicism and thereby reduce an emotion which might have a social foundation to a 'deficient and possibly histrionic selfhood'. Such criticisms moralise and render this emotion ugly rather than seek out and acknowledge envy's 'ability to recognize, and antagonistically respond to, potentially real and institutionalized forms of inequality' (Ngai:ibid.). As she goes on to demonstrate via Freudian theory, envy is actually a precondition of group identity and hostility is the ugly feeling that ultimately must be dropped or reversed if one is to become involved in collective belonging. Politicians' critical reflections on the riots generally failed to consider or else chose to reject the possibility that any envy expressed there might arise from the felt daily existence of socio-economic inequality; instead it seemed obvious that this was an envy rooted in individual avarice and lazy entitlement.

Mainstream political responses were mostly less concerned with placing this very frightening outrage in social context and more focused on spotting the clear markers of the underclass, who not only evidentially existed but was also increasingly conspicuous. Nascent debates about the declining opportunities for social mobility, the lack of secure employment, challenged family and communal structures, and so on were overwhelmed by reports which chose to mark out and codify 'deviants'. These were individuals who, much to the consternation of politicians, were apparently no longer content to live in isolated pockets on the margins of the social and at the edge of public visibility. Here spatial and bodily tropes of proper and improper behaviour in public space were used to mark the underclass out as a rude intrusion on middle-class (often white) urban and suburban respectability.

Charlie Taylor (2012), an advisor on education and behaviour to the Department of Education, reminded readers in his piece for the *Daily Telegraph* that 'we' all know how to spot the underclass: 'We know them when we see them – hoods up, trousers halfway down to their knees, swaggering along the pavement in small groups, playing loud music on their phones, swearing, spitting... these are the educational underclass.' Similarly, a reader's letter to the *Independent* in the wake of the riots also stressed the overwhelming visibility of the underclass and of the underclass values paraded across the media as well as on the streets: 'We see in contemporary Britain an unprecedented glorification of ugliness, irresponsibility and underclass conduct in clothing, language, music, literature and the media while so-called middle-class values have undergone 50 or more years of cynical erosion' (McGregor 2011).

Meanwhile *Prospect* magazine's David Goodhart (2011) argued in his blog and article on the riots that underclass attitudes have emerged and hardened via an 'Anglo-Jamaican tragedy' created by the resentment articulated in black popular music originating from the Black American ghettoes of the 1980s (see also Malik 2011). He contended that: 'The nihilistic grievance culture of the black inner city, fanned by parts of the hip-hop/rap scene and copied by many white people, has created a hardcore sub-culture of post-political disaffection.' And all this despite the fact that the 'war is over' in terms of the damaging race relations of earlier decades! A very small minority then expressed the highly controversial view that black culture had somehow contaminated a white, probably underclass population, with historian David Starkey observing, 'what has happened is that a substantial section of chavs... have become black' (in Quinn 2011). This dubious equation involved making cultural attributions, with Starkey remarking that 'nihilistic gangster culture has become the fashion and black and white girls and boys operate in this language together' (in Quinn 2011). This explicitly offensive statement is indicative of the ongoing discursive production of white classed and 'failing' subjects through an alignment with 'other' racialised categories (see McClintock 1995). There is an imputation here that a 'natural' cultural order (an impossible conjunction) has been undermined and that 'differences' of black and white have been eroded, and for the worse rather than the better. In his essay 'The Spectacle of the other' Stuart Hall (1997) offers four different models to assist in understanding how the 'other' becomes the object of fascination and/or condemnation, including one developed from structural anthropology and the work of Mary Douglas, which clearly addresses how cultural classifications operate. As Hall (1997:330) notes, this structural model proposes that 'stable cultures require things to stay in their appointed place . . . what unsettles culture is "matter out of place" – the breaking of our unwritten rules and codes'. Hall goes on to explain that the strategy undertaken when the social order is under pressure is to close down, stigmatise or expel anything which threatens the core; but paradoxically that which is expelled also becomes culturally fascinating. Hall concludes by quoting Barbara Babcock's (1978:32) famous assertion that 'what is socially peripheral is often symbolically centred.' The history of the underclass, then, is one in which a social group spied only with peripheral vision is nonetheless the object of intense scrutiny.

The language of the underclass is a fresh articulation of older discourses describing variously the unruly mob, the criminal urban underworld, a racialised outsider class and, most consistently, the undeserving poor (see Gidley and Rook 2010). So, too, the notion that these types of people 'have always been with us' as a social problem (what used to be referred to in the nineteenth century as a 'social residuum') persists in debates which suggest that riots of this type are eternally recurrent (see Welshman 2006:7–8). This is evident, for example, in journalist Mary Ridell's (2011) observation that the English riots were 'the most arcane of uprisings and the most modern', pointing perhaps towards what many saw as the novel congruence of ancient mob rule with new media communications and 'extreme shopping', described elsewhere as an 'orgy of shopping' or 'turbo-consumerism'.[2] Tellingly, observers also suggested that, while English riots have historically flared up during times of economic pressure, this violence was *qualitatively* different from that of earlier times and all the worse for it. For instance, *Times* columnist and former Conservative MP Matthew Parris (2011) observed:

What distinguishes (if anything really does) this week's rioting from the classic and time-honoured English riot is that our underclass is now so small. The white working class is disappearing; a black middle class is growing; and the residue – if human beings should ever be called a residue – cannot amount to more than about 1 per cent of our population.

A common observance was that the 'classic and time-honoured' riot of the past was spurred by class politics and the rebellion of the disenfranchised, while the current riot was symptomatic merely of poor discipline and the greed of the 'socially dysfunctional and barely employable' (Parris 2011). This division between righteous rebellion and unruly revolt is clearly bound up with an attempt to diminish the significance of the underclass figure even as it becomes central to the imagination of safely-past forms of dissent. It was inevitable too, then, that comparisons would be made with the riots of the early 1980s (and to a lesser extent of 1991 and 2001) to the detriment of the current offenders. Whereas these same commentators might well have condemned the riots of 30 years earlier as mindless violence, with hindsight they attracted a rather more sympathetic gloss. Importantly, it was confidently claimed that the 2011 riots were without *real cause* in terms of class politics, *unlike the events of the Thatcher years*. For instance, Tory Cabinet Minister Iain Duncan Smith, someone unlikely to look back sympathetically on the disorder of the 1980s which took place under his government, observed in interview: 'These riots were not riots like the ones in the '80s. These were intensely criminal activities' (*Panorama*, 15 August 2011). Others such as cultural historian Clive Bloom (2011), writing in the *Financial Times*, carefully differentiated between the trigger event in Tottenham and subsequent spreading of trouble across the country to reach a similar conclusion that the riots were not political: 'These are events devoid of political intent ... These are riots marked out by the looting of Foot Locker and Nando's – the shopping places of Britain's new underclass.'

As Zygmunt Bauman (1997 above) notes, violent flare-ups such as those of 1981, 1991 and 2011 are the common flash-points for the reinvigoration of underclass terminology in public debate, and 'law and order' becomes the rallying cry of those intent on managing the underclass. In not all cases will the offences themselves finally be attributed solely to the social groups initially blamed, but from our perspective this is irrelevant. What we are concerned with here is the speedy attribution of a disparaging class label and its cognate terms (e.g. mob, feral, idle, evil, sick) even before the social composition of the rioters is usually known. In the case of what has become known as the 'English Riots' of 2011 subsequent investigations revealed the huge diversity of motivations, the variety of rioter profiles and the impossibility of identifying either a common cause or a common profile for those taking part in unlawful activity across the 66 different areas that experienced trouble.[3] While very many perpetrators were repeat offenders, others had no criminal records; there were also many more young adults than 'youths', and a minority of rioters were from affluent backgrounds. What is important, then, is that some types of crime, some kinds of civil strife, some public acts of rule-breaking and disorder commonly attract the underclass label long before the culprits have been identified. This attachment reinforces the usual pathological associations of the underclass with poor uneducated whites ('chavs', the Irish, travellers) and other impoverished ethnic groups (e.g. Pakistanis and Bangladeshis), with black popular culture (music and the scene more generally), with disaffected youth and out of control children (the 'feral') and with conspicuous bad conduct.[4] We argue in this chapter, therefore, that a proper understanding of the way in which groups or fractions are both labelled and characterised in any particular period helps us to appreciate not so much the real material difficulties and dispositions of people living in poverty or social marginalisation or the true meaning of the consumer society, but rather the symbolic functions of the underclass as avatars of blame for social disorder, crime and declining standards of behaviour. We will argue that this is evident in the ways in which crime and disorder have been attributed to the 'non-productive' classes in both the 1980s and late in the first decade of the 2000s, and also in the insistence that the 2011 English Riots were wholly un-political and therefore largely meaningless in terms of class politics.

In order to pursue this we move on to explore key political and popular discursive features of the so-called underclass since Thatcherism. In doing so, the chapter offers a consideration of the ongoing positing of the underclass as morally dissolute, 'shameless' and socially corrosive and therefore dangerous. We explore its metaphorical location as marginal to the social but also as symbolically central (Babcock 1978:32) and its importance, therefore, as a focus of collective fascination as well as of anxiety. To pursue this we begin by unpacking the vocabulary of the underclass and its cognate terms in relation to a considered understanding of class hierarchies and the changing model of social and class relations under Thatcherism and subsequent administrations. We then go on to highlight various exemplary depictions of the criminal and criminogenic underclass since the 1990s, including its appearance in news reports and political debate.[5] Finally, we will return to the English Riots of 2011 to further unpack their depiction in the media and subsequent considerations of their political and social significance. We end by considering how so-called underclass subjects are represented not as political actors but as social subjects found guilty of aberrant consumption by 'shopping with violence'.

The 1980s: 'the underclass, so long prophesied, is now emerging'

While the concept of the underclass as a sociological category for class analysis has been strongly challenged by many sociologists (see Edgell 1993:79, Marshall *et al*. 1996, Buckingham 1999), for the media and in political debate underclass continues to be a useful term to apply to other people. As an ideologically loaded and mostly pejorative term it is also an attribution no sensible person would wish to accept for themselves or their kin.[6] Whereas it is quite conceivable that individuals might be happy to self-identify as working-class or middle-class, underclass is a label consistently pinned onto others. This is likely to be because, whether it is used as a socio-economic category (a class or class fraction) or as a social category (a social type), its connotations are relentlessly disparaging and/or unhopeful. Whereas 'working-class' continues to signify for some a persistent if weakened attachment to a politics of class respect (or at least to the practices of paid work), for the underclass no such associations exist. Whereas a political party might seek to be the party of middle-class common sense or working-class aspiration, no major political party in recent times audibly expresses an interest in being the party of the underclass. The underclass, then, is doubly exiled from both social and political cultures.

Many commentators cite Sir Keith Joseph's 1972 'cycle of deprivation' speech and his later, better-known 1974 Edgbaston speech commonly entitled 'Our human stock is threatened' as key landmarks in the redrafted cartography of class in which the persistently poor and unwaged would be located as morally suspect, criminally inclined and, importantly, as welfare-dependent (see Hall *et al*. 1978:338). In the Edgbaston speech Conservative Minister Joseph (who was later to become a key advisor to Margaret Thatcher) asks, rhetorically, whether Britain is 'willing to be destroyed from the inside' and argues for the 'remoralisation of whole groups and classes' (Joseph 1974). He goes on to indicate that the enemy within originates with unmarried mothers, whose offspring will populate what seems to be a netherworld:

> many are deserted or divorced or soon will be. Some are of low intelligence, most of low educational attainment. They are unlikely to

be able to give children the stable emotional background, the consistent combination of love and firmness which are more important than riches. They are producing problem children, the future unmarried mothers, delinquents, denizens of our borstals, sub-normal educational establishments, prisons, hostels for drifters.

As John Welshman (2006:113) observes in his indispensable history of the underclass, Joseph's solutions were mostly behavioural rather than structural or economic, and what was innovative in his thinking was the emphasis on trans-generational transmission of social dysfunction (see also Townsend 1979). Welshman explains that the longer-term significance of Joseph's speeches and the social policy research with which they were linked lay in the later connections made between the cycle of deprivation thesis, the transmission of poverty across generations and the rather melodramatic concept of the underclass, which had existed in earlier decades but came to prominence in Britain in the 1980s.

The academic theorisation and deployment of the term underclass itself originally appeared in English in the 1960s as a part of an economic analysis formulated by left-liberal thinker Gunnar Myrdal (1963), who defined it as an underprivileged class of unemployed, unemployables and underemployed who were essentially and hopelessly set apart from the nation at large. While the term was picked up in scholarship (see O'Connor 2001:242–83) and by the press during the 1970s, it was actually during the 1980s that it was thoroughly popularised.[7] US commentators such as the *New Yorker* journalist Ken Auletta (1982) helped usher it into common usage. Drawing on his own observations and available statistics, Auletta depicted a somewhat colourful underclass of former prisoners, drug addicts, delinquents and welfare regulars. Following a group taking part in a work support programme, he recorded its members' observations on a variety of issues including the welfare mentality, alcoholism, drugs, crime, unemployment, racism and black matriarchies. He concluded that there was a 'hardcore' of poor, mostly black people whose problems extended far beyond poverty and that they were generally unsocialised in any way that would be acceptable to most citizens. This interpretation of the underclass differed from that of Myrdal, who maintained that, while the underclass was essentially hapless and unproductive, it was also blameless; its subjects unfortunately caught up in economic difficulties and structurally ill equipped to take up any opportunities which might come their way. In contrast, popularisers of the term such as Auletta leant heavily towards a more behavioural, blame-oriented model. For critics such as the sociologist Herbert Gans (1995:35, see also Wacquant 2008:44) it was Auletta and other American journalists writing during the 1980s who both popularised the term and fuelled its demonising inferences. Finally, we might note that, while it is rare for sociological terms to gain a regular mention in the news, it is safe to say that journalism has in the past and still continues to substantially sustain underclass terminology through its periodic reconstructions as a descriptor for the 'dangerous classes' or, to put it more simply, for 'idle thieving bastards' (Bagguley and Mann 1992).

So, while the term underclass was deployed politically in Britain from the 1970s, frequently in the context of debates about structural (e.g. racial) inequalities and their impact on the material conditions of marginalised, often ethnic minority groups, it was not until the 1980s that it properly reached public attention (Lister 1996:2). This followed closely behind the importation of another American (albeit non-sociological) term, 'mugging', which, in the British press, became attached particularly to street robbery with violence and was cross-hatched with raced and classed assumptions about declining moral standards (Hall *et al.* 1978). As with this mugging 'crisis' of a few years earlier, US debates about the values of the socially excluded and/or the structural limitations of the labour market were also imported and reworked by British social analysts. For instance, the sociologist Ralf Dahrendorf (1987) outlined an 'erosion of citizenship' thesis in the left-wing magazine *New Statesman* which identified a series of social pathologies and a 'syndrome of deprivation' whose neglect by mainstream society cast doubt on the very social contract of inclusive citizenship (see Welshman 2006:161–2). Commentators from across the political spectrum identified an expanding group of the unemployed and 'sinking poor' who were characterised by illiteracy, football hooliganism, alcohol dependency, and so on. Thus it was during the 1980s that the term underclass eclipsed the term 'underprivileged' as a descriptor for struggling citizens who were not simply pauperised but also undeserving. As Raymond Williams (1983:324) noted, older terms such as 'underprivileged' implied some sympathy for the predicament of the poor which later terms have jettisoned. So the term underclass, which superseded it, has often (but not always) been deployed to suggest that some element of 'choice' and low morals had to be accounted for when explaining how poor people remain poor, especially across the generations. In other words, the underclass's tendency to make 'bad choices' was in itself a cause for concern.

When the politics of social class surfaced during the 1980s it was particularly around public disorder and youth culture, with the underclass becoming one of the 'key terms in the discourses grouped around Thatcherism' (Hall and Jefferson 2006:xvi). While Margaret Thatcher herself disapproved of the term (predictably because of its *class* politics connotations, which she rejected utterly), it clearly resonated with fellow politicians, including those of her own party.[8] Those on the left of the political spectrum deployed it to critique the social conditions which they argued were engendered by Conservative policies and those on the right to critique certain permissive values and standards of behaviour which they felt were weakening the overall fabric of society.[9] So, too, social commentators trying to understand some of the phenomena arising under Thatcherism, such as the so-called race riots or social protest uprisings of 1980–81, turned to an underclass lexicon. This civil unrest took place in over 30 locations across Britain. The dominant reading of the events was that they were highly racialised actions (Lea and Young 1982, Jacobs 1988, Gilroy 1987). While some news reports bewilderedly observed that whites joined blacks in the disturbances, the most 'Powellite' commentators critically condemned the 'black mobs' ranged against the 'thin blue line of the police' (Shirley 1981, Solomos 2003:146–7). Media pundits also read them against a backdrop of the ongoing underclass concerns already described; viewing them as evidence of declining social standards epitomised by easily accessible pornography, football hooliganism, idleness, promiscuity, and so forth. The fears expressed in the press were both racial and generational, conjuring nightmarish images of young people as 'stunted demons emerging from the shadows' (in Holland 1992:117).

Social critics from the left, such as those contributing to the groundbreaking collective work *Policing the Crisis*, read the state's attitude to social disorder from the late 1970s as essentially one of declassing social unrest (Hall *et al.* 1978:161, 394). For example, *Policing*, which focused on the demonisation of youth and especially black youth in the context of economic pressure in the late 1970s, underlined the way in which political discourses worked to section off the 'dangerous classes' or even declassed them utterly as folk devils who were simply gratuitously violent, disrespectful and dissolute. In the words of Michael Brake and Chris Hale (1992:48), social anxieties in the late 1970s regarding rioters, strikers, 'benefit scroungers', black 'immigrants', and so on pointed to the ways in which ' . . . crises in class relations became written as crises in authority relations' and in this move 'we can see the development of the control culture of the 1980s.' Thus, while for some commentators at the time and in retrospect the 1980–81 riots were essentially political, albeit leaderless and disorganised, for others these were individualistic and avaricious acts. In the words of Tory minister Douglas Hurd these were 'a cry for loot rather than a cry for help' (in Kim 2010:229). For Thatcher herself the motivation for these events was 'nothing more complicated than human wickedness' (Young 1989:234, see also Brake and Hale 1992:26–31). For those in her government who sought more complex explanations, the floodgates for its expression were opened by the permissive society whose tide would need to be turned by a return to 'Victorian values' and the rolling back of the welfare state (see Nunn 2002:118–19).

For those from the political left, the public order troubles of this period, which also, of course, included industrial strife and Northern Irish conflicts, were definitely rooted in class structures and therefore class politics. For example, the Marxist historian Eric Hobsbawm (1995:334) charted the emergence of the underclass as a social formation rather than a sociological concept or pejorative label during the 1980s. He viewed its development as the outcome of significant economic changes resulting in a 'cultural revolution' in which the individual triumphed over society and in which unifying social and community values were increasingly undermined. He claimed (1995:ibid.): 'This became evident in the era of neoliberal ideology, when the macabre term "the underclass" entered or re-entered the socio-political vocabulary around 1980.' For Hobsbawm (1995:340) the underclass, corralled in a netherworld beyond 'normal society', was doubly damned because it lived without material advantages and without the traditions, community and values which should have supported it in difficult times. Its presence was regarded as both an antisocial menace to law-abiding 'responsible' citizens and increasingly a threat to the capitalist economy which had historically relied on the 'habit of labour' sustained by the very families and communities whose security was being eroded (Hobsbawm:342).

The left-leaning political classes, most notably political opposition leaders, also chose to critique Thatcherism precisely on the basis that it drove profound and damaging inequalities and thus created an underclass. For instance, Liberal leader David Steel (1985), speaking in the context of very high unemployment a few years after the inner-city riots, rejected the notion that the unemployed should simply try harder to find work:

People working together to get things done for their own communities...that must be our starting point. It is no good telling them to get on their bike and go elsewhere. It is precisely the people with initiative, the self starters, who must be persuaded to stay if these communities are to thrive. Otherwise, we shall be left with a permanent underclass of those who cannot escape – the single parents, the unskilled, the ethnic minorities, the elderly – eking out a frightened existence in the twilight zones.

That same year Shirley Williams of the SDP declared, 'the underclass, so long prophesied, is now emerging...bored, threatening and without hope' (in Bagguley and Mann 1992:113). Three years later Labour Party leader Neil Kinnock (1988) warned of the increasing stratification of society, of a society 'divided into three unequal parts – a small, opulent superclass at the top; a larger class of people living in reasonable but sometimes anxious affluence in the middle...and at the bottom a third class, an underclass of people living in dire need'.

Hobsbawm (1995:304) described the economic changes of the period to which opposition leaders were referring as a time of 'veritable industrial holocaust' as the working classes and especially unskilled and semi-skilled labour 'visibly became the victims of the new technologies', of the atrophy of industrial development and a series of economic crises. Those left in its wake (and in the wake of more recent economic disasters such as the 2008 crash) became either 'displaced class actors' (Marshall *et al.* 1996:30) or an underclass, depending upon one's preferred terminology. However, for Hobsbawm (1995:305–8), the real crisis was 'not one of the class, but of its consciousness'. This was a crisis lengthy in gestation but, as indicated in our Introduction, perhaps only fully realisable in Thatcher's Britain as the pressures of neoliberal economic and social policy divided the 'top end' of the working class, who were flexible and skilled, from those at the bottom whose economic situation deteriorated. Of those at the bottom a section came to be regarded negatively as an underclass problematically subsisting on the benefits provided by their industrious and above all 'respectable' betters (see Hall *et al.* 1978:140ff).

The 1990s: from the underclass to the socially excluded

The underclass label was revived once again in Britain during the 1990s. This time it was more greatly popularised by the American social policy analyst Charles Murray (1984), whose argument, heavily sponsored by the *Sunday Times* newspaper, was with welfare as a primary cause of dependency, fecklessness and criminally antisocial behaviour. Echoing far older historical associations of the lower classes with waste and disease, he described himself as a visitor from a 'plague' area keen to discover if Britain too was being infected. In his article called 'The emerging British underclass', written at the tail end of the 1980s at the invitation of the *Sunday Times Magazine*, Murray contended that the term underclass did not refer to a '*degree* of poverty, but to a *type* of poverty' (Murray 1989:23, our emphases). Here he shifted emphasis away from the economic and material and towards discussion of flawed sociality as evidenced by character traits. Here poverty was characterised by illegitimacy, crime ('the habitual criminal is the classic member of an underclass'), wilful unemployment and the lack of the working habit for a proportion of British youth (Murray 1989:ibid.).[10] In his 'shocking' 1994 rejoinder report Murray (1994a) narrowed his focus more closely on the family unit and its breakdown as one of the primary factors in what he characterised as a deepening 'crisis'.

Murray's underclass pieces focused on the growing divide between the respectable and unrespectable classes and the criminal threat to the vast majority of the population. A week after the 'Crisis deepens' piece the *Sunday Times* published Murray's (1994b) substantial follow-up report entitled 'The New Victorians.' Whereas the first piece was illustrated with an image of five white youths on a shabby council estate, this piece presented an outside shot of a well-dressed white couple and their two children together with the tag: 'Surrey 1994: the people who are able to afford it will move further from the inner city to be safe.' Here Murray explained how the upper middle classes, the 'New Victorians', would move away and segregate themselves from the 'New Rabble'. Murray plainly itemised the characteristics of the New Victorians: they were educated professionals who were more oriented towards children and community than to professional advancement, with a 'revived interest in religion and spiritual matters' and a renewed concern for concepts such as sexual fidelity, restraint, moderation, loyalty and courage. The New Rabble, on the other hand, was comprised of the uneducated workshy who formed the 'large and lucrative market' for violent films and pornography and was 'impervious' to social policies which sought to alter its behaviour. Part of Murray's solution was to reinstate the intolerable economic penalties which had historically prevented single mothers, in particular, from becoming a viable economic unit (i.e. eliminate state support for unmarried mothers). The *Sunday*

Times showcased Murray's ideas and helped usher them into general circulation.

Hence it is from this period and throughout the 1990s that reportage, governmental and popular criminological projections onto the figure of the single mother, in particular, characterised the 'broken home' as the site of crime production and the conduit of the damaging legacy from the 1960s of moral weakness, drug abuse, lack of respect for authorities and 'deviant' sexualities (Young 1996:147). So, too, more riots in 1991, which took place in municipal centres in Cardiff, Oxford and Tyneside, continued to provide evidence for those who sought it of the 'dangerous classes' and even of the 'black underclass' despite the complex and multiracial nature of the troubles (Hasan 2000). As Beatrix Campbell (1993:97) noted, these events, which devastated rioters' own already badly damaged communities and which were fissured by gender, generation and race as well as class, tested the new regimes of public order and policing set-up following the disorder of the previous decade. Crime and disorder were presented as both the evidence and the result of underclass lifestyles.

Lone (that is, never married) mothers were singled out as formative members of the British underclass across social policy, new right scholarship and in the media (Duncan *et al.* 1999:239). As we have seen, the early 1990s actually witnessed a reinvigoration of these projections with a confluence of journalistic and governmental discourses situating the single mother, especially the never-married, 'wilfully' single, younger lower-class mother, as the breach in the social contract whose abnegation of responsibility for her children would have dire social consequences (see Young 1996:155–68). For example, government speeches throughout the 1993–94 period increasingly distinguished between the 'blameless' or 'decent' single parent (widowed or unavoidably divorced) and the hapless girl who 'drifts' into pregnancy only to end up 'married to the state', lured by the 'attractive prospect' of welfare support (Young 1996:155). Conservative policy (the Child Support Act 1991, the associated establishment of the Child Support Agency in 1993 and redefinitions of local authority housing priorities) sought to lessen these attractions and to reassure 'responsible' tax-payers that they were not being tapped to support unorthodox and feckless lifestyles.

These criminogenic families were (and continue to be) figured as the source of underclass crime (see Nunn and Biressi 2009). Overall, a high degree of consensus developed during the early 1990s uniting politicians and commentators in hostility to never-married mothers as the hub of these families (Mann and Roseneil 1994). For example, in journalism serious crimes such as the murder of infant James Bulger by two older boys continued to be addressed as underclass phenomena, with papers such as the *Sunday Times* (28 February 1993) maintaining their keen interest in the problematic culture of underclass lifestyles.[11] Newspaper spreads devoted to exposing the problem of welfare dependency underlined the dismal social consequences of women being 'wedded to welfare' (Mann and Roseneil 1996:199). John Major's call, which was made in the light of the Bulger case, to 'condemn a little more and understand a little less' was subsequently embraced by large sections of the press (see Mann and Roseneil 1996, Jones and Novak 1999:2, Conway 2010). By and large the case fed into a wider consensus about the underclass problem. This drew on moral codes and economic arguments from a range of perspectives (including Christian socialism and hard-line Thatcherism) in the calculation of the social and economic costs of state support (Mann and Roseneil 1994:193). Put most brutally by criminologist Robert McAuley (2007:153): 'successive Conservative administrations were elected because Britain's consumer society had a stake in objectifying its own waste: communities living and working in poverty.'

But, while the underclass tag continued to be used as a shorthand descriptor by social commentators in the media, by the mid-1990s it had fallen out of favour with policy-makers. New Labour came to power in 1997 and with it came a reformulated vision of British meritocracy in which the emphasis was on the energy of a new national mood which would recharge the Conservative notion of the classless society and the philosophy of equality of opportunity. Tony Blair did start out by deploying the underclass label to denote those living 'inactive lives' on benefit and without any sense of society's 'shared purpose' (*ITV Late Evening News* 2 June 1997). In this televised speech the purpose itself remained vague and unexplained, as though it was self-evident to all but those living these inactive lives. The underclass problem also became the spur to the establishment of a new Anti-Poverty Unit. In the early part of 2000 the *Sunday Times* also revived the underclass debate, asking Charles Murray to once again reflect on the underclass a decade on from his landmark article. In his piece 'Underclass+10' he observed that the British underclass, as he defined them (i.e. not merely poor, but 'unsocialised and often violent', the 'chronic criminal' and the parents 'who mean well but cannot provide for themselves, who give nothing back to the neighbourhood'), had expanded to resemble more closely in both behaviour and number their American cousins. For him the key indicators of underclass lifestyle had increased: the young male 'drop out' from the world of work, unmarried motherhood and violent crime (Murray 2001:3); with the decline of the traditional family unit as the fundamental cause of its expansion. It seemed, then, that the decade would end as it had begun, with a return by the press and social commentators to the language of the underclass.

However, it turned out that under New Labour 'social exclusion' became the descriptor of choice for policy-makers; a move which was partly due to the influence of European Union initiatives (Walker and Walker 1997:7). Generally speaking, 'social exclusion' was distinguished from 'poverty' as a descriptor because, although including low income as a factor, it also encompassed 'the inability to participate effectively in economic, social, political, and cultural life, and, in some characterisations, alienation and distance from the mainstream society' (Duffy in Walker and Walker 1997:8). For some, therefore, this semantic move was much welcomed, because inherent in the change of vocabulary was a different conceptualisation of poor people as being excluded through economic transformations *beyond their control* rather than through a stubborn, self-damaging refusal to take part in civil society. So, as with the underclass, the socially excluded are more than simply poor, but this time they are defined by their inability to access resources, to take part in social processes and also by geographical/spatial location rather than by an unwillingness to work or to be good citizens (Byrne 2005:2–3).

In speeches made in 1997 Tony Blair declared that the 'very modern problem' of social exclusion went beyond material poverty and that the greatest harm rested not simply in a damaging lack of economic security but in the concomitant injury to self-esteem, self-motivation and its likely transmission to future generations. It was therefore a matter of 'enlightened self interest' to tackle 'an underclass of people cut off from society's mainstream' (in Welshman 2006:183 and 191). Speaking to the Fabian Society in 1997, Peter Mandelson, Minister without Portfolio, opined the fatalism of 'today's and tomorrow's underclass' and went on to make the link to the preferred term of 'social exclusion'. As a consequence, the two terms arguably (and problematically) became interchangeable (Kleinman 1998:7–9). As late as 2006 Blair propounded the socially excluded message. For example, in his well-known York speech he observed of the 'deeply excluded':

Their poverty is not just about poverty of income, but poverty of aspiration, of opportunity, of prospects of advancement . . . we have to recognise that for some families, their problems are more multiple, more deep and more pervasive than simply low income. The barriers to opportunity are about their social and human capital as much as financial.... In social exclusion we are also talking about people who either may not want to engage with services or do not know how to.

(Blair 2006a)

Running alongside the commitment to raise aspiration and encourage social participation were a number of initiatives addressing the problems of 'yob culture', the setting of a 'respect agenda' and the implementation of zero tolerance measures against homeless people, who allegedly represented a public protection issue due to their tendency towards criminality (Murie 2000:116). These initiatives called for 'supervision and sanctions and support' alongside a 'tough message' for those indulging in antisocial behaviour (Blair 2006b). Projects such as Welfare to Work, the setting up of the Social Exclusion Unit and the wider attention to bringing atomised individuals back into the social fold suggested for some a worrying tendency to attribute diverse social problems to a single source (Langham in Jones and Novak 1999:viii). And, although the phrase 'social exclusion' can be used constructively to indicate the ways in which poorer people are exiled from civic life *without their consent*, it is arguable that from the late 1990s onwards social exclusion also became part of a double discourse which sought to attack 'welfare dependency' and attributed that dependency to embedded moral deficiencies (Levitas 1998, see also Fairclough 2000:57, Byrne 2005:54–7, Lund 2008:55).[12] Ruth Levitas highlighted the strategic usefulness for New Labour in deploying a term which allowed it to distance itself from the heartless Conservatism of the 1980s while holding onto neoliberal values inherent in the market, meritocracy, and so on. Indeed, it could be argued that increasingly during the late 1990s it was the 'culture of poverty' that was the trouble rather than poverty itself; a distinction which once again declassed social and economic problems in order to resituate them as problems of culture, personal values, attitudes, habits and conduct (Lewis 1971).

The underclass returns: lifestyle, consumerism, precariousness

In his investigative fieldwork into the lives of young people living as the 'socially excluded' in modern Britain, Robert McAuley (2007:158) observed that 'for our lives to make sense, we must think about crime.' McAuley's contention is that the stigmatisation of the mainly poor, mainly young as an urban underclass says far more about consumer society, its values, practices and modes of self-perpetuation than it does about young people themselves. McAuley argues, as does Hobsbawm before him, that poor marginalised communities are the inevitable detritus of late capitalism and its consumer society (see also Young 1999, Bauman 2007:40). But they are also much more than this. In his view they are also natural objects of its fear and scorn because they 'contravene the consumer lifestyle' (McAuley:159) and it is this contravention that marks them out as a class of criminals to be tackled rather than as a social class *per se*. In contrast to earlier centuries, when the majority of British people lived under the shadow of abject poverty if not in actual poverty, now the majority live a consuming life. This life needs constant valorisation and also, it seems, protection from those who would undermine it and its attendant values founded in models of aspiration, individual autonomy and the rule of (property) law.

The ubiquitous compound word 'lifestyle' sums up the all-embracing nature of a marketised neoliberal society in which every social action, desire and need can be costed and marketed (i.e. 'monetised') and its individual elements can be purchased following a decision-making process (i.e. the exercise of 'choice') in order to produce a 'lifestyle'. As David Harvey (2005:33) has observed, 'neoliberalism, in short, has meant the financialisation of everything.' In the late 1980s Mike Featherstone (1987) explained the widespread adoption of the vocabulary of 'lifestyle' as being predicated on the marketer's mantra that there are no longer rules, there are only choices, and that the choices made by consuming individuals were what determined their individuality, their self-presentation and ultimately their social identity. As such, this implied a move away from or beyond classed identities to a post-class social field in which status, affiliation and ambition arise from and are shaped by the individual practices of the consuming self and are sustained by a meritocratic model of social progress (Giddens 1991, Beck 1992, Lash and Urry 1994, Pakulski and Waters 1996). We can see how this works in advertising which asks you to buy the item 'because you're worth it' or because 'it's all about you', hectoring credit card adverts which insist 'Don't take chances, take charge' and leisure product marketing that urges 'be your personal best', 'win from within' or 'create your own legend'. From this perspective, as Mark Tomlinson (1998:2–3) explains, the social becomes 'flattened' out and individuals consume in ways which allow them to disaggregate from classed formations and other collectives.

So fashion, taste and lifestyle have become increasingly regarded both socially and by scholars as key sources of social differentiation and as important markers of social status. They are quite right about this. So too, as Jock Young (2007:65–6) explains, accompanying this was a 'whole series of connected shifts in what is valued' with status and the politics of identity being elevated above material conditions and the politics of class. For Young these shifts did not remove injustice or inequality, far from it; instead they redrew the lines between classed groups. Young (2007:56) argues 'The striking contrast between meritocratic ideals and structural possibilities occurs with greater severity, but it is experienced on a far more individual level and the patterns and shapes of class differences become occluded.' So it is Young's (2007:66) assessment that the upshot of these changes (in emphasis as well as in experience) of how social status is manufactured and maintained is that 'the lines between welfare recipients and workers become perceived much more clearly than they actually are, while the stratifications between middle and working class become less certain....' We might argue, therefore, that, if the neoliberal context of the marketised society is one of lifestyle choice sustained through consumerism, then the welfare participant, the irredeemably poor and the 'fatalistic' underclass all become an offence and a near-outrageous contravention of the prevailing social ideal. In a society of consumers 'they are people with no market value...they are *failed consumers*' (Bauman 2007:31). As McAuley (2007:166) puts it, 'These refuseniks, who "choose" not to work, who "choose" to live off the state, who "choose" a criminal "lifestyle" then become a source of "angst and dread"' (see Mooney 2009).

One way of negotiating the thorny problem of the underclass threat, then, in the context of the English Riots was to present its condition as a lifestyle choice, and this is arguably what happened (see Wiggan 2012). Many of the political and press commentaries seized once again on the underclass lexicon while severing it, perhaps permanently this time, from wider notions of political agency and class consciousness. Rioters sacked shops for branded goods, rioters were members of the underclass, therefore the riots (and the underclass) could not be read in any meaningful political way. This intellectual move, which was almost but not entirely a consensus, enabled a refreshment of underclass labels and at the same time helped the public make sense of the problem of social conflict in what were supposed to be 'post-class' times and in the context of a severe economic downturn.

It can be argued that many of the theorists whose work we have already touched on, such as Charles Murray, had before now positioned underclass subjects as *electing* to live lives characterised by non-productiveness together with an unreasonable expectation that their standard of living would be sustained by others. But since the 2000s other, more consumer-oriented discourses have also further established the underclass figure as a lifestyle category with all that this entails. Keith Hayward and Majid Yar (2006) most clearly set out how this new configuration has been produced through public discourse in their discussion of the emergence of the 'chav' in the context of crime and media culture. They argue that the decline of the underclass discourse in the UK (which as we have already noted, however, resurfaced in 2011) and the rise of the 'chav' are connected. For them the 'chav' represented a popular reconfiguration of the underclass label which, importantly, also allowed a reconceptualisation of social marginality. They maintain that, while the discourse of the underclass turned on its failed relations to production and socially productive labour, the 'chav', which is in many ways homologous with the underclass, is framed pathologically in relation to the sphere of consumption.

Hayward and Yar suggest that the underclass is not in fact currently characterised by its inability to consume (see Bauman above) but rather by its '*excessive* participation in forms of market-oriented consumption which are deemed *aesthetically* impoverished'. As we have discussed elsewhere (Nunn and Biressi 2009) with reference to news coverage of underclass crime, the criminal underclass is partly identified by its *over-consumption* (of alcohol, cigarettes, the wrong foods), its wrongful consumption (the flatscreen TV paid for while on welfare, through benefit fraud and other crime) and through the wrong aesthetic or lifestyle choices (hoodies, sports leisure wear, tabloid newspapers). As lifestyle is considered to be an embodiment of choice-making processes and part of the wider neoliberal rhetoric of 'responsibilisation', then underclass subjects are guilty of choosing to become what might be called 'aberrant consumers' by either exhibiting poor taste, consuming excessively or, indeed, 'shopping with violence' (see Bridges 2012:6).[13]

On 13 August 2012 both authors of this book were in Wood Green shopping mall in North-West London, which had been the scene of some of the more pronounced looting and unrest 12 months earlier. As we descended the down-escalator leading into the High Street we were faced with an overhead screen broadcasting CCTV footage of looters from the previous year featured as part of the ongoing Metropolitan Police's 'Operation Withern' which was set up to catch suspected rioters. The blurry images seemed to go unnoticed by many nearby shoppers but prompted a feeling of the uncanny as the unruly past broke into the present in the bustling shopping space. Both the social space and the timing of the footage were perfect, bringing together shopping and rioting one year on from the original events, recalling the consternation of those times and creating a bizarre contrast with life as usual. It was around the same time that debates about the riots and their eruption as a manifestation of 'Broken Britain' were resurrected. The feel-good success of the London 2012 Olympic Games prompted commentators to compare the moment with the feel-bad events of the previous year. The generally praised opening ceremony, which we discuss in our final chapter, was regarded as a tribute to young people and to a relaxed, sociable, multicultural Britain and the closing ceremony marked the end of a festival of sport and also, perhaps, of a pleasurable national collectivity. It was at this point, in reflective mood, that the media decided to draw comparisons between the apparent success of the Olympics as a unifying force and the social splintering of the English Riots. Commentary ranged from discussions of resources for poorer areas as promised by the Olympic bid to considerations of how the positive spirit of the Olympics might be harnessed to turn around damaged communities and disaffected youth. So for example, under the headline 'Olympic legacy? We've still got a riot legacy to deal with' the *Guardian* (10 August 2012) commented that the 'Promises of outreach and investment, better facilities and job prospects have been patchily met and sometimes not at all'. Meanwhile NBC News (8 August 2012) returned to the furniture store in Croydon which had been run by five generations of the same family before it was burnt out. Maurice Reeves, the 81-year-old owner, chose to reflect on the aid given by his local community rather than resurrecting the trauma of the previous year and spoke of the 'corny' but 'good' feeling experienced when the Olympic torch passed through the borough. News footage captured the rather cleverly named 'reverse rioting'; a campaign initiative promoted by the charity vInspired [sic] which aimed to support a 'counter-movement' rooted in positivity and community action. Its activities included helping to paper the walls of the new Reeves store with images of young people holding positive messages.

In contrast to these attempts by victims and their communities to move on and repair social damage, the outspoken Communities Secretary Eric Pickles reminded *Telegraph* readers (14 August 2012) that the 2011 unrest was 'thievery' pure and simple: 'It was Gucci-rioting, people wanting to get wide-screen televisions, phones, the latest trainers, fancy furniture and the like.' These commentaries variously signalled the ways in which the English Riots had became figured as the dark underside or counter-narrative to the reported and much celebrated national 'success' of the Olympics and an ideal of national community. It was perplexing, then, how the one nation could contain within it these oppositions; how could ordinary, mostly young, citizens be both our promised future and our broken present? How could people be shopping contentedly in the Wood Green mall where only one year previously people were 'shopping with violence'?

In 2011 Guy Standing published *The Precariat*, which was a timely book about what he termed 'the new dangerous class'. He defined the 'precariat' as a new class formation which was marked by some of the inequities of the older class structures but now newly inflected through inequalities and insecurities which were particular to the twenty-first century. He argued that large numbers of people are being pushed into this new and insecure existence. For him this expanding and primarily *youthful* class might also be regarded as 'dangerous' because it would be naturally hostile to the privileges and security visibly enjoyed by the dwindling group of the salaried and more financially sheltered workers. The 'precariat' is a global phenomenon with specific national inflections. In Britain it can be best understood in the context of the dismantlement of the public sector, the post-2008 economic crisis, the marketisation of educational and support systems and the devaluation of public spaces which once allowed shared communal life and leisure time. Moreover, as Standing has explained, new international labour markets have also weakened the power of workforces and strengthened that of employers. The result is a job market in which part-time, low-waged, unpredictable or long hours are typical, social networks are weak and benefits are rare. This environment has produced an expansion of anomie, anxiety, anger and alienation. Standing described this as a 'lottery-ticket society' in which opportunism and cynicism sit alongside an awareness that success is still predominantly measured by consumption.

Standing warns that, while this sense of precariousness can forge radical progressive political movements and activism, it may also prompt dangerous political extremism. So, too, it threatens to drift into the temporary thrill of shoplifting or petty crime, which provides (if nothing else) a 'tiny surge of achievement' (Standing 2011b:129–30). These warnings about the incendiary potential of the disenfranchised are founded partly in the conviction that so many of us might be teetering at the margins of security and the secure life. As Standing (p. 132) suggests, a marketised society makes it easy for a struggler or a failure to turn into a 'misfit' or a 'villain'. Glossing Wacquant, he lists the ' "street thugs", the "unemployed", the "scroungers", the failures, losers with character flaws and behavioural deficiencies' who become styled as public anathemas (Standing 2011:132). Admittedly, there are moments when Standing himself slips into a repetition of older underclass fears even as he attempts to peer beyond them; figuring precariat subjects as loose cannon, prone to manipulation by 'populist politicians and demagogues' (Standing:ibid.). But, importantly, his work stresses how vast swathes of people are experiencing a 'truncated status'; a kind of social and material and psychic sense of instability which might, at any time, tip into what Agamben (1998) has defined elsewhere as a 'bare life' – one lived beyond the bounds of societal recognition. The arrival and conceptualisation of the 'precariat' suggests that a new transformation of social class and class relations is underway. Whether this constitutes a reformation of older notions of the working class and the underclass is far from clear; more likely it constitutes a reformation of all of the majority classes. Standing (2011b:20) states:

> The precariat lives with anxiety – chronic insecurity associated with not only teetering on the edge, knowing that one mistake or one piece of bad luck could tip the balance between dignity and being a bag lady, but also with a fear of losing what they possess even while feeling cheated by not having more.

Perhaps it is not so much the case that one nation contains within it the contradiction of riots and reverse-riots, of robbers and shoppers, of worthless and worthy citizens, of social threat and of social promise, but rather that it contains within it an unspoken suspicion that the great majority may well be treading the same risky and uncertain economic and social path.

4
Top of the Class: Education, Capital and Choice

Inspiring the uninspired

This chapter focuses on the media's presentation of education as the key driver of social mobility, responsible citizenship and equality of opportunity. Paying special attention to political debates around educational achievement in the context of meritocracy and personal responsibility, it explores the ways in which educational choice is presented, taken up or passed by and how this then reflects critically on the perceived class status of children and their families. More generally, it considers how the values which embed current discourses on education and social mobility are reinforced, tested and sometimes challenged in lifestyle journalism, reality television and social observation documentary. In doing so it points to the pressures, conflicts and contradictions of class identity and class mobility (both up and downwards) and the ways in which these intersect with the experience of education and the individual investments which it currently demands.

In her discussion of celebrity, cultural production and public life Elizabeth Barry (2008:251) summarises the current situation: 'no longer do experts or social elites control what constitutes knowledge; this is now largely established and communicated by the popular media themselves.' She goes on to remind us that the celebrity endorser promotes not only consumption but aspiration, even to the extent of guiding our values, our levels of self-esteem and our politics. One of the lessons which celebrities teach us is that individuals make things happen and that personal success is usually the product of individual aspiration, passion, drive, talent or accomplishment and the ability to overcome obstacles of all kinds including the economic, cultural or educational.

Nowhere is the logic of this lesson more apparent than in the reality series *Jamie's Dream School* (C4 2011), in which chef, television celebrity and social entrepreneur Jamie Oliver sets up a temporary school populated by unqualified young school leavers and by 'teachers' whose impressive credentials are forged via a talent for their subject and a high level of public recognition. These teachers were flagged as '18 of the most brilliant people in Britain' (Anthony 2011); it is they who populate the 'dream' of the 'Dream School' by virtue of their unique contribution to cultural life. They included media dons such as David Starkey and Mary Beard, DJ Jazzy B, Tony Blair's former communications manager Alastair Cameron, the photographer Rankin, sailor Ellen MacArthur, actor Simon Callow, poet Andrew Motion, scientist and TV presenter Sir Robert Winston and artist and TV presenter Rolf Harris. These figures were well-known in their fields and to fairly wide audiences but almost entirely unrecognised by their new pupils, whose celebrity points of reference were quite different. Indeed, perhaps the only figure in the series universally recognised was Oliver himself, who presided over the 'school' for its six-week run (together with 'award-wining headmaster' John D'Abbro). In interview Oliver declared:

> The thing I like about the show is that it's about a massive political issue. Almost half of students are leaving school without enough GCSEs to take them on to A-levels or higher education. I guess the big question is: are there just bright kids and thick kids, or are there other ways to motivate people who have had a rough time at school? In other words, can *Dream School* inspire the uninspired?
>
> (Tucker 2011)

Oliver's credentials as a celebrity social interventionist had been established through his TV series *Jamie's Kitchen* (2002), in which he mentored 15 young people and trained them alongside professional chefs. It was consolidated in *Jamie's School Dinners* (2005), which was credited with influencing policy on school meals (but see Naik 2008), *Jamie's Ministry of Food* (2008) and *Jamie's Food Revolution* (2010). It was *Jamie's Kitchen* that repositioned him in the popular imagination from celebrity cook to both a businessman and a 'moral entrepreneur' and further legitimated an already developing public discourse that entrepreneurialism was a better solution to social problems than state intervention (Hollows and Jones 2010:308). In addition, his endearing rejection of easy cynicism in the face of seemingly intractable social problems branded him differently from other middle-class social commentators and better equipped him to tackle the 'knowledge poverty of the working class' in particular (Hollows and Jones:308–9). His visibility on the political stage is notable, with Oliver ruefully recalling that by the time of *Dream School* he had already met five Education Secretaries; suggesting a longevity in the public eye which many politicians would envy. *Dream School* ended with the youngsters visiting Prime Minister David Cameron for a question and answer session. This scene sealed the narrative ark of the series as one which travelled from individual struggles via a transformation narrative towards public engagement around social issues by non-state actors.

The youngsters involved with the programme had fallen behind at school, were labelled by some as 'tearaways', and most, but not all, were now at a loose end with few good prospects for employment. They came from a variety of backgrounds, including public (state), faith and fee-paying schools for which parents with very modest jobs had struggled to pay (Williams, S. 2011). Several of the youngsters commented on the new opportunities offered by the series, the excellent facilities provided by the school, the smaller classes and the longer-term benefits of the *Dream School* scholarships which were to support them beyond the life of the series (Crosland 2011, Williams, S. 2011). Real school teachers were rather more sceptical, with one observing that, 'It was good to see passionate, accomplished people trying to inspire those without passion, but this was a showpiece. It wasn't anything like a school – it was just big fun party time, like *Celebrity Big Brother* or *The X Factor*' (Murray 2011).

Dream School arguably offered a distorted but by now familiar replica of putative successful learning in education and future achievement in the world of work. This model is located entirely within an individualist framework of talented, charismatic but unqualified teaching and students who are expected to learn the value of hard work and individual aspiration via celebrity role models and mentors. It is essentially the pedagogy of the talent show. As TV satirist Charlie Brooker (2011) acerbically noted:

> The audacity of *Dream School* is truly inspiring … the first episode opened with Jamie recounting how he left school with no qualifications. The British educational system failed him, just as it fails millions of others like him every year. Now he wants to make a difference. Not by campaigning against education cuts – which might be boring – but by setting up his own school. Not one staffed by actual

teachers – which might be boring – but by celebrities. And it won't be open all-year round – which might be expensive – but for a few weeks. Thus our education system will be saved.

Far from being a long-term project, *Dream School* was a once in a lifetime opportunity devised by a television production company with Oliver at the helm as a social entrepreneur. As such, it was in keeping with a strand of 'life intervention' reality programming, as described by Ouellette and Hay (2008), which has brought about the 'neoliberalisation of social work through reality TV'; a strand which teaches people to tap their abilities to attain 'normalcy, happiness, material stability and success' (Ouellette and Hay 2008:64, 67). The series itself constantly came up against the problem of its exceptionalist logic, which, like the talent show, sought to identify the potential in the lucky few who, in turn, must demonstrate their commitment and passion for success against the odds. Despite these artificial, not to say experimental, conditions, Oliver's bafflement (foregrounded by the editing of the programme) was apparent when, for example, circumstances prevented his students from thriving and from grasping those offered chances. When 18-year-old Latoya arrives in tears with her sick baby and is told that she can't continue at school because he has chicken pox, Oliver laments, 'this is about life chances and her life chances are set back a bit more now,' and later he observes thoughtfully that 'real events change things for each student.'

Television reviewers were generally divided as to which aspect of the series was the less edifying: the frequently uncooperative teenagers playing up to the camera or the often inadequately prepared celebrities who tried to 'make a difference'. Ironically, and perhaps unfairly, bearing in mind the celebrity foundation of the show, criticism of the youngsters focused on their own attachment to celebrity culture and easy money. One journalist reported: 'Asked by actor Simon Callow for a person with whom they could identify, one said Bill Gates (fair enough), while another teenage guy said Katie Price. The Shakespearean actor was busy looking for an exit: "They're unruly, not disciplined, wanting money, success and power. They just wanted money" ' (Stephenson 2011). A number of journalists condemned this attitude as symptomatic of a wider mind-set of lazy entitlement to respect and to a good life without the willingness to put in the requisite work. Moreover, the teenagers were condemned for not even knowing what constitutes a good life in the first place; for being more attached to notions of apparently unearned 'respect', money and their mobile phones than to respect for others, cultural enrichment and a passion for work. *Dream School's* ambitions, then, were both to reveal to students what the good life actually is and to make them ready to lead a productive work life. Oliver observed in episode 5 (in which work experience and planning for work are highlighted): 'If you've got someone who's fairly rounded, can cook and buy for themselves, they can express themselves in poetry in one form or another, they've got opinions in politics...for me as an employer, I'm interested in that.'

In moments such as these *Dream School* came up against the long-held contradictions in the ways in which the purpose of education is conceived and, in fact, it usefully amplified them for a contemporary audience. As James Donald (1992:4) explains in his illuminating study of education, popular culture and governmentality, the post-enlightenment liberal notion of education is riven with tensions because it bears the paradox that individual freedom (the freedom to think, to choose, to become a fully-functioning citizen) is thought to be attained via the 'submission to education'. Debates about the purposes of education frequently battle with the essential tension between education as a pathway to personal development and the good life (through a *taste* for good food, poetry, effective citizenship, etc.) and education as socialisation and as the mode of delivery for work-ready labourers (through 'employability'). The idealism of *Dream School*, which was appealing for some and irritating for others, was stymied by the need to negotiate and overcome, in only a few weeks, various obstacles to these twin goals of personal emancipation and socialisation, including individual resistance (a type of individualism to be condemned) and social inequality.

The political terrain upon which this challenge took place was that of neoliberalism. As others have already demonstrated (Becker 2006, McCarthy 2007, McMurria 2008, Ouellette and Hay 2008), reality TV makeovers, perhaps more than any other formats, sit well within a neoliberal framework of choice, entrepreneurialism and self-reliance and act as popular platforms for their propagation. Democracies work '*through* the liberty and aspirations of individuals. Rather than silencing and constraining their desires and self-governing capacities, technologies of the self have attempted to attune them to political objectives' (Donald 1992:142). This affiliation to self-government and its attachment to personal development as an adjunct of productivity, effective citizenship and especially employability is dependent on the understanding that social differences (class, gender, 'race' inequalities) are obstructions which can be overcome through individual passion, drive and hard work.[1]

Our reading of *Dream School* also supports Nick Stevenson's assessment of the ways in which primetime reality entertainment is challenging the boundaries between entertainment, politics and education. As Stevenson (2010:351) explains, quoting Thomas Frank's assertion that 'dreaming of a better world is now the work of business', business competition and talent shows are evidence that the sites of pedagogy have been extended well beyond the realm of formal education into the domains of popular entertainment and new technologies. He observes, too, that much of the dramaturgy of these shows operates through the 'threat of exclusion' via shows which invite mostly working-class participants to compete for success and which remind its subjects that many of the shows' mentors and role models made it despite their own rather humble origins. In *Dream School*, many, if not all, of its pupils, have experienced exclusion from their own schools, and it is made clear that, while they are not competing against each other to achieve success, they are competing against the expectations of others that they will continue to fail.

For critics, the politics of social difference which was played out in the conception and execution of *Dream School* (in which students were deliberately chosen to represent diverse class and other backgrounds and teachers were parachuted in from radically different social worlds) was fairly invisible and the politics of class was deemed especially irrelevant. However, in the series itself the language of 'us' and 'them', of disadvantage and opportunity, was deployed strategically by all concerned, and the iconography of class difference was evident, if rarely remarked upon. Oliver himself, dressed down in sweatshirt and jeans and speaking Essex 'mockney', embodied what Cora Kaplan (2004:101) has referred to as the 'retro-social performance' of class identity that now has to stand in for the real thing. It also positioned him as a well-meaning intermediary between the sometimes unworldly or inept or stressed teachers and 'the kids' (see Charlesworth 2011). As such, his role included managing pupils' and teachers' perceptions of the class distinctions at play in the classroom and beyond. Pupils defensively or aggressively condemned teachers for talking 'posh' or talking down to them or for being naïve, and seemed acutely aware of the social distinctions which marked them as outsiders in their own real and now experimental classrooms. They directly asked human rights lawyer Cherie Booth how she had lost her Liverpudlian accent and challenged her as an 'upper-class' person about her view of the 'rights' of 'working-class people'. They also had pragmatic views of their own future life chances. So one boy tells young mother Latoya quite bluntly that she has few prospects: '17 – got a kid with no way of supporting it. Trapped. End of discussion.'

The iconography of these social distinctions was evident when, for example, volunteer teacher and former Poet Laureate Andrew Motion is filmed in his book-lined study musing on his inability to reach his students, when Starkey presents a gift of his own book to a somewhat bemused student or when Oliver observes of an education in classics: 'if it's good enough for Harrow and Eton it's good enough for *Dream School.*' The markers of social distinction here are the traditional ones of cultural capital and good taste, and they often sit uncomfortably alongside the more practical lessons learned about cooking, sailing or biology. Despite an eclectic mix of classroom content and an ongoing rhetoric of social equality, it is evident that there is one social class, in particular, that has something to prove. For instance, in the final episode Oliver explains that the teenagers have been pitched in a sports event against a 'posh private school'; a pairing which symbolically establishes the competition between social classes. Again, in an earlier episode Oliver confronts one of the students about her bad behaviour and asks her rhetorically, 'what do you think that the posh people in education, in universities or in politics will think? Segregate them [people who won't learn] and teach those who want to.' In this way, despite the series' commitment to recruit students from across social classes, it continues to tap into notions of a competition between classes for resources, life chances and, perhaps most importantly, recognition and respect.

Despite some residual and under-explored sense in the series that life chances are more easily grasped by those whose material circumstances, cultural and social capital best equip them to hold out their hand, public criticism was levelled at the children themselves for deficiencies in individual character and the degraded climate of indiscipline at home and at school which had rendered them into either characters from *Lord of the Flies* (Anthony 2011) or 'truculent dunces' (Deacon 2011). Alice Thomson (2011), writing in the *Times*, was exceptional in raising social class as a factor in their unsuccessful schooling, if only to dismiss it as an unnecessary distraction:

> It's not a question of background or class. The 20 children...are allowed mobile phones in class. Of course they can't concentrate when they are Googling and tweeting but the adults, who include Alastair Campbell and Cherie Blair, are too terrified to take them away. These children don't lack self-esteem but have a huge sense

of entitlement and no respect for others; they have never learnt to take control of their lives.

Her argument was that over-indulgence was a cross-class or non-class problem, with middle-class parents equally culpable for pampering their youngsters. She noted:

> Eastern European au pairs are amazed when children stick out their feet to have their Velcro shoes done up. In Switzerland they teach children responsibility at school so when they grow up they don't need signs saying: 'This beverage may be hot'. But not in Britain. Our children are growing up far too slowly if at all. We've ditched Just William for Diary of a Wimpy Kid.

For Thomson the only thing that can guarantee success is an individual's hard work; the key characteristics which high achievers share are that they are 'robust, resilient and resourceful'. Oliver, in interview, pursues the same lines of explanation. He posits that schools have somehow failed these children, but also notes an absence of stamina and aspiration in the kids, traits which allowed him to succeed despite his own very poor educational achievements:

> When you're unleashing students into an economy where there's trouble with jobs, the ones who haven't got academic verve, they need to have a basic approach to physical work. You need to be able to knock out seven 18-hour days in a row – you need to know what real fucking work is.... I had that experience.
>
> (Tucker 2011)

Having noted the hard work and difficult environment faced by secondary school teachers, Oliver asserts, 'Dream School is questioning everything about schools that we know, including whether you need traditional qualifications to be a teacher – I think we both know that's a no.' The series arguably explored the idea already being aired in political debate that education can be deprofessionalised and/or even privatised through the introduction of non-teachers into a privately established alternative to school. As in many of the programmes featuring Oliver as mentor, teacher–trainer and role model, the message was one of individual responsibility, with the onus on young people to seize every opportunity. For example, in the earlier Jamie's Kitchen nearly a thousand unemployed young people applied for 15 training places in an environment in which, argue Peter Kelly and Lyn Harrison (2006:8), they were deemed to be suffering from the consequences of their own individual (in)actions. This is because success in the current marketplace of work is marked by the development of a robust selfhood, and it is this individual ability to endure workplace turbulence that is supposed to protect people from the 'risk of social and material oblivion that hangs over individuals in a globalised risk society' (Kelly and Harrison 2006:9).

Sharp elbows and the competition for resources

The model of what constitutes the cause and the solution to educational failure and poor employment prospects as set out by Oliver in interview and in *Dream School* generally chimes with broader popular and even political discourses which suggest that individual actions by non-professionals (children, parents, school governors, volunteers, entrepreneurs) and the responsible exercise of choice build the foundations of a successful, fulfilling life. In other words, where the public sector must play a leading role in education provision and preparation for work it should do so within the framework of choice-orientated values which characterise the private sector. *Dream School* and the wider discourses upon which it draws are based on the conviction that merit and hard work will be recognised despite humble origins, that collective (public and welfare) solutions to educational failure are unrealistic and that the formations of class, gender or ethnicity from which children, families and even educators emerge are inconveniences rather than major obstacles. Within this logic, the solution to social problems lies robustly outside the state and in the hands of citizens. This conviction is nicely summarised by Conservative MEP Daniel Hannan, who observed, '... families are a very good way of delivering services to the next generation. They are much better at delivering education and healthcare and social security ... than the state is'.[2] Here the onus is on families themselves to make education work.

The problem, as Sally Tomlinson (2005:165) has argued, is that 'educational policies, both deliberately and by default, have since Thatcher's first government in the 1980s, increasingly favoured groups already privileged or seeking privileges' (see also Ball 2003, Furlong 2007). In this context the middle class, in all its variegation, became the major beneficiary of market competition for the best schools, resources and funding. In terms of the political discourses of the responsible exercise of choice, the assumptions are that the middle-class family, in particular, must be the model to emulate in terms of its reproduction of socially responsible and productive citizens in the context of a marketised education system. But even so, Tomlinson notes, during the last several decades even those middle classes have had to strive harder to maintain their sometimes precarious hold on the social advantages they might once have taken for granted.

The assurance, as expressed by Hannan, that families have the capacity to 'deliver' education and to deliver it more effectively than the state is part of what Val Gillies (2005:835) refers to as the 'individualization of social class', which, in her view, fails to recognise the material and social grounding on which raising children happens. Drawing attention to the politically influential work of Beck and Giddens, who characterise late modern social actors as moving beyond old class identities and affiliations to become self-directing citizens, Gillies sketches a welfare agenda under New Labour which was concerned to empower individuals to take 'responsibility' within an openly meritocratic framework. In this context the socially excluded are to be regarded as 'failures of self-governance' (Gillies:837). Consequently the high ground of achievement will be ceded to those who can adhere to and exploit the middle-class norms of effective self-management and robust individualism.

According to Gillies (pp. 838–9), disadvantage has been reconceptualised in educational policy so that class mobility arises from being 'the right kind of self' and the factors which support achievement are rooted in parental involvement, role models, self-esteem and the strategic recourse to social networks. Her own fieldwork suggested that the terrain upon which parents supported their children was fundamentally uneven, so that working-class parents were supporting children to manage perceived injustice, instability and hardship while middle-class families could deploy resources, social and cultural capital more directly in the service of scholarly achievement. Middle-class parents were especially adept at constructing their children as bright, 'unique' or distinct from others, and even when their behaviour was difficult or their learning slower than expected it was important that their talents be recognised and nurtured (Gillies:843–7). Meanwhile, working-class parents were more concerned that their children 'fitted in', were polite, affable and avoided trouble. Here the marking out of the exceptional from the ordinary becomes a middle-class strategy totally in keeping with current meritocratic models and, it could be argued, with media culture's emphasis on the public figure or celebrity as a uniquely talented individual whose background is relevant only as a marker of how far they have progressed.

Gillies instructively illustrates both the degree of commitment middle-class parents (and especially mothers) evidence and the high degree to which they are equipped to support that commitment. She uses as an example the account of a mother whose nine-year-old was struggling with literacy and becoming increasingly disruptive at school. In this case the mother paid for a private dyslexia assessment and stressed that it was her daughter's high IQ and maturity which actually caused her to be difficult in the classroom. Gillies (p. 847) argues that, as a lawyer and as a member of the Parents and Teachers Committee, she was also ideally positioned to act as advocate for her daughter's 'special exception and entitlement' and understood the grounds upon which these claims could be made convincingly.[3]

The resourcefulness of the middle classes in exploiting the possibilities of state education to their fullest was signalled in 2010 by David Cameron, who pointed to the capacity of the 'sharp-elbowed middle classes' to pick up on education services such as the state-supported Sure Start programme offering childcare for toddlers (Hope 2010). He observed: 'There is a criticism sometimes with Sure Start that a great new centre is established and the "sharp-elbowed" middle classes, like my wife and me, get in there and get all the services.'[4] Alongside the distracting debates about whether the Camerons themselves were, in fact, middle class (rather than upper class) and therefore qualified to comment, this triggered disputes about the assertiveness of middle-class parents which, anecdotally, reinforced the findings of Gillies and others that some middle-class parents were adept users of state services to the detriment of others. These debates also worked to categorise, often humorously, varieties of middle-classness via their attitudes to enterprise and *active* involvement in overseeing their children's progress. For example, on the back of the 'sharp-elbowed' debate the *Telegraph* published an extract from a quiz featured in *The Middle Class Handbook: An Illustrated Field Guide to the Changing Behaviour and Tastes of Britain's New Middle* (Benson and Armstrong 2010) which pointed to initiative and the mobilisation of public resources as the hallmark of middle-classness today (Armstrong 2010). The following scenario was established:

Q. You hear that a local comprehensive has new funding, a sharp, dynamic head teacher and exciting new premises. Do you:

A. Think it's nice that the kids from the estate have a chance at a decent education and sign the school fees cheque as usual.

B. Send your kids along for a term or so because mixing with all classes and creeds is as much a part of education as the exam results.

C. Organise a mass e-mail petition of middle class parents in your area to swamp the school with applications and effectively win control.

Answers

Mostly As – You're not yet middle class. Keep at it.

Mostly Bs – How quaint? One of the old middle class. You might even have guilt.

Mostly Cs – Congratulations. You've elbowed your way to the front of the class. As your children no doubt will. Now . . . who needs this untidy aristocracy lying around?

The quiz slyly suggests that the traditional notion of the middle-class trajectory of social achievement, where one simply pays for a top quality education and leaves it to professionals to deliver it (writing the cheque as usual), is an abnegation of responsibility and that sending your child to a good state school is idealist (i.e. rather quaint). By implication, both options are styled as outmoded, un-modern and rather fusty and increasingly out of step with the drive to sustained social mobility through individual action. The right answer to the quiz is to roll up your sleeves and monopolise those state resources.

The choice-directive or choosing to choose

Middle-class advocacy and entrepreneurialism function within an education framework which posits a marketplace of 'choice' that can be exercised by parents who make the effort to become fully involved in their children's schooling. However, educationalists have argued that parental choice can only be fully practised if it is informed by experience, expectations and the 'capacity to compete' (MacDonald 2006:92). Middle-class competence, enthusiasm and social advantage all contribute to the effective and active exploitation of the choices available. The many guidelines available to parents via governments, charities, self-instruction books and parenting websites underline the onus on families to take responsibility for their children's successful journey through the education system. The influential parenting community website mumsnet.com, for example, issued 'a lively look at education planning' called 'From embryo to eighteen: How to survive the education highway', which offered a checklist for parents topped with an image of a baby wearing an academic mortar board.[5] The five-page overview covered issues from pre-conception ('consider the pros and cons of September birthday babes') through to school leavers ('work, gap year, university or for an unlucky few re-sits. A number of crammers offer students the chance to improve their grades'). The advice, with links to further information, signals the parental work of, in Hannan's words above, 'delivering education.' The advice for parents of 2–4 year olds is worth quoting at length here:

> Give thought to the school you want your child to attend and the education programme you wish them to follow. If you are serious about a good state school check to see if you are living in the right catchment area and that you fulfil the admissions criteria. If your preferred establishment is a faith-school make sure Sophia and Serge attend Sunday School. Volunteer for flower and coffee rotas at your local Church and make sure people, particularly the Priest, notice you doing so. If Eton or Harrow are on the agenda choose your pre-prep with care. We cannot stress enough what a waste we think tuition is at this stage but that has never stopped pushy parents from indulging.

The citation throughout the mumsnet.com document of numerous strategies to support children in meeting educational milestones (tuition, spotting talent or learning difficulties, home preparation for key stage tests, exam crammers, etc.) points to the erosion of distinctions between the private/domestic sphere and the public sphere. They also highlight the increasing burden on parents to equip their children for a successful educational trajectory and hence for life. The consequence, argues Diane Reay (2008:642) in her analysis of the discourse of parenting under the Blair administration, is that parents become 'teaching adjuncts' whose efficacy is partly rooted in their financial capacity. It is now 'incontestable' that the economic impact on families has been substantial, as evidenced by an exponential growth in private materials and tuition for home learning, to the extent that parents spend more per annum on textbooks than their schools do (Reay 2008).[6] This level of investment, together with a political and popular discourse of parenting which stresses parental responsibility and choice, would suggest that existing educational inequalities will become further compounded as those best equipped to rise to the occasion do so. Moreover, the classed (ethnic, gendered and material) processes of parenting become muffled as education is championed, in a somewhat circular fashion, as both a field of opportunity which all parents have a responsibility to maximise and as the solution to the inequalities of social class in the economic field.

At its most visible the choice-directive, as we choose to call it here, is manifested as a competition for the very best resources among a few focused and clever people who are perfectly aware of the life-changing opportunities that the best education will afford their children. For instance, the Cutting Edge documentary *Too Poor for Posh School?* (C4 2010) followed the journey of three boys as they underwent a relentless battery of tests (IQ, debating, maths, sports, etc.) and interviews for a scholarship to London's Harrow School. This is a private boarding school which has educated future prime ministers, diplomats, business leaders and so on, and which to date usually charges £28,000 per annum in fees. Here the 'poor' boys are shown in direct competition with each other (rather than with all applicants) for the only funding aimed solely at families of modest income. The scholarship's sponsor Peter Beckwith states to camera: 'Whoever wins these scholarships is going to be socially engineered' and hence they are aimed at 'families with ambition and drive and the courage to change their whole lifestyle'.

Many parents and children are perfectly aware of the long-term commitment that competition for the best schooling entails. For example, the Cutting Edge documentary *Parental Choice* (C4 1997) which was broadcast at the outset of the New Labour government tracked the attempts of six families to get their children into grant-maintained schools via highly competitive examination; revealing the time and resources needed to exercise 'choice' freely. One parent observed ruefully that the school they were interested in (Latymer) marketed itself and its products (e.g. selling the previous year's exam papers), highlighting the way in which even the process of applying had been monetised. She also speculated that without the expense of a private tutor their child would have little chance of passing the entrance tests. Another described how her daughter had to be trained by private tutors for two years to overcome the disadvantages of applying from a state rather than independent (fee-paying) school. Others observed the profound social and cultural differences that moving to Latymer would entail. For instance, Craig, a black British boy, observed warily: 'The building was like church...and...there weren't no Indians, no mixed or black, just lots of white people.' Later, when he fails the examination, he discloses that he is not really that disappointed because 'Latymer is a posh school, lots of smart, smart people go there.'

By the end of the programme we learn that only one of the six children featured gained entry to Latymer (Catherine, who received intense tutoring), and one other (Craig) got into his second-choice school because the family decided to move house to fall into the correct catchment area. All of the parents reflected sceptically on the rhetoric of choice and whether they were, in fact, free to choose. One mother observed that the 'choice' offered is a 'negative choice', that is, to try to avoid a poorly performing school, while a father wonders whether there are less tangible obstacles in the way of the choices apparently on offer.[7]

> It's like looking at this picture with a gauze over it, whilst it appears quite clear and precise I have this underlying feeling that we've not been told everything about the qualifying process. I still have the feeling that there's another underlying political qualifying level that we are not told about.

On the whole what the programme revealed, albeit anecdotally, was the high level of parental work involved in opting for 'choice' over the default position of simply taking a place at the local school. Catherine's mother, for instance, seemed exhausted, having supplemented her daughter's tutoring with her own time before and after school. Others, as the quotation above suggests, laboured under the sneaking suspicion that, despite their best efforts, they had not fully grasped the rules of the game or that they had been excluded for reasons beyond their control. Finally, as Fiona Devine (2004) has illustrated, 'middle-class' parenting in terms of the transmission of security, privilege and further upwards social mobility is also fraught with risk and uncertainty. Not all middle-class parents originate from middle-class families, not all are equally equipped to support their children, and many may be working hard simply to prevent their children from 'falling' rather than rising to greater heights in terms of profession, income and other markers of social status. Nonetheless, her comparative qualitative research concludes that 'Without doubt, the empirical evidence has shown that family economic resources are crucial to the reproduction of middle-class advantage' (Devine 2004:178).

The parent-citizen and the deployment of capital

A number of critics (e.g. Biressi and Nunn 2008, Ouellette and Hay 2008, Ferguson 2010, Gambles 2010) have considered the ways in which the popular media have taken on board, amplified or explored political expectations of the parent as pedagogue or trainer and of the family (and private initiatives) as the source and solution to social inequalities. Here it is purported that poor citizenship skills (i.e. not inculcating educational values in children) and the failure to properly take up educational opportunities contributes to the economic problems arising from unschooled and undisciplined young adults who go on, in turn, to have 'problem kids' themselves. Cultural critics have also indicated in discussions of television series such as *Supernanny* (C4 2004–) and *Honey We're Killing the Kids* (BBC3 2005–) how the solutions offered come in the form of what might be described as privatised support or 'para-welfare'. As with Jamie Oliver in *Dream School*, the 'experts' who advise parents in programmes such as *Supernanny* or via self-help books often reject or disavow professional qualifications in favour of practical experience and disciplinary strategies which seem to chime with commonsense notions of how to solve children's behavioural problems.

Journalist and social policy researcher Richenda Gambles (2010) proffers the examples of Gina Ford (Oliver's preferred guru for infant care) and *Supernanny*'s Jo Frost as popular pedagogic models who, despite professional experience as a maternity nurse and nanny, position themselves outside the professions and align themselves with parents. For Gambles, models such as these operate interactively with government's (in this case New Labour's) promotion of parents as the motor of social and economic improvement and the private sphere and privatised culture as the realm where this would rightly take place. She cites a 2007 DfES document which notes approvingly, 'parents are demonstrating a growing appetite for discussion, information and advice, as we see from the increasingly vibrant market in television programmes, magazines and websites.' She also recalls MP Beverley Hughes's observation that the popularity of *Supernanny* supported her own view that parents welcome 'an extension of the opportunities for parents to develop their expertise' (Gambles 2010:703).

The choice-directive, which positions parents as autonomous agents in the education market-place (albeit supported by the guides and media instruction praised by the government and cited above), is most effectively undertaken by willing parents equipped with social, cultural and financial capital. Often these are intertwined in complex ways.

For example, in the *Parental Choice* documentary discussed above one father explains that he heavily encourages his son's participation in the expensive hobby of go-cart racing because he needs to become more competitive in everything he does, including educationally, if he is going to succeed in life. Other children are filmed receiving dance or music lessons as well as in formal preparation for exams. As we saw with mumsnet.com, overall, many forums stress the strategic importance of engaging with informal social networks, knowledge exchange and community activities to help parents make their educational preferences a reality.

Social and cultural capital are themselves rather loose, contested and difficult to define concepts, but ones which make sense as part of an explanatory model of the undertow of competition between the classes for resources, including in education. Derived from the interests of policy makers and political sociologists rather than directly from the market or the public realm, these concepts came to the fore in the late 1980s with the circulation of French sociologist Pierre Bourdieu's observations that conventional economic theory was overlooking other dimensions of economic and social life, specifically those of cultural and social capital (Bourdieu 1984, Bourdieu and Wacquant 1992). In other words, and put simply, individuals draw on a range of educational, cultural and social assets (such as personal networks) in addition to those derived from income, investment or inheritance, and it is all of these taken together which contribute to social difference among and between individuals.

In its most neutral or at least politically uninflected form, *social* capital has been described as those 'features of social life – networks, norms, and trust – that enable participants to act together more effectively to pursue shared objectives' (Putnam 1995:664–5). As David Halpern (2005:10, author's emphases) explains in his comprehensive account of the rise of social capital as both a policy model and political philosophy, most forms of social capital are composed of a '*network*; a cluster of n*orms, values and expectancies* that are shared by group members; and *sanctions* – punishments and rewards – that help to maintain the norms and the network'. These broad-brush definitions suggest a self-sustaining, relatively benign and highly functional social mechanism which allows cooperative action and collective progress: a mechanism in tune with the call for a social entrepreneurial agenda of civic responsibility.

But, as the term suggests, social capital, although rooted in human relationships and often tied through bonds of trust, shared values and good will, is explicitly *economistic*, with Charlie Leadbeater (1997:67ff), for example, describing a 'virtuous circle' for the development of entrepreneurial social organisations in which social capital is inherited, invested (together with other forms such as financial and human capital) and made to pay 'dividends'. Also, as Halpern and others have pointed out, not everyone has access to the right or best networks, nor is everyone equally well-equipped to draw on their benefits, and these inequalities of access and advantage are drawn along classed and other lines of social difference. This is what Robert Putnam (2000:350ff) refers to as 'the dark side of social capital'. In other words, some people have far lower stocks of social capital and lack the skills to build on those they do have, or else they are excluded through intolerance or prejudice. This original lack or exclusion results in a cycle of disadvantage and prevents them from accessing the employment, educational, medical or social benefits which would make social mobility more achievable.

The accumulation of *cultural* capital (and the confidence it helps build) has also long been recognised as a necessary adjunct of social mobility, and hence, in *Jamie's Dream School*, the social experiment includes a speedy inculcation of traditional cultural knowledge and reference points (with Shakespeare and Latin alongside photography, music and science). Sociologist and founder of the Open University Michael Young (1958:176–7) observed in his famous educational satire *The Rise of the Meritocracy 1870–2033* that those from outside the elite classes:

> came from homes in which there was no tradition of culture. Their parents, without a good education themselves, were not able to augment the influence exercised by the teacher. These clever people were in a sense only half-educated... when they graduated they had not the same self-assurance as those who had the support and stimulus of their families from the beginning.

Young's novella or fictional treatise, which was subtitled 'An essay on education and equality', was obviously written in a different era in which high culture was universally recognised, common culture was shared and cultural values were also fairly commonly agreed upon. His future-set speculations envisaged a society in which special tests and scientific knowledge of IQ and aptitude would decide whether an individual could move through the social classes and which jobs they would be best suited to perform. Young speculates that this society's attempts to promote individuals according to their merit and their intelligence rather than, say, the social position into which they were born would simply prompt the affluent middle classes and establishment families to seek new ways to shore up their failing children or to further propel those who were already successful. What is remarkable about his treatise is his prediction of the strategies which the 'elite' classes, as he refers to them, would adopt in the face of attempts to equalise access to social mobility. In doing so, he signalled the *adaptability* of individuals in the face of new threats to privilege. Importantly, from our perspective, Young also points to the paradox of meritocratic culture, which defuses class politics through schemes aimed at equality of opportunity but without necessarily removing those social divisions which fuelled that class-based activism in the first place. He (1958:124) commented wryly that 'since bottom agrees with top that merit should reign, they can only cavil at the means by which the choice has been made, not at the standard which all alike espouse.'

Paul Barker (2006) has observed that with hindsight the sociology, if not the science, of Young's book rings true with the dissolution of a comprehensive educational system and its replacement, albeit unevenly, with a more meritocratic model of education.[8] The features of this model were evident in the post-Thatcherite implementation of testing, the widening range of selective and specialist schools, the identification of 'gifted and talented' children and the rhetorical promotion by the Blair government in 2004 of the 'opportunity society' (Barker 2006:42, Tomlinson 2008). Blair's (1996) well-known 1996 Ruskin College speech set the tone and pointed to the intersection between education and collective economic progress:

> Since I became leader of the Labour Party, I have emphasised that education will be a priority for me in government. I have done so because of the fact – increasingly recognised across our society – that our economic success and our social cohesion depend on it. An Age of Achievement is within our grasp – but it depends on an Ethic of Education. That is why in my party conference speech I said that my three priorities for government would be education, education and education.

In Sally Tomlinson's (2008:68) view, the government's conviction that success must be earned and its provision of separate pathways for the variously talented rather than one pathway for all required that:

> all members of a society have a duty to invest in their own human capital, which will…improve national economic productivity in a

global market. Since all cannot acquire the desirable jobs in a high skills economy, there must be meritocratic competition between individuals who have different abilities and aptitudes – softened in government publications to a language of different needs and aspirations.

It has been argued (Dench 2006:12–13) that New Labour's promotion of meritocracy thereby took an 'imperative form' through increasingly centralised schooling, accreditation and targets as well as via a rhetoric that achievement equated to individual financial success and increased visibility in the public realm. As Young suggests above, this was a rhetoric whose reasonableness seemed to defuse opposition rooted in class politics; in Barker's (2006:42) words, 'It seemed to be what people wanted.'

Under the 2010 Tory–Liberal Democrat administration, education provision promised to depart further still from the inclusive (and not entirely successful) model of comprehensive schooling, with the academies conceived by New Labour (schools independent from local authorities) being further encouraged and also being supplemented by a new 'Free Schools' policy. This new and, at the time of writing, small-scale and rather controversial initiative gives groups of parents or teachers, faith-based groups, and private organisations the chance to set up a state-funded school. As Mansell (2011:92) observed, 'Critics worry that the free-school policies give each institution too much control over student admissions, that free schools will benefit financially from the funding mechanisms at the expense of the remaining local authority schools, and that the policies will diminish local democratic accountability.' Proponents, on the other hand, point to the enhancement of choice for parents in the selection of type of education their child receives and enhanced standards as local authorities are forced to cede control to teachers and parents and to compete with them for pupils.

More dream schools

For those parent-citizens with the full range of social capital, with time and possibly money (or the skills to attract it) and a suitably bullish and entrepreneurial attitude, the choices apparently on offer are further extended as opportunities multiply for them to become involved in the delivery of schooling. At its most entrepreneurial this might be referred to as the 'high-end' of parental advocacy in terms of the resources, confidence and savvy-ness deployed in the pursuit of the best education tailored for the particular needs of one's offspring. Exemplary, if highly exceptional, was the well-reported case of barrister Annabel Goodman, who decided to suspend her career and use her savings to set up a tiny fee-paying school in Worcestershire, which was filmed for the Wonderland series of documentaries as *The Woman Who Bought A School For Her Son* (BBC 2008). This daunting project was undertaken explicitly to rescue her dyslexic 13-year-old son from an education treadmill in which he had already struggled through six state and three independent schools. In interview with the *Daily Mail* (Wilkes 2007), Goodman observed:

> Jacob has been in a state school for the last couple of years.... They have been very supportive but it was a comprehensive school and there were 1,200 children there with 30 pupils in the smallest classes.... Staff were totally under-resourced, under-funded and although they tried very hard to deal with Jacob's special needs, they were simply unable to do so.

The documentary which followed the progress of the school in its first year under Goodman's headship revealed the phenomenal financial and emotional strain of getting the project under way as well as the pressures on Goodman's two sons as they settled into their mother's new school.

Whereas Goodman's lone initiative appeared somewhat risky and eccentric, in the years since, parents have been increasingly encouraged to participate as formal deliverers of schooling. As noted above, following the new Coalition Government education policy, the launching of Free Schools was made possible in England from September 2011. The Department for Education promoted the Free Schools as follows:

> Free Schools are all-ability state-funded schools set up in response to what local people say they want and need in order to improve education for children in their community. The right school can transform a child's life and help them achieve things they may never have imagined. Through the Free Schools programme it is now much easier for talented and committed teachers, charities, parents and education experts to open schools to address real demand within an area.[9]

These would contribute, in the words of Michael Gove, to 'a state education system in which parents are in control'.[10]

Mark Lehain (2011), writing in the *Guardian* newspaper, signalled the hard work needed simply to gain approval for the establishment of a Free School:

> All of these groups [Free School applicants] have been through a process that is demanding and time-consuming – intellectually, practically and emotionally. They have had to create robust plans to prove that their schools will deliver a high-quality education. Communities have had to be engaged to support the proposal. Parents have had to sign up to express an interest in sending their children to the proposed school.

These new schools, forty launched to date (September 2011), are diverse in origins and aims and include former private schools, faith schools, schools with rather traditional or alternative curricula, and so on. Unlike the academies, they can be very modest in size, with as few as twenty pupils, and with a far smaller start-up cost. The most prominent in terms of media coverage was the West London Free School, partly because its founder was Toby Young, son of Michael Young (above). Promoted as a 'comprehensive grammar', Young's (2011) new school aimed to draw on older, once-shared values of culture such as those already signalled in the social experiment of *Dream School*. Young declared:

> I believe that all children can benefit from learning Latin, from seeing the plays of Shakespeare and from studying our island story. To deny them that opportunity on the grounds that those things are 'elitist' is inverted snobbery. We'll never dismantle the English class system if poor children are herded into media studies classes and forced to watch *EastEnders* while the children of the rich are introduced to the best that's been thought and said. That's not social justice, it's social apartheid.

Earlier Young (2009) pointed to the intellectual heritage of his father and how Free Schools would redress the reinforcement of unfair social divisions through education which his father had so roundly condemned: 'Today there are two types of comps: the good ones in middle-class suburbs and affluent rural areas, which are comparable to old fashioned grammars, and the rest...My hope is that "comprehensive grammars" can address this problem, honouring my father's inclusive philosophy, but without the unhelpful egalitarian baggage.'

In its first year (2011), 500 applied for its 120 places in an admissions procedure in which half the places were allocated by proximity to the school and the rest by lottery (Garner 2011). With a number of Free Schools already over-subscribed, it remains to be seen whether these, together with the range of provision already on offer, will constitute a genuine extension of choice through diversity or represent increasingly divisive educational resources. From our perspective, however, what is significant about these newer interventions is the continuing commitment to 'choice' as the driver of educational reform and as a seemingly obvious and incontrovertible benefit to parents and children. This is underpinned by a thoroughly marketised understanding of culture in which competition naturally offers choice and choice will naturally drive up standards in educational provision despite the material inequalities of those children who have to participate in it.

We suggest that the introduction of a lottery for entry to Young's Free School is, on reflection, especially intriguing because it points to a contradiction at the heart of the choice-imperative. David Cameron, speaking of the importance of choice in the provision of public services, has called for the replacement of a 'take what you are given' culture with a 'get what you choose' ethos, which is promoted as vital to making the UK fairer and more competitive.[11] But in many cases, as seen in the Cutting Edge documentaries and mumsnet.com document discussed above, the choice to 'apply' for what is perceived to be the better or the best school is, for many, the choice to 'compete' for a place or to elect to play the game. Whether entry to the school of choice is achieved by lottery, proximity, house relocation, additional tutoring, passing entry tests or the development of a competitive edge in life, it is class privilege, as well as skill, luck and determination, which will count towards that success. But the explanation offered for this success is likely to be one of responsible parental commitment.

Poor choices

So, parents have become increasingly burdened as they worry about the consequences of making the wrong choices or of making no choices at all (just taking what is offered) in terms of the damaged life chances of their offspring. Despite the fact that children are not *consumers* of education (education is, after all, compulsory by law) and very far from being autonomous citizens in their own right, they are also addressed in *Dream School* and elsewhere as, at the very least, *emergent* consumers who must also learn to take on the choice-directive. In other words, children will also be expected to make the right choices for themselves and their futures. But we should end by reminding ourselves that for some people any choice-making seems impossible, because the very notion of choice is posited on an agency they do not feel that they have.

Philosopher Renate Salecl (2010:140) suggests that wrong choices as they are conceived of socially make us feel ashamed, leading us to focus on ourselves rather than focusing on the 'cracks in the social order'. She notes, for example, that 'in times of reality television ... being poor can be misunderstood from the outside as an optional condition'. We can see how *Jamie's Dream School* and other social engineering reality television academies such as *From Ladette to Lady* or *American Idol* do, albeit inadvertently, reinforce this misunderstanding of choice or 'optionality' as always available, rationally accessible and wholly rewarding. But the tensions in these shows between the push to make responsible, pro-social choices (to be diligent, responsible, motivated, etc.) and the pull of resistance, bafflement, apathy or incapacity are also revealing.

This tension is legible, for instance, in another more recent Cutting Edge documentary called *Rich Kid, Poor Kid* (C4 2008), which explored the ways in which the poor can be regarded by others as the agents of their own downfall and how the poor regard their own predicament and the range of choices available to them. As a kind of social experiment, it brought together two girls who, although only living yards apart, were socially polarised. In one scene 17-year-old Natalie (the poor kid) is filmed desperately trying to sort out the last-minute paperwork required in order to find her younger brother Gaby a primary school place. Eventually she is confronted by the film-maker, who asks to know why Gaby is in the situation of not having a school to go to in the forthcoming autumn. Natalie becomes upset and defensive, but persistence reveals that a place should have been applied for some years before. In this scene we witness Natalie's shaming and the embarrassment of that moment. But eventually Natalie rallies round to defend herself by explaining that she already cares for her mentally ill mother, that she has to be the head of the family and that she herself was still only a schoolgirl when her brother's paperwork needed to be done. The film begins by holding Natalie to account for her disorganised family practices, but then goes on to expose the cracks in the social order through which she and her family have slipped through poverty and illness. By the by, it also demonstrates how, for many citizens, the choice-directive in education can be a nonsense, as it is obvious that Natalie and her mother were ill-equipped to sort out Gaby's schooling or to pursue the speech therapy tutoring that he seemed to need to support him in school. They were certainly in no position to 'choose' a school.

Salecl (2010:147) argues that it is highly problematic to regard choice-making as entirely rational, and we must bear in mind that the imperative to choose is in keeping with economic theory and consumerism and all that this entails. With regard to education and the ways in which it is understood in contemporary culture, this supports a model in which differences of class, cultural capital and material wealth are repressed and choice-plus-merit becomes the driver of social mobility and economic well-being. The end-logic embedded in this model is that, as indicated in the 'sharp-elbowed' middle class quiz (above), if state education doesn't work then it is up to individuals to 'opt out' or to take it over or to capitalise on the flaws in the system.

Let us end here with a brief return to *Dream School*. In one of the more intimate scenes a female student is asked by the classicist Mary Beard what she would like to do with her future, and the girl replies that she would like to have lots of money. Clearly Beard considered this to be the wrong answer. When Beard asked her again, urging her to forget about the money, she then replied that she would like to become a lawyer, a response which Beard received more approvingly. The moment is a poignant one and cross-hatched with unanswered questions. Why was it wrong for a girl with no money to want it? Why was it easier for her to imagine having money than to imagine becoming somebody important or doing something significant? In any case, in the context of the series these two last objectives, which would involve what might seem to be radical transformations of the self, appear to be out of reach. After all, if one can't even identify what is important in life (not the money, but the achievement of earning it) then how might it ever be attained? It is arguable that this and many other 'wrong' responses on *Dream School*, in which the students' aspirations seemed irrational or unrealistic (and hence mocked by critics), were fully understandable when the youngsters were faced with questions which assumed agency, positive futurity and an element of choice: things which the youngsters (probably rightly in most cases) felt that they did not have. If the responses seemed foolish, well, then, so did the questions. They also reinforced a common understanding of who is eligible to be an expert in living a successful life. As Roger Hodge (2008:362) has observed: 'If your life is one marked by lower educational attainment, lower income, and lower class, you are less likely to be considered an expert about anything, even your own life.'

5
The Ones Who Got Away: Celebrity Life Stories of Upward Social Mobility

As in Chapter 4, this chapter addresses public narratives about choice, social advancement and individual achievement, but this time through a consideration of celebrity life stories rather than educational attainment. Here we explore life stories as a resource for understanding the politics of class and aspiration and its attachment to the language of ambition, merit, chance and opportunity, consumption and work. These are unpacked via celebrity autobiography in particular; focusing on the manufacture of celebrity life stories as paradigms of social mobility. We make this choice on the same basis that Karen Sternheimer (2011:12) chooses to examine celebrities in the context of the American Dream: because 'they highlight contradictory notions about class, status, and upward mobility' and can be mobilised and read as evidence that we have an open class system based on 'one's own talent, skill and specialness'. Hence, this chapter concentrates on biographical stories of the *upwardly* socially mobile and the socially successful and the ways in which they are articulated across a range of media forms, including autobiography and memoirs. We do so because we are keen to understand how marketable life stories, and especially first person narratives, contribute to the social production of knowledge and help nourish a consensus about the possibilities for social mobility and escape from an often difficult or constricting early life. By definition, then, we have selected formats in which the subject of the life story takes an *active* part (thereby excluding, for example, unauthorised biography). We might call these 'authorised' life stories; that is, ones in which the public figure or celebrity has willingly participated, either through writing their own story or by agreeing to feature in biographical narratives such as the observational documentary.[1] We choose these because, while we understand that autobiographies and other authorised life stories are manufactured, commercially driven and often fairly standardised, we still wish to examine them as narratives of individuation and individual achievement; as narratives which are doubly loaded when their protagonist invests in their own narration.

It is well known that celebrity autobiography, in particular, as a form of genre publishing actually complicates definitions of authorship because it is so often the product of collaborative writing processes employing co-authors, editors, ghost writers and researchers.[2] It is also often journalistic in its mode of delivery, sometimes presenting the life story 'as told to' the writer and resulting from transcripts of recorded interviews together with press archive material, and so on. Moreover, it is well understood that the life stories of public figures as depicted on television and in the press (such as 'bio-docs' and interviews) are also collaboratively produced, especially within the context of the celebrity industry, where the development of the celebrity's public profile is economically driven (see Rojek 2001:10–11, Turner 2004:34ff). From our perspective this collaboration is not problematic, as we are not interested in scrutinising the stories of individual public figures as *repositories of individual memory* about social mobility. Instead we wish to chart the *common vectors of social mapping* which take place in and across a range of mediated life stories as they speak publicly about the courses of social mobility (Bromley 1988).

In the best tradition of cultural studies, we wish to acknowledge the individual's contribution to the production of their personal life story while at the same time reading it as representative of many stories and in the larger context of class structures and material culture. Roger Bromley's (1988) ground-breaking study of popular autobiography and biographical fictions is most salient here, as he establishes the balanced approach needed to negotiate the interlocking complexity of the autobiographical voice, the formulaic structures in which it features and the wider political and social terrain it inhabits. As he explains in the lucid introduction to his own study:

> The eye witness is never a simple 'I'; individual testimony is always social [...] recall is necessarily selective; selectivity is a matter of social and political determinations which is why *forms*, the habits of phrasing, and the use of formulaic repertoires in these writing will be a central part of the study.
>
> (Bromley 1988:13)

A common feature in the repertoire of celebrity life stories is the 'rags to riches' or 'rise-to-fame' trajectory. As will be outlined below in more detail, this may include the subject's self-identification as a classed individual, a sometimes painful alertness to social difference and the charting of effort, aspiration and achievement finally leading to success in the public realm. Here we will be exploring the myth-making of social mobility rather than its reality, while acknowledging, without cynicism, that these myths are fashioned by individuals from lived experience and (co-)authored by real people with a genuine investment in telling their stories as they recall them. We also do so purposefully in the context of the social reality of class difference, social stratification and social change. In other words, we are interested in pursuing how the life stories of the famous and well-known intersect with the wider rhetoric and reality of class categories, class consciousness and social advancement.

The consistent characteristic of the material we have selected for examination is that it all features prominent public figures, all of them famous nationally, and all of them choosing to insert themselves actively into media culture or at least to cooperate with the media in telling their life stories.[3] Some subjects deliberately locate their life stories in the landscape of class experience and others do not, but all of them underline, in one way or another, their *difference* or uniqueness as individuals by virtue of having a story to tell which they believe others might wish to read and, indeed, pay for. This quality of uniqueness is a prerequisite for the commercial value and popular appeal of most life stories of famous people and public figures. As Graeme Turner (2004:37) observes, while the celebrity industries would no doubt appreciate a production-line, perfectly reproducible celebrity product, 'the whole structure of celebrity is built on the construction of the individuated personality.' The methodological decision to focus on biographies of mostly well-known figures (rather than, say, the working-class memoirs of 'ordinary' people) is thereby also based on a central aim of this chapter, which is to understand the rhetorical structures of social mobility as they are played out in the *public realm* and as articulated in the media industries.

The chapter begins by charting some of the earlier, mostly sociological, work on the rise of celebrity culture and celebrity biography. In doing so, it highlights some of the ways in which the emergence of celebrity icons has been read both culturally and sociologically, the emergent definitions of the celebrity and the value judgements involved in forming these definitions. It then picks up these judgements in the context of more recent cultural analyses of celebrities as icons of social mobility before moving on to establish how we understand celebrity-hood in the current moment. The chapter then focuses on the authorised life stories of the celebrity entertainer as narratives of social advancement and individual exceptionalism.

Celebrity biography: production and consumption

It is almost customary at this point to invoke Daniel Boorstin's (2006:81) judgement made in 1961 that celebrity is a vacuous category in which the chief claim to fame is fame itself. In his estimation the celebrity who emerges from the world of light entertainment, in particular, is *de facto* non-serious and without cultural value; a view still commonly articulated today.[4] For celebrities, especially those who achieve fame without the more obvious talents of the sporting champion, the politician or the artist, for example, this vacuous-ness is also read as the evacuation of authenticity and 'realness'. And, as will be discussed below, the issue of authenticity is especially problematic for those seeking to grasp the classed nature of celebritisation. This is because class identity itself, especially in its lower or working-class forms, has frequently been measured against benchmarks of authenticity, a characteristic which is the very opposite of the perceived fakery of contemporary celebrity personas (Hoggart 1957, Dodd and Dodd 1992:121, Bidinger 2006:155ff).

Daniel Boorstin (2006:79) observed that celebrity is no longer a condition of being (of being talked about, of being celebrated) but of personhood: '*the celebrity is a person who is known for his [sic] well-knownness*' (emphasis in the original). This now much-repeated assertion is supported with reference to his historical research into the proliferation of star biographies appearing in the popular magazines of the early to mid-twentieth century. He cited these publications as evidence of the historical shift away from the media focus on the achievements of great individuals towards a new emphasis on light entertainment, personality and celebrity, arguing that they exemplify a turn away from the public engagement with human greatness ('heroes').

The growing convergence of proliferating celebrity life stories (whose protagonists are frequently figured as society's winners) and an interest in consumption and social aspiration was also established prior to Boorstin by sociologist Leo Lowenthal in his much-cited 1944 content analysis of celebrity ('entertainment') biographies in the popular American magazines of the 1940s. Lowenthal's project observed the tremendous increase in biographies to date, with a rising tide of celebrity coverage including autobiographical sketches, résumés, biographical feature articles and books. Lowenthal also described a proportional shift in magazine coverage away from people in the 'serious' professions such as business and politics (designated by him as 'idols of production') to those in the world of entertainment, media and sport ('idols of consumption'). The argument was made that this swing also represented a decline in popular interest in biographies which connected people's personal lives to history and to the forces of production and of work and a growing curiosity about celebrities' private lives, consumer practices and leisure. In other words, leisure and consumption rather than work increasingly formed the primary matter of public interest (Granter 2009:163). As Lowenthal (2006:132) observed: 'consumption is a thread running through every aspect of these stories' and hence the consumption of celebrity life stories is effectively circular, as readers' own leisure time is spent consuming stories of consumption and non-work. Lowenthal (2006:131) summarised: 'They [readers] receive information not about the agents and methods of social production but about the agents and methods of social and individual consumption. During the leisure in which they read, they read almost exclusively about people who are directly, or indirectly, providing for the reader's leisure time.'

In our own time the binary opposition between the serious idols of production and the trivial idols of consumption has dissolved as politicians, business leaders and innovators have increasingly been personalised, packaged and celebritised. These include mainstream politicians who have increasingly recognised the need to communicate with the public in more intimate and informal ways, whether by choice or perforce. Others are business leaders and entrepreneurs who undertake political or charitable work; people who are strongly influential, economically powerful and mostly unaccountable. Conversely, there are also many examples of celebrities from the entertainment and leisure industries who have contributed to public life through politics, charity work or social entrepreneurial activity. Overall, the celebrity is an increasingly prominent figure in the landscape of social aspiration because the 'expansion of celebrity status' is dependent upon its association with both capitalism and the 'democratising sentiments' of an apparently accessible culture (Marshall 1997:25–6). As we have noted elsewhere (Nunn and Biressi 2010a), 'the celebrity figure spans the fields of the individual and the collective, the popular and the political and thereby offers a model of personal success which reinforces the idea of individual achievement and social success as attainable by all.' In doing so, it also necessarily breaks down the boundaries between these fields by offering hybrid politico-celebrity figures.

In addition, even the non-politically active celebrity is legible politically. So for example all of the celebrity figures examined later in this chapter can be read, and often willingly present themselves to be read, as exemplars of certain kinds of publicly endorsed social success, and their life stories are frequently deciphered as such. As Renate Salecl (2010:44) has observed, 'there has been a major change in the way that the individual identifies with social ideals under late capitalism,' which is evident in the paradoxical stance in which people are both required to be self-made and at the same time choose to (and are encouraged to) emulate models derived from celebrity culture. This chapter will look more closely at celebrity life stories to enquire into the nature of these social ideals.

P. David Marshall (1997:10) argues that for celebrity studies the strengths of critiques by people such as Lowenthal (often arising from or affiliated to the Frankfurt School) lie in their development of a linkage 'between theories of the individual and their integration into the meaning of capitalism'. But at the same time their emphasis on mass manipulation inhibited a more complex understanding of audiences (who, for example, are understood to simply 'receive information') and their relationships with celebrities and celebrity culture. More recently researched histories of celebrity consumption are arguably more nuanced in identifying the *active* hope for social mobility that this shift towards celebrity culture mobilised and directed for audiences. For example, Karen Sternheimer's (2011) account of a century of celebrity culture and its imbrication with the American Dream of social mobility explored how stories of the stars helped Americans to understand and interpret their own experiences of opportunity, inequality and social frustration. In doing so, she discovered how early film magazines promoted the advantages and the fantasy of becoming middle-class through advertising and through profiles of the stars' middle-class (rather than, as now, often excessively elite) lifestyles. For example, even at this early stage (the 1910s), magazines sold the promise of financial security and easy money to their readers via opportunities for employment in the exciting new culture industries. Adverts appeared for correspondence courses promising that readers could become self-taught successes as screenwriters, songwriters and so on (Sternheimer 2011:43). Having charted the changing shape of celebrity culture through the decades and across genres up to and including reality television, and its articulation of social mobility in various socio-economic contexts, Sternheimer (p. 239) concluded, 'As a collective fantasy, we are active participants in both the American Dream and the meaning of celebrity culture.'

Importantly, from our viewpoint, Sternheimer's archival research stresses the importance of consumption as the driving force of celebrity culture without negating the need to understand celebrity in the context of social class and its moralistic attachments. She (2011:12) observed: 'Ultimately, celebrities' lifestyles reveal the material blessings of wealth, and those that go broke spending reaffirm the Horatio Alger notion that poverty is the result of poor individual choices, rather than systematic inequalities.' Put simply, it is possible to decode celebrity biographies and the models of aspiration their life stories propose both in terms of the consumerist society and as negotiations of classed identities. This joint approach offers productive insights, for example, into the phenomenal appeal of recent talent shows, which can be read both as ideal machines for consumption and consumerism (as commodities in themselves and by offering models of the consuming self) and as narratives which situate contestants within the context of social class and class advancement. In terms of the latter, the ideal winner of, say, *Any Dream Will Do* (BBC1 2007) or *Pop Idol* (ITV 2001–03) or *Operatunity* (C4 2003) is someone whose story is one of evident social mobility despite their modest (read 'poor' or more often 'working-class' or 'ordinary') origins.

Having noted this, the complexity of the celebrity image, of social advancement and its iconic significations (via consumerism especially), has been treated by some as evidence of either the redundancy of social class as a factor in the organisation of social structures and/or its growing irrelevance as a conceptual tool for understanding social mobility within a consumer society. Moreover, the view that celebrities are socially useless and in some cases form a 'powerless' elite (Alberoni 2006) has contributed to the argument that celebritised culture is better conceptualised via tropes of production, distribution and especially of consumption rather than, say, as part of status systems (but see Kurzman *et al.* 2007) or class taxonomies or even cultural labour. If we were to subscribe to this view, we would have to concede that, even if we stubbornly insist that social class is meaningful in the *social realm*, we might well reject it within the context of celebrity culture analysis. After all, we might ask ourselves, if celebrities are 'artificial' or constitute a 'new category of human emptiness' (Boorstin 2006:74, 90) or are simply animated brands that do no essential work in the world, then what can their biographies usefully tell us about the real and dirty business of social class?

Whether or not we agree with Boorstin about the essential wrongness of celebrity ascendancy (in his view evidently signifying a decline in standards and values) compared with the more traditional public actor who achieves fame through obvious endeavour, talent, skill or even genius, the celebrity is certainly a troubling, tricky and significant subject for the serious critic of culture and society. This is partly because, as already noted, the celebrity embodies a consumerist ethos (which earlier 'heroes' did not), especially by virtue of their affiliation to branded leisure and mass entertainment. Also, as with more traditional idols, celebrities continue to inspire emulation with all of its attendant ideological problems. Zygmunt Bauman (2011:18) asserts, for instance, that 'the driving force of conduct is no longer the more or less realistic desire to "keep up with the Joneses", but the infuriatingly nebulous idea of "keeping up with celebrities".' This is a rather poignant and especially fruitless aspiration when, in his view, the chances of living a satisfying life are declining rapidly for the many casualties of profit-driven, consumer-oriented society.

So, from this viewpoint, scholarly attention to the phenomenon of celebrity via consumption and consumerism in particular, albeit condemned by Boorstin (2006:80) as an 'oversubtle' approach, can be defended in terms of the changing form and content of popular biography and with regard to its longer historical economic and political arc. The celebrities studies critic Chris Rojek (2001:13–16) has built on this approach through an influential mapping of this trajectory. Rojek (p. 12) maintains, in summary, that three major historical processes fostered the emergence of the celebrity as a public preoccupation: the democratisation of society, the decline of organised religion and the commodification of everyday life. These macro-changes led to the generation of a new or alternative ideology 'of the common man'. For him this ideology underwrote the extant political system and nourished business and industry, thus 'contributing immensely to the commodification of celebrity' (Rojek:13). Celebrity-hood is often orchestrated around the centrality of consumption to contemporary ways of living in and organising the social world and 'celebrities are significant nodal points of articulation between the social and the personal' (Rojek:16). Rojek doesn't engage with class and material inequalities in relation to celebrity culture (that's not his primary concern), but, like others (above), he does identify real social damage as a result of the proliferation of celebrities:

> If celebrity society possesses strong tendencies to make us covet celebrities, and to construct ourselves into objects that immediately arouse sentiments of desire and approval in others, it also creates

many more losers than winners. The celebrity race is now so ubiquitous in all walks of life that living with failure is oppressive for those of us who do not become achieved celebrities.

(Rojek:15)

What we take from Rojek and other critics and historians (as cited, and also including Foster 2005, Karl 2007, Redmond and Holmes 2007:189ff, Cross and Littler 2010, Tyler and Bennett 2010), whatever their moral judgement or critical evaluation and whether they choose to pursue questions of consumption, of class or of both, is a recognition that celebrity (and celebrity culture) is equally in and of the world rather than a thing apart. As such, it must be considered to be socially and politically (as well as economically) significant. We would argue that the view of celebrities as wholly inauthentic, and consequently somehow beyond class and outside the social, is a fundamental misunderstanding of their positionality. By placing them outside class analysis we risk losing sight of the ways in which class difference is being articulated in the current moment and the ways in which social inequalities are explained and justified. If social status is made rather than merely inherited, and financial success is theoretically available to all who really want it enough, then celebrity culture is playing its part in conveying how these should and can be achieved.

Celebrities working to keep it real

In our world of big names, curiously, our true heroes tend to be anonymous...the person with solid virtues who can be admired for something more substantial than his well-knownness often proves to be the unsung hero: the teacher, the nurse, the mother, the honest cop, the hard worker at lonely under-paid, unglamorous, unpublicized jobs.

(Boorstin 2006:90)

As noted above, for some people celebrities seem to personify a functionless existence unless mass entertainment and the promotion of consumer goods are regarded as positive contributions to the social good. Indeed, even their functionlessness feeds into entertainment culture. See, for example, the flurries of press coverage showing how to calculate the most pointless celebrity (e.g. Thomas, D. 2007). Annoyingly, some celebrities also appear to undertake well-paid work without labour; for celebrity work is generally masked over or represented as both easy and fun (Bell 2010:79).[5] Arguably, as a consequence, celebrities and their publicists often have to make the case through autobiography, interview and other recourse to their life stories that they have, indeed, *earned* their success and their prosperity. In other words, they have to work towards authentication and the assignation of significant value, often through attachments to characteristics of 'realness', labour and classed notions of authenticity.

If 'true heroes', in many people's estimation, are (public service) workers such as those described by Boorstin, then it makes sense for celebrities to forge associations with these kinds of people. They may do so, either by visibly 'giving back' to the community through charity work or political activism (see Littler 2008) or by emphasising their continuing attachment to their own more humble origins, to family, and thus staying true to themselves. The latter is difficult to achieve as Jo Littler (2003) explains in her critique of musical artist Jennifer Lopez's video *Jenny From the Block*. This video tells Lopez's own rags-to-riches story while stressing her continuing connections with her friends from the Bronx. But Lopez's claim to 'keep it real' is bound up with contradictions. First, her realness is about what she has taken from her original culture (authenticity) rather than what she can contribute and, second, her claim to remain unchanged is likely to be received with scepticism, perhaps even by all but her most ardent fans. In this analysis Littler offers a nuanced reading of the markers of fame, intimacy and post-modern reflexivity, as they are articulated in celebrities' accounts of their own lives, without jettisoning the politics of class or a lively engagement with debates around material inequalities and meritocratic myths. Ultimately, summarises Littler (2003:13), 'referencing the "moment before" fame is in part about money, work and class.'

Society issues warnings against celebrity ambition and taking the benefits of fame too seriously. As noted in our earlier discussion of the critical reception of *Jamie's Dream School*, talent shows are especially problematic as routes to social mobility because they appear to offer deceptively easy access to social advancement. As celebrity production lines they seem to act as an unhelpful distraction for younger people in particular, and specifically for working-class children, who turn away from more serious and viable ambitions. In ways similar to Boorstin's critique above, affluent celebrity-hood (as personified by models, music artists, footballers, etc.) continues to be unfavourably contrasted with 'real' jobs whose value is allegedly being undermined by celebrity icons. As one Teacher's Union member declared in conference when condemning the impact of celebrities on the aspirations of working-class boys (Paton 2010): 'Getting up, going to work, doing a good job, looking after your family, not being a drunkard, living within your means, not running up debts, looking after your house, are all part of the role that needs to be presented as important and worthwhile.'[6]

In similar vein, commentators from the conservative press perceive celebrity-hood as a worrying attraction for the lower social orders, observing, for example, that for 'children from working class families, where aspiration is considered middle class, choices in life consist of becoming a celebrity, working in a shop or becoming a mum' (cited in Jones 2011:218). In reply perhaps to persistent criticism such as this, newly-minted talent and reality show celebrities, especially those from modest social backgrounds, choose to underline the labour of celebrity work and their vocational attitude towards it. For example, Olly Murs, a self-identified 'working class boy from Essex' and former call-centre operative who achieved success through *The X Factor*, professed:

> I used to wonder how professional footballers get up in the morning. What's your motivation to play football when you're getting paid £10 million a year? But I see it now. I'm not earning anything like that, but entertainers get paid ridiculous sums too, yet we love the job. If you love what you do, whatever your job is, you don't care about the money.[7]

This positioning, as someone who has money but does not care about it, who has work but it is work they love, who has been given a lucky break but works hard to sustain it, is a tightrope act which negotiates both consumerist imperatives and classed investments and aims to satisfy both. Talent show celebrities have been praised by their fans and promoters precisely from the perspective of their success as classed role models; they strive to counter accusations of the celebrity performer both as not 'really' working and also as a negative role model.[8] For instance, Laura from Oxford posted her support for *The X Factor* winner Joe McElderry on the *Daily Mail* website in the following terms:

> well Joe is very sweet and talented – he is the best of being British and he is working class. Lets [sic] face it, no use going on about the great British of the past – 100 years ago the aristocrisy [sic] of this country would have had a Joe type down the mines or in the trenches and he would have been dead by 30 years old – face it!!![9]

In sum, there are profound contradictions in the ways in which celebrities are positioned in relation to 'real' work, to the extent that they may be found to simultaneously underwrite and undermine the rhetoric of hard graft. This is beautifully exemplified in the BBC3/BBC Radio 1/online show *Up For Hire Live*, which was stripped over four nights in October 2011. Aimed at a young audience, it debated rising youth unemployment and demonstrated how to secure an occupation using a combination of social experiment (through televised work placements), real job vacancies with chains such as Starbucks and Argos, consultations with entrepreneurs and online resources. The first show focused on the hard grind of entry level roles and built a consensus that young people had to knuckle down and take any job to step onto the career ladder. Early in the first episode, presenter Richard Bacon asked reality show winner and TV personality Stacey Solomon whether talent shows sent out the wrong messages to young people by raising expectations that success can come without hard work. In reply, Solomon defended her career choice and emphasised the hardship of surviving the auditions and undertaking reality tasks for her post-talent show appearance on *I'm A Celebrity: Get Me Out of Here* (ITV 2010). Despite this nod towards a social concern with the negative influence of celebrity culture, the series consistently mobilised celebrity advice based on the life stories of youth-friendly entertainers. This included pre-recorded sound bites and live chat with a host of reality stars, comedians and broadcasters. In addition, each night the live panel also featured two celebrities alongside one industry specialist to respond to the issues highlighted.

Both the criticisms and defences of celebrities as indicated above are often articulated in the everyday language of class difference, and sometimes, too, in the older language of class politics. As Imogen Tyler and Bruce Bennett (2010:375) observed when setting out their own agenda for critiquing celebrity culture: '[...] in contradistinction to claims that the concept of social class has lost its analytic value in the context of contemporary consumer society and the growing ideological purchase of meritocracy and choice...class remains central to the constitution and meaning of celebrity'. They go on to demonstrate that the proliferation of celebrity biographies and autobiographies, of background stories and the public scrutiny of celebrity conduct and deportment is in fact fundamentally rooted in class fascination. Indeed, it indicates the 'increasingly central function that celebrity plays within wider social processes of class-making' (Tyler and Bennett:377). Working in line with this conviction and in the interests of unpacking some of these processes, this chapter now goes on to consider, in some detail, entertainment celebrities' self-told stories in order to work through some of the typical features of successful social mobility as commonly set out in the media.

Drawing on Chris Rojek's (2001:18) modelling of celebrity-hood, the next section will mostly exclude 'ascribed' celebrities; that is, those who inherit celebrity through family lineage, such as actor–manager dynasties. We make this move because we wish to focus on life stories of *conspicuous* social mobility rather than success supported or sustained by family or institution, where the mechanisms of promotion can be fairly obscure. In these cases the implications of these stories as narratives of class and social advancement would need separate attention. Instead, we will focus on 'achieved' celebrities, 'attributed' celebrities or blended celebrities (those combining skills or talent and managed media attention), such as those who have attained fame through the entertainment industries in comedy, variety shows and chat show hosting. We will also reference 'celetoid' life stories; taking celetoids to be a variant of achieved celebrity-hood as a 'media-generated, compressed, concentrated form' (Rojek 2001:ibid.). This last category is best exemplified, in our view, by reality show and talent show contestants. Attributed celebrities and celetoids are more obviously the products of the expansion of the mass media and the conglomeration of the media industry interests (e.g. broadcasting, journalism and the book trade) and there is a notable history of concern about their status and their influence as role models of social ambition, consumption and achievement.

I dreamed a dream: celebrity origins

Autobiography and life-writing is without doubt a very popular genre in UK book publishing, with autobiography making up 28 per cent of the non-fiction market between 1998 and 2005 (see Feather and Woodbridge 2007). It could be claimed that the notable commercial success of *celebrity* autobiography, in particular, was mostly due to the growing convergence of television and the book trade, which grew together, consolidated and diversified during the 1990s (Sutherland 2002:163). In the UK there was also an observable spike in the number of bestselling celebrity autobiographies coinciding with the recession, with notable sales successes for memoirs by established entertainers during 2008–09.[10] Cultural critic Mark Lawson (2008) attributed this to a decision by readers that they would rather spend their limited budgets on being entertained than on the pricey ingredients needed for the recipes offered in celebrity cookbooks. This may well be the case.

We would also add that many of the books he cites (Kay 2006, O'Grady 2008, Parkinson 2008, Walters 2008) were written by older or well-loved entertainers rather than newcomers and commonly chronicled their journeys away from working class, materially limited origins (see also Barkham 2007). The essential elements for the appeal of these stories are nicely summarised by Ebury Press Editorial Director Charlotte Cole when describing the reason for its acquisition of a memoir by actor Sue Johnson: 'Sue's memoir has all the stuff of a bestseller: a gloriously-recounted working class childhood in the 1950s and '60s, in Liverpool no less, and – in Sue's mother – a central figure who haunts the narrative . . . . Sue's story is a rich and emotionally-satisfying read all her own' (in Allen 2011). It may be no coincidence that, when readers themselves are cutting back on spending, and even perhaps revising their own ambitions and values during an economic downturn, they turn for diversion to stories by well-loved figures who have escaped their own unpropitious beginnings without sacrificing the values that contributed to their development as characters and as 'personalities'.

So the popularity of the celebrity life story has been attributed to two somewhat subjective factors: the 'likeability' of the biographical subject and the regaling of a story in which the protagonist conquers immense personal difficulties such as a tough childhood, a career disaster, mental illness and imprisonment. Former Time Warner director Alan Sampson was quoted as saying: 'It's not so much about revelations. The public now expects obstacles overcome' (in Rees 2003). As indicated, these obstacles were often of a highly personal nature and seemed to meet an audience demand already evidenced by the so-called misery or dark memoirs of the late 1990s and early 2000s. These included the best-selling *Angela's Ashes* (McCourt 1998), an Irish-American narrative of appalling childhood poverty, and the American child-abuse trilogy written by Dave Pelzer which commenced with his early experiences of atrocious maltreatment at the hands of his mother.[11] Such was their popularity that booksellers set aside new 'painful lives' shelving sections to help customers locate their new favourite genre. Literature scholar John Sutherland (2002:169) spied a thematic connection between stories such as these and successful British celebrity life stories. His evidence included the biography *Billy* (Stephenson 2001), which was a 'life study' of the comedian Billy Connolly authored by his psychotherapist wife. This described a bleak childhood and subsequent bouts of substance abuse and was the number one non-fiction hardback of that year. Another success was an autobiography by the famous footballer and alcoholic George Best entitled *Blessed* (2001). For Sutherland these narratives were essentially stories of survival, and especially of overcoming self-destructive tendencies. Indeed, the book trade even went on to massage the evolution of misery memoirs into new hybrid categories of 'celeb mis mems', which included celebrity memoirs such as Kerry Katona's (2006) *Too Much, Too Young* and Kim Woodburn's (2006) *Unbeaten: The Story of My Brutal Childhood* and 'misery sport' memoirs, such as *Being Gazza* (Gascoigne *et al.* 2006) and *Black and Blue* (Canoville 2008) (see Bury 2007, Bell 2008).

We suggest that this celebrity emphasis on the self and the transformation of the self takes place in the context of a confessional and therapeutic culture which shapes recollections of suffering through individual psychological and emotional moulds. As such, it also arguably deflects attention away from bigger collective stories of survival from material deprivation, class or race prejudice and the disadvantages with which this is associated. Even when class (and other) disadvantages and class difference are highlighted by celebrity entertainers, this is usually undertaken within a very narrow remit, wherein class injury is relevant solely or mainly as a marker of how far the protagonist had progressed. The huge commercial success of soap star and entertainer Shane Richie's autobiography *From Rags to Richie* (Richie and Crawford 2003) became the model to emulate.[12] Its Amazon product description highlighted its narrative arc of humble origins, success, failure and more success, and prioritised Richie's origins as the son of dustman and later as a Pontins Bluecoat [holiday camp] entertainer.

> The son of a dustman, Shane Richie has come a long way from the rough streets of London's Harlesden. As *Eastenders'* loveable rogue Alfie Moon he is now the 'darling' of every soap fan in Britain, but it has been an incredible roller-coaster ride as he twice fought his to way the top. Shane grabbed the trappings of fame with both hands, sleeping with a string of women and indulging in the champagne lifestyle to excess.

The chapter headings, mostly using quotations and delivered in the vernacular, set the tone of a working-class and sometimes tabloid or demotic style of address. Titles such as 'Hello, mister, my name's Shane', 'People like us can't afford to have dreams', 'Cracking up', 'Didn't you used to be Shane Richie?' and 'To the Moon and beyond' mapped the highs, lows and greater highs of a celebrity career. They are also reminiscent of Walter Greenwood's (1933) poverty exposé *Love on the Dole* and the auto-ethnography of cultural studies pioneer Richard Hoggart

(1957), whose own chapters also deployed the working-class voice with headings such as 'There's no place like home', 'Putting up with things' and 'Living and letting live'. Importantly, however, the celebrity self-told story mobilises the protagonist's origins as the marker of how far they have travelled rather than as a reflexive political engagement with the past and with class difference. Richie's own story begins with his conception (the result of a drunken 'knee-trembler') followed by his family's immigration from Dublin to London in search of work (with passing references to prejudice against Irish immigrants). Typically for the genre, his account of a poor and difficult childhood, partly lived in the refuge for battered wives which employed his mother, is related with wry humour and a warmth which could be described as working-class romanticism. His mother had a 'heart as big a number 18 bus' (Richie 2003:9), rats were large enough to be mistaken for rabbits and the topsy-turvy life of the refuge was anarchic fun. Richie never discusses class inequality or class politics. His few direct mentions of social class (in this case 'working class') refer to the opportunities for work with soap opera, stand-up comedy and realist theatre which were welcoming forums for working-class entertainers. It is clear, however, from the generic conventions cited here that this is recognisable as a working-class story of social advancement.

A more recently established forum for working-class success in the entertainment industries is, as already noted, the talent show. Singing star Susan Boyle (2010) maintained in her autobiography *The Woman I Was Born to Be* that for the reader her story should begin with her first appearance on *Britain's Got Talent* (*BGT* ITV 3rd series 2009), although for her, of course, it actually began much earlier with her birth in a village in West Lothian, Scotland, in 1961. Susan Boyle is the superstar singer 'discovered' in a talent show. Her story is from rags-to-riches and ugly-duckling-to-swan all rolled into one. She begins by recalling 'that moment' when she should have spotted something auspicious but failed to do so; the occasion of her rendering of 'I dreamed a dream' from the musical *Les Misérables* (itself based on a novel of social advancement and struggle and adapted as light entertainment). Her audition performance, which patently defied the expectations of the judges, was rapturously received after its first broadcast on YouTube.com, and her subsequent rising trajectory has had to accommodate commonly made judgements of her as both exceptional and ordinary: exceptional in her talent and her persistence and ordinary in her background and her appearance. Susan Boyle's (2010:120) autobiography established the talent show as the only possible launching pad for a woman who can sing but is otherwise ill-equipped to deliver to the conventional expectations of the producers and audiences of the entertainment industries: 'It was the only route to success that someone like me knew.' Hence, her account of her own dogged persistence recalls her auditions for *Opportunity Knocks* (BBC1 revived 1987–90), *My Kind of People* (ITV 1995) and *The X Factor* (ITV1 2004–) and underlines their crucial role in providing a platform for 'ordinary people' such as herself.

This narrative of determination to succeed was, however, already complicated by what was perceived to be her social oddness, with reports of mental health problems, disabilities, spinsterhood and an unusually restricted and isolated life (signified by her living with mother and her unemployed status). This, too, was compounded by her appearance, which was relayed by commentators as profoundly unkempt, ill-managed and unattractive. Overweight, badly dressed and unglamorous (and so already marked as 'lower-class'), she 'embodied social failure' as it is commonly read and crudely understood through her back-story (Duffett 2011:180). Subsequently, then, as Mark Duffett (p. 181) argues, her story became one of 'romantic longing as an outsider coming into celebrity'. Somehow, despite all the social obstacles Boyle encountered, such as her struggles at school (not helped by 'cognitive disabilities'), her unhappy unemployed days during the 1980s and her depression, her narrative becomes one in which she moves from being 'different' to being 'special', from being a 'loser' to a 'winner' by virtue of her remarkable voice. Boyle effectively (and affectively) straddles the gap between ordinary and exceptional. In the chapter entitled 'Special', for example, she recalls (p. 61) how, following a religious pilgrimage, she returned to school and performed her first public solo to great acclaim: 'I had a gift, people kept telling me afterwards.' Increasingly her story becomes reconfigured from social failure to one of destiny, to becoming 'the woman I was born to be' as well as one of talent and striving (see Holmes 2010).

Each celebrity autobiography is by definition unique because it markets a specific life story to fans, but at the same time the selection, ordering and presentation of past events are likely to be familiar to any regular readers of celebrity marketing material. Boyle's book is no exception here, and it is not difficult to identify common features simply by comparing it with the products of other talent show celebrities. For instance, whereas Boyle 'dreamed a dream', *The X Factor* (ITV 2004–) winner Leona Lewis (2009) reveals in her book what happens when 'dreams come true'. Whereas Boyle's life is read as a 'Cinderella story' (p. 187), Lewis's 'life is a real-life fairytale' (back cover). Boyle's story begins by reflecting on her 'journey' since her initial media success and Lewis's (p. 11) memoir, headed 'The Journey Begins,' starts with the announcement that she has won the competition. But these coincidences of description are rather more than the iteration of cliché (although they are that, of course); rather, '[t]he life remembered in these books is done so within the context of present fame; it is a teleology towards the current position of the writer' (de Groot 2009:36). As such, they are also only the most obvious features of the formulaic repertoires that embed celebrity success stories in particular social and political explanatory frameworks; frameworks which commonly insist on certain interpretations of social advancement and exclude others. As we shall see, these interpretations only allow for certain rather proscribed readings of the determining role of social class in the achievement of upward social mobility.

The humble beginning, and its establishment through recollection and family album, is a common feature of the celebrity memoir. Often engagingly told without self-pity and even with wry humour, the *pastness* of 'lower-class' living and sometimes even of poverty is doubly emphasised through the reader's knowledge of the author's present success. Susan Boyle's narrative is exemplary. Readers learn that she was the ninth child delivered by her mother in a period of 23 years. As Boyle tells it, her parents were devout Catholics who refused to terminate the pregnancy despite the dangers identified to mother and child, both of whom suffered from illness subsequently. Her father was working as a miner when they relocated, following her birth, to a council house with more room (three bedrooms for ten people, as one sibling had died long before). This social and economic setting, little commented on in any detail, is amplified by the book's inclusion of early monochrome and then later coloured family photographs of Boyle as a child standing in the paved yards and simply furnished living rooms of her early years, followed by images of Boyle in later years as she tries to pursue her ambition to perform.

Again, the recollections of comedian, former drag queen and talk show host Paul O'Grady (born 1955) are often both humorous and anecdotal, with the humble setting of his origins the signs of a largely individualised social condition. His best-selling autobiography *At My Mother's Knee* (2008) spanned his childhood as the son of Irish immigrants growing up in Birkenhead through to the death of his father; all in the years before he became famous. It was reported that by September 2010 O'Grady's book had sold 772,987 copies in Britain (Egawhari 2010). A weightier affair than the volumes already cited,

O'Grady's book made space to present a family memoir in a historical context which included his own relations' reminiscences of the Second World War, political unrest in Ireland and amusing stories of 'making do' with limited resources. Only then did it move on to his own seemingly haphazard trajectory through schooling and early working life. As in the other stories already cited, class distinctions and class difference, while frequently acknowledged through anecdote, are inscribed as an individual condition to be experienced stoically and with good humour. In this way poverty and deprivation 'exist by themselves, part of another time, discontinuous with all other moments' (Bromley 1988:39). Another example of the same move, but told in a tougher, less affectionate tone, may be found in the autobiography of stand-up comedian Roy 'Chubby' Brown (né Royston Vasey), *Common as Muck!* (Vasey 2006). Brown achieved scandalous fame for his vulgar, often misogynist and homophobic jokes, which attracted a mainly white working-class audience (see Medhurst 2007). In this narrative Brown draws very strategically on this persona, interspersing his recent experience of cancer and a newly happy home life with recollections of a 'colourful' earlier life from his working-class origins in Yorkshire. These difficult times included spells of prison, living rough and working in the merchant navy before his break into the entertainment industry. Here monochrome photographs of his early years are frequently anchored with humorous, slightly bitter observations. A picture of his father wearing a flat cap and holding a glass of beer is labelled 'My dad. We buried him with a pint in his hand, but we all loved him' and another, of his old home town, is labelled 'The good old days (my arse!)' (Vasey: between pp. 116–17). To draw on the subtitle of entertainer Tommy Steele's (2006) autobiography *Bermondsey Boy*, these histories are already presented and understood to be 'memories of a forgotten world', but in Brown's case it is a world he is more than happy to leave behind.

As already noted, the teleology of the celebrity biography moves towards the now and the current moment of celebrity-hood (de Groot 2009). This is reinforced by the number of 'instant' celebrity memoirs designed to capitalise on sudden fame and make the most of what is likely to be the transient quality of maximum public recognition. As Kurzman *et al.* (2007:363) argue, 'Celebrity is status on speed. It develops quickly, not over generations as in Weber's theory. It decays quickly, rather than accumulating over the years.' Even though many popular biographies are speedily produced and start with the 'nowness' of the person's current fame, there is also an imperative to 'historicise the celebrity' (de Groot 2009:36). This arguably helps to counter the ephemeral nature of celebrity-hood (perhaps not always successfully), sets up the individual in place and time and establishes the social distance they have travelled. This manoeuvre, already long-running in auto/biography as a genre, also fits well with new hybrid genres in which public figures are invited to return to their roots or to explore their family origins or even their genetic inheritance. Series such as *The House I Grew Up In* (BBC R4 2007–), *Who Do You Think You Are?* (BBC 2004–) and *All Roads Lead Home* (BBC2 2011) all variously position the celebrity as a seeker after their own history and origins, and many of these episodes ask the protagonists to reflect on how lucky they were not to have been born in an earlier era of class inequality. For Anne Marie Kramer (2011:434), this move goes beyond the 'contemporary mythologisation of the familiar rags-to-riches story. Given that the celebrity is presented as "living" history they also represent the embodiment of historical experience and memory.' At the same time, we could argue that, as Roger Bromley (1988) has demonstrated in another context, this autobiographical recourse to the historical is often actually a recourse to a more generic 'pastness' which often lacks what we might call the grit of historical materialism. This is most evident in written celebrity autobiographies in which the past is both generalised (as poor but happy, poor and repressive, or middle-class and stifling, etc.) and then made specific by virtue of its anchorage to the life of one very singular individual who, as we already know, will move on and away to better things. Overall, the beginnings of these kinds of celebrity biographies reassure readers that the limitations of social class are firmly behind us.

'How did I get here from there?': celebrity endings

Older celebrity autobiographers do sometimes make reference to the strategic importance of education (often via an account of their experience of the now long-defunct 11 plus exam) or of other kinds of state support in driving their own social advancement. But even the books which do this are still mostly legible (at least by contemporary reviewers) as individual tales of triumph over adversity. The institutional supports which are known to lift people out of poverty, such as education, training, and a healthy and safe environment to live in, are accorded minimal importance when compared with individual 'passion' or drive to success. Agony aunt, novelist and distinguished social campaigner Claire Rayner (2003) asked, perhaps inadvertently, the most important instrumental question about social advancement, which is 'how did I get here from there?' In her autobiography of that title 'there' was an impoverished and difficult childhood, which she managed to overcome to live a successful and productive life. The book was widely reviewed, praised and highly commended for being 'inspiring', 'positive', 'uplifting' and 'empowering' as well as for its candid revelation of her neglect and mistreatment during her precarious early years.[13] As such, its marketing and reception were typical in playing down the wider field of class difference and class injury which Rayner herself recognised and highlighted in the memoir. In reviews little mention was made of the story as an account of the state-supported social mobility which had enabled her to play such a prominent role in public life in her later years. Yet Rayner described her training as a nurse as a crucial prop to her own independence and social advancement, allowing her to gain an education and equipping her to earn her own money. As a media personality, her account of getting away from social deprivation is exceptional in giving credit to the ideals of the welfare state and the values of collective social progress which she championed all her working life.

'How did I get here from there?' asks Rayner. But where is the 'here' of current success and media visibility? What are the lessons learned by the protagonist; lessons which will in turn be humbly offered to readers for their own enlightenment? For Rayner, her ultimate arrival and achievement lay in her increasingly important position as a spokeswoman for 'ordinary people' through her role as a health and welfare campaigner. But for the reader, of course, 'here' is also a location of financial comfort and public recognition. To emulate the celebrity's social and economic success, readers are mostly encouraged to stay true to themselves or to dearly held values, to work more and to complain less. At the end of her autobiography Susan Boyle (2010:317) recounts the advice given to her by a friend: 'You are writing your story Susan. It's about achievement and belief in yourself.' The now-ness of celebrity autobiographies often resides not only in their current accomplishment but in their retrospective reflections of lessons learned about the psychology of the self. As we have explained, these are rarely critical reflections on the classed (or even ethnic) experience of individual social advancement but instead focus on 'survival', the maintenance, discovery or return to one's true self, the sustenance of family values established pre-celebrity or the recognition that some things are more important than fame and wealth. Stacey Solomon (2011), for example, reflected on her sensible management of money despite her fame and how her family values have helped her to keep her feet on the ground. Soap star Patsy Palmer (2007 cover notes) offered an account of how she 'chose to survive' domestic dramas and various addictions to finally rediscover herself in the chapter entitled 'Finding Julie' (she was born Julie Harris). *Big Brother* (C4 2000–) winner for 2006, Pete Bennett, offered a story which took him from a 'rough' south London council estate, through 'low life' encounters and addictions and via the roller-coaster of fame, to finally return to his former, better self. He revealed, 'all the time I am getting closer and closer to normality, finally back to being the real Perfect Pete' (Bennett 2006:291). Bennett's *Big Brother* housemate Aisleyne Horgan-Wallace's (2009:231) book, which charted difficult years of homelessness and her experience of a dangerous street life, concluded that 'we can all turn our lives round and make them better.' Her book also finished with a list of charities to help young people, those with addictions, and so on. These underlined the non-state solutions available for social welfare and the generic connection between personal distress and the celebrity autobiography as self-help manual. Craig Phillips (2009:282), the much-liked winner of the first UK *Big Brother*, and someone who has subsequently sustained a solid media career, concluded with an address to the reader: 'Remember, you can achieve anything you want to with hard, honest work, dedication and, most importantly, by just being yourself.' This hybridisation of celebrity with self-help, life-coaching and therapy culture is further complicated by the often unspoken and subtle influence of the American motivational movement, which promotes active *desire* for success as its own launching pad to achievement. Here positive thinking is presented as the key to success and its inverse (failure) is therefore inevitably inscribed to personal deficiencies in this regard (Ehrenreich 2009). Many of these volumes suggest that anything can be achieved if the passion is there to succeed.

In the British context, while self-help is usually expressed in a fairly low-key way, family values are strongly highlighted as integral to a fully rounded and ultimately successful character. For instance, talk radio host and tabloid journalist Jon Gaunt (2007), in an autobiography which segues back and forth from his traumatic childhood to his various career highlights and failures, finally produces a story which is far less about his advancement from poverty to financial comfort and public recognition (although it is that) and rather more about his reconciliation with his father. Hence, his memoir concludes with a scene at his father's deathbed when he finally concedes that he should accept the loving support of his family. Gaunt (2007:242) recalled his father saying: 'Jon you prick, accept the love, the support...you're a man, a father, a husband and more importantly a son.'

Likewise Roy Brown, having survived critical illness, the break-up of a relationship and the discovery of long-lost offspring, finds himself in similar terrain through a happy personal relationship and by being at the peak of his career. Andy Medhurst (2007:199) argues that Brown is an important figure because his popularity is a 'flagrant testament to the persistence of class as a meaningful category' and his comedy routine is 'determined...to speak up for its disregarded constituency'. Brown acknowledges this as he describes how he built up an act based on the lives and especially the language of 'common people'. Outside his stage performance Brown's life story is also one of a self-consciously classed experience, with a clear narrative of escape from a difficult, chaotic family and a town so poor that crime wasn't even worth committing because there was literally nothing to steal (Vasey 2006:25). 'The stage had been my salvation,' observed Brown (Vasey:ibid.). In conclusion he chooses to reflect somewhat more critically than some of his peers on how his comic persona and personal success both provided him with an escape route from poverty and social exclusion and also increasingly confined him to a mouthy stereotype of working-class masculinity:

> I've watched dozens of Grangetown lads who were just like me when I was younger [...] drop like flies, cut down in their prime by cancer, heart attacks or violence. That was their miserable life. I was part of that brigade, part of that shitty existence, but Chubby showed me a way out...He saved me from myself and brought me the kind of success and riches no Grangetown lad could ever reasonably respect. There's some people who say money's not everything, but you try and get something without it.
>
> (Vasey:368)

Over the course of his autobiography his story is remade as one in which he realises that he has now worked hard enough and progressed far enough emotionally (rather than economically) to dispense with his character Chubby at will and become the person he is today. Like many of the other memoirs scrutinised in this chapter, his story of a classed journey away from endemic poverty and socially structured disenfranchisement becomes refashioned as an emotional journey. As he learns the importance of family life above all else, Brown concludes (Vasey:369), 'Helen [his wife] and the kids had replaced Chubby...he used to rule my life because I felt I owed him everything. Those days were over. Chubby had become just a bloke with a mucky mouth and a silly suit.'

6

The Upper Classes: Visibility, Adaptability and Change

This chapter addresses the representation of the British upper classes and the mediation of their social practices and values. In doing so it seeks to explore the ways in which the upper classes are accommodated and condoned within an unequal society despite the often-repeated conviction that success should be achieved through merit both within and also across generations. For some readers, a chapter on the upper class might seem less than pressing, as there is a perception that this social bracket is rather small (perhaps being confined to those with titles, for example) and therefore without significant economic or political power or even cultural influence. This view is entirely understandable, because the upper classes in Britain are indeed small in number (even when the non-aristocratic rich are counted; see Abercrombie *et al.* 2000:183). They can also be rather oddly invisible except in their most institutionalised, ceremonial and archaic of forms; that is, in the shape of the monarchy, those with titles and their social set and through the annual publication of Honours Lists and the like. Indeed, since the second half of the twentieth century at least, the aristocracy and what has been referred to as the landed gentry (those land-owning classes who could live off the income of their estates) have been portrayed as a dying breed. They have been seen to struggle to adapt to social change; juggling the economic pressures of maintaining stately homes and country houses or turning to trade with work in business, in the City of London, and so forth. Moreover, the post-World War Two years have witnessed a decline in class-based deference for the aristocracy and even for the royal family (Rosen 2003:39–40). Depictions of turmoil and social dysfunction in the royal family during moments of media exposure, such as those seen during the 1980s with the marriage and separation of the Prince and Princess of Wales and the Duke and Duchess of York, also served to

118

undermine, if only in the short term, popular notions of the centrality and relevance of the royal family to national life.

Having said this, it has nonetheless been argued that overall the media, which are mostly under upper-class (albeit non-aristocratic) ownership, continue to depict the upper classes as non-threatening or even as beneficial to British life, business and culture (Roberts 2011:177). When the media do choose to debate their role more questioningly they still do so in the context of mass, mainly uncritical coverage of the *monarchy*, which, in itself, ultimately *underlines* rather than undermines the continuing importance of the upper classes to national life (Blain and O'Donnell 2003:30).[1] Moreover, there is far more diversity and political weight to the British upper classes in terms of their contribution to British life, culture and the economy and to its political institutions than these reports of royalty, both major and minor, would suggest. The upper class is in fact far broader, more variegated in character, more resilient and more stable than might be assumed from its depiction in the media. As Ken Roberts (2011:169) explains in his informative overview of the modern upper class, the current upper classes are the product of the blending of old (aristocratic) and new (business) money which was realised during the nineteenth-century industrial period and which continues to this day (see also Anderson 1992:19). Also, it is worth noting that, while the aristocracy are no longer at the core of this influential stratum, their influence still extends well beyond the pomp, ceremony and provision of elegant backdrops which help fuel the tourist, movie and fashion industries. As Roberts (p. 172) notes, there are few sociologists who doubt the presence of a separate and distinctive upper class, and this category is characterised not only by its exceptional wealth but also by its ability to both consolidate and also to renew itself as a social group. In other words, it has a remarkable continuity precisely because its members do not form an entirely 'closed group' but incorporate others who have become seriously wealthy, primarily through business and other originally middle-class enterprises. Thus, entrepreneurs such as Sir Richard Branson and Lord Sugar, global politicians such as Tony Blair, bankers and financiers, media conglomerate owners and even prominent figures from the entertainment and fashion industries such as Sir Paul and Stella McCartney could now be regarded as upper-class alongside the 'blue blood' royals and other titled elites (Harvey 2005:31).

So we might say that the upper classes now are constituted of a diverse range of the idle rich, the famous, the charitable, the titled and the industrious. Entertainment celebrities rub shoulders with social entrepreneurs, royalty, politicians and CEOs. In some ways what we might consider to be their less important activities are highly conspicuous, as these continue to be covered in the society pages of glossy magazines, celebrity magazines and the national press. One example should suffice. In November 2011 the London *Evening Standard* published a full-page lavishly illustrated article called 'London's powerful come to our party' (Spanier 2011:3). The article gleefully recorded that 'London's most influential people' gathered to celebrate the launch of the *Standard*'s annual guide to the rich and powerful; with guests forming new friendships as they sipped cocktails and nibbled canapés:

> Cabinet ministers including Iain Duncan Smith and Francis Maude rubbed shoulders with Ken Livingstone [former mayor] and Holly Valance, star of *Strictly Come Dancing* and girlfriend of property developer Nick Candy...Metropolitan Police Commissioner Bernard Hogan-Howe and best-selling *Wild Swans* author Jung Chang swapped tips on literacy with Sue Porto, boss of children's charity Reading Help...The doyenne of divorce lawyers, Tory peer Baroness Shackleton, mixed with Labour QC Baroness Kennedy...BBC London TV presenter Riz Lateef swapped notes...with Michael Acton Smith, creator of [online game] Moshi Monsters. Other guests included [designer] Ron Arad, Kids Company charity founder Camilla Batmanghelidjh and *Tatler* editor Kate Reardon.

This mixture of the 'great and the good', the famous and the politically influential is typical of the current scene. While elites are evidently visible when attending launches and charity fund-raisers, this mingling of charity workers, celebrities, lawyers, politicians and entrepreneurs also arguably obscures the actual class distinctions which structure these relationships and the real relations of class power in which they participate.

The resurgence and refashioning of the aristocracy and the gentry in particular, as part of this more diverse, celebrity-oriented milieu, is nicely encapsulated in the title of Peter York and Olivia Stewart-Liberty's (2007) upper-class lifestyle guide *Cooler, Faster, More Expensive: The Return of the Sloane Ranger*. This book was the follow-up to the renowned *Sloane Ranger Handbook* (Barr and York 1982), which wryly observed the upper classes at play and (to a lesser degree) at work: style-watching, charting their *mores*, their fads and the ways in which they exclude social outsiders. The original handbook went through 14 reprints between 1982 and 1997 and chronicled the lifestyle of 'Sloanes'.

The term Sloanes was a reference to the geographical location around Sloane Square, on the boundaries of the exclusive London districts of Knightsbridge, Belgravia and Chelsea, which was frequented by the wealthy upper classes. The 2007 *Return* declared that during the intervening 25 years of social change two factors had radically altered the 'Sloane' identity and lifestyle. First, the deregulation of the City in 1986 fundamentally disrupted old boy networks and prompted the established upper classes to raise their game in response to the incursion of the so-called yuppies (young urban professionals) into City culture. Second, Princess Diana's prominence until her death in 1997 paved the way for upper-class glamour, celebrity and media-friendly charitable work. For Sloanes and commoners alike, Diana, in particular, is an important transitional figure in the refashioning of upper-class elites, in Heather Nunn's (1999:94) words, 'linking the nostalgia of "traditional" structures through charisma, pageantry and an aristocratic manner to a "modern" populism...' which was more palatable to contemporary society.

So, despite their continuing presence in media culture and in society, the upper classes, most of whom are essentially very rich and powerful, seem to be an under-researched group by Anglophone sociologists.[2] There are explanations for this oversight. Michael Billig (1992:2, 7ff) attributes the sociological neglect of the royal family, for instance, to a confident conviction that, while its continuing presence may involve many complications (constitutional, fiscal, etc.) it is not regarded as constituting a *major social problem*. In other words, neither the government of the day nor the results of British social attitude surveys seem to call for a critical engagement with the 'Problem of the Monarchy'. Moreover, as Paul Ward (2004:22) notes, historically 'representation of the monarch as head of the national family helped to over-come internal social and geographical divisions'. The perpetuation of this construct of the monarchy as a familial and healing unifying force continues to be enacted through large-scale public events; state occasions such as weddings, anniversaries and the London 2012 Olympic Games. For example, the Royal Golden Jubilee Festival in 2002 sought to involve 'the people', regardless of their social class or ethnic background, in a renewal of civic pride and faith in British institutions which had been historically coded as white, monocultural and elite. As Jo Littler and Roshi Naidoo (2004:337) observed with some scepticism: 'It was predictably presented as good for "the people" rather than being good for the institutions under threat from diminishing faith in their legitimacy...'

So, too, the upper classes beyond the aristocracy (i.e. the richest members of our society) also enjoy a relative lack of critical scholarly analysis, seeming to inhabit a world apart. Andrew Adonis and Stephen Pollard (1998), tracing the development since the mid-1960s of the new elite originating from the legal, corporate and financial worlds, designated these, in particular, to be a 'super class' which sits apart from mass society (see also Lansley 2006:138ff). Both Adonis and Pollard (1998:68) and Ken Roberts (2011:171) indicate that as recently as the 1980s the ascendancy of this group as a super-elite was poorly anticipated by sociologists. This was due to a consensus that opportunities were opening up across the once exclusively upper-class professions and that there was increasing room at the top for meritocratic success. In fact, suggests Roberts (p. 191), the vitality of the upper classes and the robustness of their institutional boundaries continue to offend middle and working-class investment in notions of meritocracy; in short, their strength lies in the ways in which they reinforce their own privilege once it has been accrued. Others, such as Andrew Milner (1999:77), have proposed that inquiries into structured social inequalities have neglected the culture of the upper class 'in part because of its assumed visibility in the dominant institutions, in part because of the relative difficulty of securing access to its truly private affairs'. At the same time, it is well known that continuity is maintained and reinforced by the adherence of the upper class to established practices around schooling, the deployment of extensive social capital, inheritance within the family, in-the-know cultural practices and the exertion of influence. The spaces in which these connections are made and influence exerted are naturally private, exclusive and obscured from view. As Abercrombie *et al.* (2000:188) note, despite apparently changing times, the upper classes across the generations continue to populate the most desirable and/or influential professions and institutions such as business and finance, civil service, the army and the church. These positions are not so much won through open competition as 'sponsored' through a lifetime of family and social connections.

So we might say, for the purposes of this chapter, that the upper classes include all of the aforementioned groups, which taken together form an 'Establishment' whose visibility is only partial but whose influence is probably incalculable (see Oakland 2001:10–15).[3] In this chapter we will explore the conundrum of how the upper classes, who wield significant power and influence and who are generally economically robust and socially assertive, are so often portrayed as in decline or as a diverting distraction (as in the *Evening Standard* report) or as largely irrelevant or as mostly benign. This is, of course, when they are portrayed at all. In many cases the upper classes (such as financiers, bankers and captains of industry) are largely invisible unless they choose not to be, protected as they often are by a *cordon sanitaire* of security, gated residencies, private transportation and highly exclusive leisure activities. The chapter begins, then, by exploring one fraction of the upper classes, most often regarded as in decline, that is, the monarchy and the aristocracy. We consider their current significance as keepers of the national heritage and emblems of national identity and therefore conventionally beyond class-based critique. We then go on to consider the often-repeated assertion that celebrity is now the 'new aristocracy' and its implications for how we understand the upper class more generally, their (in)visibility and their influence. As has been argued elsewhere, the Princess Diana years were pivotal in the media re-visioning of the upper classes paradoxically both as celebrities and as ordinary people (Blain and O'Donnell 2003). These were also the years when the aristocracy and its social set appeared to become more democratised and middle-class, arguably as a reaction to the public support for Diana as the 'People's Princess' as well as being due to a longer historical process of public repositioning (Davies 1999, Nunn 1999). We consider all that this democratisation entails as they are repositioned both as 'normal people' and at the same time as trend-setters in terms of fashion and lifestyle and as opinion formers in spheres such as charity work and fundraising.

The chapter concludes by examining the ways in which popular culture is reinstating upper-class taste, conduct and values and asks how this might both colour and muddy our understanding of the social role of the upper classes in Britain. In doing so, we consider a spate of TV programming, self-help books and popular journalism in which 'experts', often from very privileged and even aristocratic backgrounds, work to instruct others in the attainment of social skills, self-presentation, diet and lifestyle. Looking at examples including *The Duchess In Hull* (ITV 2008) and *From Ladette to Lady* (ITV 2005–10), we discuss how the cultural capital of taste, deportment, self-discipline and tasteful consumption has been repackaged for the edification of reality show participants, cook show viewers, and readers of lifestyle and self-help guides. Overall, these inquiries are pursued in order to map out some of the ways in which the upper classes are both highly conspicuous (as institutional icons, celebrities and lifestyle experts) and yet oddly liminal; with their power and influence somewhat obscured from public scrutiny. As Perry Anderson (1992:30) explains, deploying the Gramscian language of the old left from which cultural studies scholarship is increasingly estranged, the 'hegemonic order' (the cultural as well as coercive and financial authority that one power bloc holds over another) exhibits a rather 'bizarre' or even 'absurd' morphology, but is nonetheless effective for all that. Anderson maintained (1992:31) that the oddly hierarchical, pseudo-feudal character of English society, still visible today as an expression of and instrument of aristocratic power, acts as 'perhaps the most successful of camouflages of class structure: by simultaneously intensifying and displacing class consciousness, it tends to render it politically inoperative . . . '

The business of aristocracy

It has been argued, despite earlier over-hasty diagnoses of aristocracy's demise, that Britons have now finally arrived at a time when aristocrats, in terms of their traditional status, social roles and political power, are 'little more than a fragmented memory' (Doyle 2011:77). British historian David Cannadine (1990, see also 1994) described a period around the 1880s as the final peak of aristocratic ascendancy, after which the position and influence of the established families declined rapidly, due to a number of causes, reaching a nadir in the years after World War Two. Aristocratic decline has commonly been evidenced by a diminution of direct political involvement, a waning of political influence (which has been ceded to the money-making classes), an inability to seize the new opportunities of the industrial revolution (Doepke and Zilibotti 2005) and beyond, and a dilution in popular deference towards those born into privilege (see Rutherford 2005:83). This last perception is nicely summarised by historian J.M. Bourne (1991:385), who claimed: 'We are all meritocrats now. Fashion, modes of speech, the professionalization of sport, rock and roll, television have all been profoundly unaristocratic . . . the aristocracy has been marginalized in many of the most important areas of British social and cultural life. Its survivors have become quaint.'

The quaintness of the upper class emerges in the stereotypes of eccentricity summoned up for the BBC's (2011) British Class Survey. The survey presented 'famous faces' (reflecting a fixation on celebrities as social commentators) endeavouring to answer the question 'what is the upper class?' Their insights into the constituents of upper classness included: 'lots of tweed', 'I imagine they eat pheasants and ox at Christmas', 'names such as Peregrine, Jasper or Devere', the 'upper class were [sic] lazy, incompetent buffoons', 'if it's small, covered in fur and runs they'll try and shoot it', and so on.[4] This really was a case of the uninformed describing the already mispresented. This unhelpful typecasting was not untypical in proposing that the 'upper classes' (in fact, more often the aristocracy and gentry in terms of these labels) are idiotic, un-modern and largely irrelevant and/or belonging to the distant past or the rural present.[5]

In the public (and indeed historians') eye aristocratic attrition has also been symbolised, and even proven, by the growing inability of titled families to maintain their stately homes, their heirlooms and their estates and their increasing redundancy as political actors in civil society. Since the 1960s, at least, the British media has highlighted the decline of aristocracy together with a few exceptional reversals of fortune which enabled a minority to survive or even thrive, financially if not politically. So, for example, the 1974 The Destruction of the Country House exhibition held at the Victoria and Albert Museum epitomised the perception of an upper class in crisis. So, too, documentaries such as Alan Whicker's *The Aristocracy Business* (Yorkshire TV 1968) and documentary series such as *The Aristocracy* (BBC2 1997) and *Crisis at the Castle* (BBC4 2007) and TV drama such as *Brideshead Revisited* (ITV 1981) and its film version (2008) all contributed to largely critical or nostalgic (or indeed both together) examinations of the aristocracy. These arguably all testified to the changing fortunes and shifting perceptions of the importance of the aristocracy (see also Higson 2003). In addition, influential cultural critiques such as Robert Hewison's (1987) *The Heritage Industry: Britain in a climate of decline*, which was part of the so-called heritage debates of the 1980s (see McGuigan 1996:116ff), argued that national decline was in part attributable to a regressive patrician ruling class (see Littler and Naidoo 2004:331–4).

A number of British situation comedies also sent up the upper classes as outmoded and ill-equipped for the modern world. For example, the immensely popular sitcom *To the Manor Born* (BBC1 1979–81) found humour in the predicament of an upper-class widow forced to sell her estate to a supermarket millionaire of 'foreign extraction' (see Rhodes and Westwood 2008:96). Meanwhile, affectionately sketched characters, such as Harry Enfield's (BBC2, then BBC1 1992–98) unintelligent former public schoolboy 'Tim nice but dim' and the *Fast Show's* (BBC1 1994–97, 2000) lonely and repressed Lord Ralf Mayhew, figured upper-class men as out of the swim of contemporary life. More recently, shows such as *Country House Rescue* (C4 2008) continue to offer stories of the decline and mismanagement of Britain's heritage by peers, the landed gentry and, more often, new money as they attempt to sustain their lifestyle through income generation.

In counterpoint to many of these, the case has also been made that aristocratic wealth, if not direct political power, rallied from the 1980s (an argument also made in part 3 of *The Aristocracy*, subtitled *Survival of The Fittest 1970–1997*) and has been sustained ever since. Indeed, the case could be made that those who had managed to weather earlier financial storms actually benefitted from kinder taxation and greatly increased property and asset values (Lansley 2006:101ff). In 2010, following a land ownership audit, it was reported that a third of Britain still belonged to the aristocracy and the landed gentry, with land ownership being a key benefit in attracting subsidies, minimising tax payments and generating income (Cahill 2010, see also Abercrombie *et al.* 2000:183). Respected architectural historian (and aristocrat) Giles Worsley (2005) has been adamant that the much-lamented decline of aristocratic fortunes (and with them the country house) has been reversed and that this has not been fully acknowledged in current scholarship. For him the evidence includes the consolidation of wealth via tax breaks, City financier income and so on, as already mentioned above, together with the ingress of new wealthy families and even the commissioning of new-build country houses. Worsley (2005:435) explains that, while the country house is no longer a 'political powerhouse' (only three senior government ministers officially occupy country houses), it still functions as a marker of status and social standing while at the same time acting as 'camouflage' for owners' serious wealth. Looking across the board, Worsley (2005:ibid.) concludes, 'the essence of the country house today is privacy, escape, space, security, the chance to entertain friends and engage in country sports, without social or economic commitments to the neighbourhood...'

Nonetheless, for those who have held on to their estates or, indeed, seen them flourish, an inverted relationship to wealth and possessions is still insisted upon wherein it would be vulgar to be wealthy for wealth's sake. Princess Diana's brother Charles, now Earl Spencer (2010), writing in *Vanity Fair* magazine about the erosion of aristocratic wealth, approvingly quotes the conviction, 'We belong to our possessions, rather than our possessions belong to us. To us, they are not wealth, but heirlooms, over which we have a sacred trust.' He adds: 'This remains the mission statement of traditional aristocratic families today.' In Robert Hewison's (1987:72–3) words, then, since the 1980s 'private ownership has been elided into a vague conception of public trusteeship.' The development of new revenue streams through tourism, the accumulated value of heirlooms (in Hewison's words a 'discrete source of funds'), together with the accumulating capital value of land, seem to have shored up the position of many aristocratic families. For those in the limelight and who are very industrious and able to diversify, it is possible that a mini-industry can be sustained by a single family, requiring a mission statement no less. To take Earl Spencer as a prominent example, he has authored four books to date on the Spencer family estate and military history, presented history documentaries, presided over a museum dedicated to Princess Diana's memory, renovated the Althorp family seat, which is situated in 550 acres of parkland (open to visitors, paying guests and for catered events), runs a reproduction furniture company, launched a literary festival, and so on.

The view of the aristocracy as preservationists of what Stuart Hall (1999) calls 'the National Heritage' has been reinforced by the dominance of institutions such as the National Trust, English Heritage and the Historic Houses Association, all of which contribute to the support of stately homes, their upkeep and marketing. These partly survive by stressing their relevance to contemporary civil society as well as windows into earlier social and national history. Thus, recently, the heritage industry has latched its claim to benefit Britain to an engagement with dominant political discourses around the Big Society and economic recovery. For example, English Heritage declares, 'The historic environment is the Big Society in action, helping to build communities and giving people a real investment in the past, present and future of where they live and work.'[6] Heritage, then, is promoted as part of the solution to a socially 'broken Britain' and to its broader economic recovery, and it has indeed proved to be commercially successful, albeit without involving the more 'broken' members of the 'broken society'. Since the recession of 2008 all three bodies have seen their public membership and visitor numbers rise as middle-class families opt for affordable days out in charming surroundings that summon up the values of a bygone age. Chair of English Heritage, Baroness Andrews, noted in response to these burgeoning numbers, 'The heritage sector provides a life-line for the nation's past. Heritage is the very thing that makes England special in the eyes of the world and can help to underpin the economic recovery.'[7] Membership of these institutions offers a middle-class 'club' experience which allows members to participate in sustaining certain social values, taste and the popular memory of class deference (Smith 2006:153). Laurajane Smith argues (2006:154) thereby that this leisure activity constitutes above all 'a certain vision of being middle class'.

It also, of course, sustains a certain vision of the upper classes as caretakers of national culture and offers them a life-line as they work with charities to provide public access to their property (see also Urry 1995, Smith 2009). Moreover, as Simon Stewart (2010) demonstrates, the dominant classes (upper and middle) have also effectively come together to make up what he describes as 'defensive formations' around issues such as opposition to the fox hunting ban, the Countryside Alliance and the Campaign for the Protection of Rural England (whose Patron is the Queen). This activism is often presented as preserving a traditional (shared) way of life and a common British, or more often English, culture (see Lowenthal 2004:137, Woods 2004). Stewart (2010:177) notes that, while motives may be laudable, including, for example, an emphasis on the interests of the rural dispossessed, 'this is where dominant groups express their exclusivity aesthetically, and conceal economic concerns (the defence of property and land owning exclusivity) in the romantic language of rural protection.' This romanticism is arguably rooted in an organic notion of blood, property and soil beneath which class distinctions are somewhat buried. Patrick Wright (1985), a key contributor to the 1980s 'heritage debates', points to the broader ideological implications of the harnessing of aesthetics to the national preservation of private property. He observes that 'the inalienability of the Trust's property can be regarded (and also staged) as a vindication of property relations: a spectacular enlistment of the historically defined categories of "natural beauty" and "historic interest" which demonstrates how private property simply *is* in the national public interest' (Wright 1985:52). Here the heritage industry is criticised for protecting an already entrenched commitment to the Briton's inalienable right to private property and of property itself as the safeguard of national identity. This commitment is also served up and further amplified by numerous visually appealing television documentaries about British ancestral seats, their heirlooms and artworks, the gardens and surrounding landscape, including *Treasure Houses of Britain* (History 2001), *English Heritage* (BBC4 2010) and *Royal Upstairs Downstairs* (BBC2 2011). Most recently *To the Manor Reborn* (BBC 2011), featuring Penelope Keith, who starred in the popular comedy to which its title refers (above), charted the refurbishment of a 500-year-old country house in Wiltshire in a four-part series that married arts and crafts skills, observational documentary and promotional material for the work of the National Trust. Anyone who is heavily critical of such admirable and apparently benign endeavours can only appear begrudging or resentful.

The royal family at work

While there may be some who regard aristocrats as quaint or out of touch (or even as an annoying but probably minor drain on society), in the long view, the monarchy at least appears to remain popular and is regarded even with some fondness. Moreover, there are, of course, royalists among the population who have attracted very little scholarly attention but whose presence should not be dismissed (see Rowbottom 2002). The spectacular and overwhelmingly positive media coverage and marketing of the wedding between William and Catherine, now the Duke and Duchess of Cambridge, may be taken as evidential; so, too, the trend in well-received British films about royalty such as *The Queen* (2006) and *The King's Speech* (2010). With this cultural, rather than social or economic, context in mind, MP and historian Tristram Hunt (2011:167) observed in a think tank essay for the Institute for Public Policy Research that 'however much modern, cosmopolitan, secular progressives might shudder at the longevity of the royal family, its global reach remains remarkable.' We might ask, then, how it has come about that in a union of four nations, where common culture is 'profoundly unaristocratic' and social inequalities continue to deepen, the monarchy, which is characterised by its wealth, privilege and access to leisure (see Hall 1992), continues to attract support.

Andrzej Olechnowicz's (2007:280–1) important research tracks four strongly competing explanations for the survival and popular support of the monarchy even in times of deepening social divisions. First, there is the socialist view that the popularity of the monarchy and social inequality are mutually dependent and self-perpetuating: where one is, so will the other be, and therefore the monarchy cannot be tackled as a problem in isolation. Second, there is the view that the national significance of the monarchy overrides any concern about its social significance (Nairn 1988, see also Billig 1992). Third, people regard society with some satisfaction as a seamless, albeit hierarchical, web (see Cannadine 1998) in which each person has their place. Fourth, it may be that as privatised, family-oriented individuals we have increasingly dispensed with any collective class consciousness or awareness of the real extent of social inequality (here he references the work of Giddens). Olechnowicz (2007:282) approaches all of these explanations with caution, pointing out, for instance, that this last argument can be refuted by empirical counter-evidence produced by British sociologists which shows that people are in fact quite aware of structural social inequalities and the unfair wielding of privilege and social advantage. Finally, Olechnowicz's thesis offers an excellent and very clear analysis of the changing pattern of public opinion regarding the royal family. He (2007:301) concludes that there has probably been no time in the last 130 years in which the majority of citizens have believed that Britain would be better off without it. In sum, Olechnowicz (2007:ibid.)

notes that an 'incongruity between resentment of social inequality and popular support for a privileged institution cannot be wished away.'

Clearly, the massive media coverage of the monarchy's activities must also play a part in their cultural prominence and social acceptance, creating significant psycho-social pressures to conform to their support or else remain rather out on a limb (Olechnowicz 2007:301–2). As Stuart Hall (1999:26) observes, 'if you do not recognise yourself in the national story you are excluded.' This is especially so when high profile events such as a royal wedding or funeral alter the very character and tempo of the day and even the calendar (additional bank holidays were created for the Golden Jubilee in 2002 and the wedding of Catherine and William in 2011). Indeed, we need to take into account that since the late 1990s the public has witnessed the increasing promotion of the Mountbatten-Windsor family as people working for the state and hence working for citizens (not subjects). Supportive portraits of labouring royals, mostly written by the usual suspects (either authorised or by 'insiders'), abound: see, for example, Anthony Jay's *Elizabeth R* (1992, and accompanying BBC documentary), Jonathan Dimbleby's (1995) 'insider' biography *The Prince of Wales*, James Morton's (1998) account of Prince Charles' 'professional job as heir to the throne' (cover notes) and Robert Hardman's (2007) *Monarchy: The Royal Family at Work* (with another accompanying BBC documentary). Coverage such as this helps sustain the perception of the royals as salaried or income generating, rather than being hugely rich from inherited wealth or drawing from the public purse. In these accounts the royals are portrayed as generally adaptive and 'fit for purpose' in changing times (Marr 2011) with Prince Charles both 'born and worthy to be King' (Nicolson 2003:139). This is also evident in the consistent media coverage of the Queen's diary of public engagements, the family's ongoing charity work, Prince Charles' business initiatives and social entrepreneurism, and most recently Prince William's massively publicised marriage to 'commoner' Catherine Middleton, the daughter of multimillionaire parents who, it is frequently reported, both started out in life as flight attendants.

In Michael Billig's (1992:118) words, 'there is an ideological job of settlement to be done' to ensure that any class-based resentment at royal privilege is contained. Clearly there are functions to be undertaken by members of the royal family as designated by their legal stipulated role. But, in terms of the public perception of whether or not the royal family is pulling its weight, there is, as Billig notes, a twinning of personal and class morality at play. In other words, the royal family needs to demonstrate *through their individual persons* and *everyday actions* that they are up to the job. Tristram Hunt (2011:169) promotes Prince Charles' 'practical monarchy in action' as answering any criticisms rooted in class morality: it is here that a 'welfare monarchy' sustains a charitable entrepreneurism and helps justify its continuance (see Prochaska 1995). But Hunt also recognises the personal advocacy dimension of public work which, he suggests, Prince William would be better placed than his father to sustain alongside the business of charity. Hunt commends William for 'wielding a Diana-like populist touch – put to good effect in sleeping rough for the Centrepoint homelessness charity – the young Prince has already bought into this model of civil society monarchy'. Here public relations (putting to good effect), public duty (a model of monarchy) and celebrity charisma (via Diana) converge to form an ideal representation of royal public work which is practical, dutiful and in touch with ordinary people. This supports Neil Blain and Hugh O'Donnell's (2003:177) argument that the media (and royal supporters) easily recognise the market value of Prince William as Diana's son, reproducing much of her value in him: 'in whose features she can so plainly be read'.

While Diana was lionised for her charity work, this *per se* did not make her unique. Her selling point was in seeming to diminish the distance between royalty and commoners through the conveyance of public intimacy. Writing in the 1980s, Judith Williamson (1986:78–9) commented on scenes of Princess Anne visiting the starving in Africa that 'there is something deeply disturbing about this image of privilege showing concern for the poverty on which, in part at least, its wealth has been founded.' In spite of this obvious incongruity, these scenes of the rich visiting (and even bedding down with) the poor are plentiful; augmented with a host of celebrity fundraising events and reality shows such as *Famous, Rich and Homeless* (BBC1 2009) and *Secret Millionaire* (C4 2006–). In current times we have become accustomed to these unlikely juxtapositions of rich and poor whose social inequalities seem to be smoothed over by good intentions, publicly expressed emotion and celebrity appeal. In the case of monarchy these initiatives work to show 'the human face of hereditary rule' (Williamson 1986:88) as well as the social usefulness of monarchy.

As noted above, this human face is also a familial face. In Billig's (1992:90) words, 'the job of the Royal Family is to be a family.' As Billig demonstrates through interviews with ordinary members of the public, their tolerance of the privileges of an hereditary elite is predicated partly on the royal family conducting its family matters with dignity (and, we might add post-Diana, with a feel for 'normal' modern life and contemporary values; see also Lawler 2008). This 'normal' modern family is essentially an ideal of the middle-class family, and the royal family have actively engaged since the 1960s, at least, in the representation of themselves as upper middle-class. One of the often cited landmarks in this process of self-presentation is the 1969 BBC documentary called *The Royal Family*, which was commissioned by the Queen (Pimlott 1998, Rosen 2003, Bastin 2009). This was undertaken in order to prepare the public for the investiture of her son Charles as Prince of Wales. Director Richard Cawston recalled that he was engaged to film the Queen and her activities across the year and demonstrate through her own industriousness the role that Charles would himself inherit (in Rosenthal 1972). The film was also notable for its relatively intimate family scenes, such as a barbeque at Balmoral, and for its blending of the public and domestic. As such, it marked a significant stage in the ongoing transformation of the Windsor-Saxe-Coburg-Gotha dynasty into the Mountbatten-Windsor family of today. Richard Hoggart (1995:201) called this transformation 'the Woganisation of the Windsors' with reference to the popular, unthreatening, affable middle-brow family entertainer Terry Wogan: a shorthand phrase for their 'picture-postcard version of petit-bourgeois life: chintz, gladioli, the dogs, the framed photos of the family'.

Clearly by the 2000s the younger members of the royal family could not realistically hold on to the staid middle-class dogs-and-chintz image that had made town and country, Colefax and Fowler and Laura Ashley interiors so popular in the 1980s. But, as supporters and critics alike have noted, neither could they entirely jettison the national emphasis on the solid family as central to their continuing popular support. Consequently, the presentation of the royal family as middle-class and 'just like us' continues today, albeit inevitably adapted to make sense in changing times. This camouflage is far from easy to sustain, especially during times of austerity and when consumerist values are necessarily under review for 'real' middle-class families. An example would be Tristram Hunt's (2011:174) attempt to envisage a credible future for a working monarchy. He ends his own treatise on the subject with these words for the Duke of Cambridge and future King:

Building his own family, sustaining his marriage, will also be for William a deeply progressive act. For few events affect the life chances of children more than growing up in a safe and secure environment. As he seeks to do so, to make the personal political, he will provide a more honourable model of duty and service than did the baby-boomer generation of royals which preceded him.

What can this mean? Clearly this supports the notion that the royal family must also be an ideal-typical model family for the nation's benefit. But, if we take 'progressive' to mean action in favour of change, reform, progress or improvement, how does sustaining a marriage become a progressive act and make the personal political? Hunt advises the younger generation of Mountbatten-Windsors to differentiate themselves from the recently much-maligned baby-boomers. In political debate these have been blamed for a post-recession blight in job prospects and housing, attributed in part to their selfish and over-indulgent lifestyles and the benefits they accrued from rising property values (see Willetts 2010). These actions have been held responsible for damaging the life chances of future generations, because it is their children who will be 'squeezed' further in a post-recession environment. But how can the fall-out from a banking crisis, a world economic downturn and a self-indulgent older generation affect a family where life chances are supported not only by immense wealth but also by long-held dynastic connections? History already shows that the extra-marital affairs and eventual divorce of William's parents Diana and Charles, which could in some families precipitate a social fall, failed to impact on his and his descendants' life chances. Here Hunt reiterates and refreshes an ideologically convenient longer narrative mythology of the royal family as essentially middle-class (just like us) when they are not (see, for example, Homans 1998:44, Olechnowicz 2007:31). As such this is simply dishonest.

Since the late 1960s, when Richard Cawston's film was made, the royal family, the aristocracy and the rich upper classes have undergone a series of image modifications. First, their celebrity status and global media appeal were enhanced through the coverage of the wedding between Charles and Diana in 1981, which was reportedly viewed by a world-wide audience of 750 million people, and that of William and Catherine in 2011, whose audience figures are likely to be far higher when web-streaming is taken into account.[8] Second, as already noted, Diana's emergence as a world-wide figure of fascination and scrutiny was a significant landmark in the restaging of the aristocracy as glamorous, celebrity-oriented and above all, perhaps, caring, and much retrospective coverage of her continues to refer to her as an object of admiration. Third, the incorporation of Catherine Middleton into the royal family will again positively modify the royal image because she can be regarded as commoner turned princess, with all of its aspirational (as well as gold-digging) connotations (Church Gibson 2011, Coward 2011, Miles 2011). If marriage has traditionally been regarded as a vehicle for upwards social mobility, then Catherine's marriage refreshes this notion for modern times; representing the most aspirational marriage possible (a fairy tale come true) and at the same time contributing towards the presentation of the royal family as contemporary rather than anachronistic. Also, like Diana, with whom she is inevitably compared (and whose engagement ring she now wears), she may be regarded as an antidote to what constitutional reformer Anthony Barnett (Barnett and Bourne Taylor 1999:51) called the British 'cult of miserabilism'. In conversation about Diana he once observed that the larger public admired her because she 'made it': proving 'you can be an English rose, make a mint and do something for AIDS awareness. The aristocracy had never before lent itself to encouraging people to identify with England as a land of opportunity.'

Upper-class life-stylists: the knowledge, the gift and the rules

Over time, redistributions of power and wealth have seen the descriptor 'aristocracy' attached to new figures of influence. For example, in the nineteenth century the emergence of phrases such as the 'aristocracy of wealth' and 'aristocracy of talent' (Gooley 2010:76) were used to denote new and emergent groups with the authority to inform public opinion and to intervene in politics. By the late twentieth century a new 'aristocracy of celebrity' had also emerged, as evidenced by the growing political and social influence of mostly very wealthy people from the entertainment and sports industries. It has been observed that by the twenty-first century a 'new aristocracy', comprised of these high-visibility celebrities together with people in business and finance, have deployed their elite status to influence policy, and thus may even distort democratic processes (Mullard 2004:36). Indeed, John Lahr (2002:299) has gone so far as to describe celebrity as 'democracy's substitute for aristocracy'. Current cultural and social critique focusing on the presence and importance of the aristocracy in British culture reveals the belief that the influence of aristocrats, minor royalty, socialites and the landed gentry has been thoroughly usurped by celebrities. It has been noted by marketers, for example, that the shaping of taste, personal behaviours and attitudes is now in the hands of the 'new aristocracy' of celebrity (Higham 2009:159). The transformation over the longer term is also revealing. A century ago, magazine journalism rarely employed celebrities to market fashion and cosmetics, and royalty was the benchmark of fashion to which all would aspire (Church Gibson 2010:128). Now celebrities predominantly fashion public taste and help form opinion on subjects of national and even global concern. This means that they, too, are the subject of the adulation, affection and, at other times, cheeky disrespect which the old aristocracy formerly attracted. It has even been argued that the democratisation of the media has led to a new egalitarianism which allows celebrities to be lampooned in the twenty-first century in much the same way as aristocrats were by the satirists of previous centuries (Burns 2009:19).

This is not to say that the aristocracy and the older established upper classes are no longer looked to as arbiters of taste; far from it. Although they may be less ubiquitous and evidently less numerous than entertainment celebrities, they continue to make incursions into cultural life, to be seen at landmark social events as covered by the press and to help form notions of taste and aspiration for particular constituencies. Indeed, the 'successful' aristocracy are those who have themselves been effectively celebritised as well as monetised or who can market their tastes and their lifestyle; a good example of this is Earl Spencer's reproduction furniture-making outlet, where the furniture is explicitly marketed as copies of pieces in the Althorp collection. As noted at the outset of this chapter, we would make the case that popular culture and lifestyle journalism is actually reinstating upper-class taste, conduct and old-time values via home interiors, food and personal makeover features led by 'experts' who include the established upper classes and those who instruct and school them. These experts are often from very privileged and even aristocratic backgrounds, and they monetise their knowledge and cultural capital by instructing others in the attainment of social skills, self-presentation, diet and lifestyle, and so on.

The trend in upper-class, mostly female-oriented, leisure and lifestyling made its mark with the advent of the makeover show *What Not to Wear* (*WNTW* BBC2 2001–07). The makeover is essentially 'the transformation of self with the help of experts in the hope or expectation of improvement of status and life chances through the acquisition of forms of cultural and social capital' (McRobbie 2004:97). In short, this and similar shows were part of what Irmi Karl (2007:2) describes as 'a public class re-education project through body politics'. *WNTW* was fronted for the first five series by Trinny Woodall and Susannah Constantine, women with distinctively upper-class pedigrees, who together descend on a woman badly in need of a fashion makeover and train her to dress well. Here the participant is taken into a mirrored room where the experts discuss her assets, her 'problem areas' and her underwear. Then she is shown what to wear and given a budget to shop under the new rules. Intermittently the pair intervene to point out where the shopper is already slipping up until, reformed, we see the newly fashioned woman. The show closes with an update to see if the participant has managed to sustain her new look in real life. Here recidivists and refuseniks are roundly condemned. The whole show is styled as a humorous but vigorous no-nonsense assault on the taste and deportment of mostly less socially elevated, less confident women. Trinny and Susannah's horse-play, single-sex posh-school humour, with lots of references to 'tits' and 'bums', seemingly fascinated and delighted audiences.[9] As Frances Bonner (2008) explains, the problem of the class gap in shows featuring Trinny and Susannah also constituted their unique selling point. For many, the appeal lay partly in mocking the 'posh totty' experts and partly in appreciating their literally hands-on and refreshingly unembarrassed involvement with other women's bodies. For critics, the evident 'class antagonism' of such scenarios was politically unacceptable, with Angela McRobbie (2004:100) arguing, for example, that 'both the presenters and the audiences are assumed to know that no harm is intended and that, in post politically-correct times, this is just good fun .... And the message is that the poor woman would do well to emulate her social superiors.'

McRobbie is crystal clear that these shows victimise the women who participate in them and that they are the subject of 'symbolic violence' rooted in class enmity, albeit sugared over with declarations of good intentions. It is certainly the case that participants undergo some wounding as part of the process of the transformation experience, which is often manifested through tears and explained as a working through of emotional problems such as low self-esteem. But they are also given the gift of lifetime rules in return: as Bonner (2008:549) notes, 'The requirement to dress in the terms advocated by the presenters is a requirement about living properly, about not being an embarrassment to friends or family, not letting the partner's desire flag, not failing to look right at work.'

This submission to the experts in exchange for the gift of rules which will last a lifetime is distinctively different from the earliest class-difference makeover shows. Appropriately, perhaps, it is claimed that the first makeover show was the American series *Queen for a Day* (1956–64: NBC), which, despite its title, did not elevate the deprived wives and mothers featured into debutantes but instead lightened their load with gifts such a domestic appliance, a hearing aid, a wheelchair for a disabled son, fashionable clothing and a vacation. Here, the contestants, many living just above the subsistence line, were invited to tell the host in detail how poor and needy they were by describing their intensely difficult lives and emotional problems (Scheiner 2003, Cassidy 2005:184ff). Competitors were swiftly eliminated until only five remained in what was generally a distasteful scenario of exhibition-neediness not very far removed from current programming such as *Extreme Makeover: Home Edition*. In a melodramatic tone, with contestants frequently in tears as they recalled appalling social circumstances, the winner was elected by audience approval as measured in applause. With 'Pomp and Circumstance' playing in the background, the winner would be draped like a coronation queen in a red velvet robe and crowned on a velvet-upholstered throne. As Marsha Cassidy (2005:193) notes, the show 'explicitly tied the reconstitution of distressed women to material goods and beauty'.

The difference between this studio-set series and the makeover shows of today is that now the woman deserving of a makeover is guided by an expert so that she can be a queen for life rather than queen for the day or for the length of her all-expenses-paid vacation treat. On the face of it, shows such as *WNTW* are more caring and benign (or at least well-intentioned), even therapeutically inflected, and the 'gifts' of good taste, of style and general well-being are surely more enduring than the consumer goods given to the winner of *Queen for a Day*. However, there is something troubling about the recourse in current times to the upper class as life tutors who coach other people to class-pass or present themselves as better spoken, slimmer, better-dressed and more tasteful versions of themselves.

Other, more recent, series also guide lower-class subjects in food and lifestyle discipline or etiquette and feminine behaviour in order to equip them with either useful or decorative life skills. One of the best known is *From Ladette to Lady* (ITV 2005–10). The synopsis on the production company website encapsulated the privileging of once-outmoded upper-class values not simply as the motor of a lifestyle transformation but also as its object:

[the young women] move into Eggleston Hall, a traditional finishing school, brought back to life for the purpose. The girls' clothing will be binned and replaced by traditional daywear as their institutionalisation begins. There will also be numerous challenges which will have to be completed successfully in order for them to avoid elimination ... the tasks will include attending a dinner dance and a country house weekend, cooking a cordon bleu dinner party, wine tasting and dressmaking. Will the girls be able to walk in their new shoes, choose Champagne over Babysham and cope with the eccentricities of high society life to pull it off and reveal a true female sensibility?[10]

This is essentially a Pygmalion scenario in which mainly working-class women are schooled by the upper class to pass as something other than their current social selves. As Deborah Philips (2008) has noted, the series explicitly referenced *My Fair Lady* (the musical version of George Bernard Shaw's play *Pygmalion*) by drawing on its music and deploying the 'reveal' staircase sequence used in the film version featuring Audrey Hepburn. Oddly, too, even though the instructors at Eggleston Hall provide only a crash course in class-passing, the aim is to 'reveal a true female sensibility', a nonsense which actually reveals the irresolvable tension between artifice and authenticity which is at the heart of the reality makeover. So, too, it suggests the ongoing promotion of the association between older social values, upper and upper middle-class comportment and sanctioned forms of femininity. In George Bernard Shaw's famous play Professor Higgins, taking notes as he observes street-seller Eliza Doolittle, remarks: 'You see this creature with her kerbstone English: the English that will keep her in the gutter to the end of her days. Well, sir, in three months I could pass that girl off as a duchess at an ambassador's garden party.'[11] As an upper-class life-stylist Higgins remakes the cockney working girl (whose surname openly links her with the idle 'undeserving poor' also cited in the play) and, theoretically, improves her life chances (although purely as a self-serving social experiment and to win a wager). As Philips (2008) argues, *Ladette* presents the Eggleston finishing school as a marriage-making hothouse in which feminine upper-class skills and pursuits equip 'girls' for a socially advantageous marriage. Importantly, she notes that, while the skills and setting seem hopelessly anachronistic and outmoded, the dominant discourse of the programme nonetheless:

> serves to confirm and to reaffirm the culture and superiority of aristocratic and upper class mores. The staged social events are populated by groups the programme's voice over and characters accept as (in the language of the programme) 'outstanding members of the community'; defined as those with titles, the hunting and country house community.

Clearly *Pygmalion* was destined to be a source of inspiration for makeover television. It informed makeover programme concepts some years before *Ladette*, and explicitly so in the series *Faking It* (C4 2000–05), which focused on equipping candidates to pass as somebody radically, often socially, different. Hence, an early episode charted the transformation of working-class northerner and 'modern day Eliza Doolittle' Lisa Dickinson Gray into 'Lady Lisa'. This was to be effected by a voice coach, a grooming, etiquette and posture teacher, and the *Daily Mail*'s society journalist Tim Walker. Like all of the instructors, Walker makes it clear that he has the knowledge that Lisa lacks: 'I chronicle society... I know what it is, I know the things she should be doing and the things she shouldn't be doing.'

As Joanne Morreale (2007:97) observes, properly executed, the subject in *Faking It* 'becomes the self they have been taught to enact'. She describes the process in which they are remanufactured as 'life-style immersion', including living with one of their mentors, acquiring a new look and learning to self-monitor their own impersonation before entering a work or social situation in which they must remain undetected as an impostor. Here working-class 'naturalness' is connoted as both endearing and dangerous. In the episode featuring Lisa Gray, entitled 'From shop girl to it girl', she is warned that when she laughs her old accent could reappear and betray her true social origins, and Walker observes that she simply won't be 'accepted' with 'that accent'. When she confesses that she enjoys drinking beer Walker comments: 'I had a nasty feeling you were going to say that... it's got be champagne and wine.' Her mentors are also keen for her to go to art galleries and the like, not because the upper classes have enquiring minds but because they are educated (this is styled as 'cultural appreciation' in *Ladette to Lady*). Overall, Lisa is urged to perform 'upper class-ness' for the four weeks of her training, even when alone, in order to learn to become convincing. After the dinner party in which she was supposed to pass, reviews by fellow guests offered a confusing mix of observations. One diner laments the fact that Lisa felt she had to change her accent to be accepted (she was charming enough without this), while another found her out because she didn't draw on a back-story of equine or other upper-class pursuits. Overall, Lisa is only partially successful in passing in high society, and this in itself becomes a lesson in class-based authenticity and the fixity/mutability of class structures. Her judges commend her for being charming and real despite her attempt to pass, and her mentors comment sympathetically on her fierce attachment to a 'northern cocoon' of family life and family values that have made her who she is (and by implication prevented her from fully transforming into someone else). Lisa herself reflects, perhaps ruefully but apparently defiantly, that 'I will always be a Lancashire Lass.' Finally, and with some relief, she rejoins her family, but expresses her gratitude at being given an opportunity which shows that she can achieve anything she wants to.

In series such as *WNTW*, *From Ladette to Lady* and episodes such as 'From shop girl to it girl', the upper classes impart knowledge and instruction. No compromise is made by 'society' to accommodate a class interloper while they are expected to work hard to at least 'pass' and preferably even adopt the values and appearances of upper-class femininity. The lack of hospitality shown here for class outsiders (who are subject to intense critical judgement), then, is quite different from that played out in series such as *Geordie Finishing School For Girls* and *Peckham Finishing School for Girls* (both BBC3), in which upper-class girls are allowed to retain their classed identities while learning about and often participating in the lives of working-class girls. The working-class hosts of programmes such as these may be wary, but they are also welcoming; even when they are expected to take direction from others living privileged lives quite different from their own.

We conclude, then, with a final example of the makeover programme as the vehicle of the upper-class lifestyle gift: *The Duchess in Hull* (ITV 2008). In this two-part programme Sarah, Duchess of York, is welcomed into a working-class home to help a poor family improve their health and well-being. The Duchess visits the Sargeson family: 'an overweight, cheerfully tattooed family on one of Hull's roughest council estates' to 'help them to eat healthily on £80 a week' (Pile 2008). Amusingly, none of the family even recognised their famous surprise visitor, although afterwards mother Tonia Sargeson disclosed that she had felt 'overwhelmed' to learn that a member of the royal family had visited her home. The Duchess's personal credentials for this enterprise included her successful association with American Weight Watchers and the co-production of five books about weight-loss and lifestyle, including *Dining with the Duchess* (1998) and *Reinventing Yourself* (2001) – all evidence, too, of her own ability to adapt to and survive in changing times. Her qualifications as a home economist were rather less convincing, as she was reportedly living beyond her means and with large outstanding debts remaining to be settled. From this perspective, it seemed unlikely that she would be able to advise on feeding a family healthily for £80 per week. But ultimately, we would argue, it was not her life-coach skills which merited her appointment. Instead, she was qualified to advise the Sargesons because of her higher social status as a member of the royal family and as a member of the celebrity set. To explain her fame, and therefore her reason for advising the rather bemused Sargeson family, she tells them: 'The Queen was my mother-in-law,' 'Diana was my sister-in law.'

As an upper-class expert in the global celebrity circuit, the Duchess would seem to have little in common with her makeover subjects and with most viewers. However, like most celebrities, she also laboured to build a contract of trust and proximity which might overcome this. Personal revelation and intimate confession was the obvious mode of establishing this (see Nunn and Biressi 2010a). Hence, the programme devotes a lot of space to following Ferguson and telling her own story. She is clearly the key protagonist in this show. Despite the goodwill shown by all parties as the series progressed, the makeover project was clearly used to rehabilitate Ferguson's career as much as the Sargeson family's lifestyle. She is invited to give an account of her life in which she recalls her own experiences of inadequacy, her struggles to become confident and to love and accept herself for who she is and her commitment to her family. Her own learning curve and her deep love for her family both become, in turn, a further authorisation of her role as an expert whose help the Sargesons clearly need. These also work, of course, to camouflage her position of upper-class privilege, to defuse any discussion of the classed structures in which she and the Sargesons find themselves embroiled and to divert attention from the social inequalities in which they are all entangled. If anyone is really qualified to counsel others on survival, adaptability and change, it is perhaps the Sargesons themselves rather than their elevated royal visitor. As journalist Stephen Pile (2008) observed: 'Mitch and Tonia [Sargeson] had much to teach all of us, never mind Sarah Ferguson. They have been married for 22 years and, despite poverty and long-term unemployment, they have not only kept their family together, but also decided to adopt a seven-year-old in need.' But it seems that in these times of austerity it is the middle and upper classes who have been approved to train, educate and guide us in life skills and personal values.

7
'Are You Thinking What We're Thinking?': Class, Immigration and Belonging

> I need to know that my voice matters; indeed the offer of effective voice is crucial to the legitimacy of modern democracies....
>
> (Couldry 2010:1)

> Home is an intensely evocative concept.... Indeed, such concepts, pregnant with nostalgia, emerge at their most insistent at a time when it is recognized that, perhaps, they are no longer secure in the world.
>
> (Silverstone 1999:88)

This chapter focuses on 'tinderbox' moments in which the public discussion of immigration, race and ethnicity became noticeably articulated to social class and turned on certain assumptions about what 'ordinary' people, and especially white working-class Britons, might believe about immigration and the multicultural society. To focus on this we consider media debates, political interventions and campaigning, and public conversations arising from the general and local elections which took place in 2005–10. Through these exemplars the chapter explores how the white working class have become the container or reservoir for a range of persistent notions of inherent, uneducated racism. We will make the case that as such they function as a kind of distraction from, or masking of, the ways in which prejudice, anxiety and unwelcoming attitudes are more broadly circulated and institutionalised in politics and culture.

From this perspective we are also interested in the question of voice, that is, the processes which purport to offer a voice to certain constituencies and the ways in which some voices are denigrated, undervalued or dismissed (see Couldry 2010, Standing 2011b:113). We consider especially moments in which the media, politicians or an individual elects to speak on behalf of 'ordinary Britons' and/or of the white working class. We also consider what happens when the white working-class subject, in particular, is asked to speak publicly about home, belonging, community and politics, and the ways in which this can become, or can feel like, a kind of double-edged invitation. We consider how the invitation to speak and to express an opinion in public can render the speaking subject a hostage to fortune as the views expressed become circulated, amplified, co-opted and/or elaborated by others and by the media.

This consideration of voice is also framed by the idea of home both as a defensive structure and also as a potential site of welcome and hospitality. Here home will be the organising concept which helps us to think through contemporary media debates about race, ethnicity, the immigrant and the asylum seeker and how these intersect with frequently aired assumptions about class, and especially the white working class. To conclude the chapter we will shift the perspective to talk about the powerful emotional dynamics at play when individuals open up their home to a stranger in the presence of the media and how the state of contemporary feelings about class can be inferred through mediated relationships of encounter with the racialised stranger. In keeping with our discussion of the contradictions and emotional landscape of class, we want to think about the messy experience of encountering others in a mediated life-world and how home and neighbourhood are spaces for exploring these encounters. Here we want to discuss the negotiation of otherness through representations of the white working class in their home spaces. We do so because whiteness is, in many national popular and especially populist discourses, implicitly how both British identity (see Schwarz 2011) and working-class identity are understood.

Overall, this chapter analyses representations which bear the weight of the political moment in which race and immigration overlie questions of class and sometimes collide in interesting bursts of conversation which may provoke embarrassment, recognition, dismay or outrage, or even a reconsideration of long-held personal views (see Balibar 1991). In a way, then, this chapter is about voice, about territory, and particularly about home and about the ways in which the home can be treasured, policed, defended or opened up to others who are not like ourselves.

Borders, belonging and 'saloon bar' Britons

Real Britons, while tolerant about genuine asylum seekers and sympathetic to honest economic migrants, are exasperated at the way this government has lost control of Britain's borders…

And, yes, these same 'saloon bar' Britons also worry that our hard pressed hospitals, schools and housing stock cannot cope with this unprecedented influx.

(*Daily Mail*, 15 February 2005:14)

On 28 April 2004, responding to heightened public debate about immigration, asylum and entitlement, Prime Minister Tony Blair stated that 'we will neither be *fortress* Britain, nor will we be an *open house*' and that there would be a 'top to bottom' rethink of immigration policy (Gibson 2006:694, emphasis in the original). These and later declarations made by government and opposition moved to reassure voters that their concerns about immigration were being taken seriously. This reassurance seemed much needed when in May 2004 ten new central European nations acceded to the European Union, which allowed increased labour mobility and unrestricted access to the British labour market for new tranches of workers (House of Lords 2004: Chapter 2).[1] New Labour also had to negotiate electoral 'moments of dramatic significance' (Dunleavy 2005:9) such as the surge in support of UK Independence Party and the far right British National Party (BNP) during 2004 European and local elections. Patrick Dunleavy (2005:7) has argued that 'the BNP's significant support in 2004 reflected the resonance of immigration and asylum issues with some voters, along with some anti-Muslim sentiment'. Alongside a rise in support in significant areas such as Yorkshire and Humberside and the West Midlands, 'research in 2004 also showed that up to one in four British voters said that they could envisage voting for the BNP in the future' (Dunleavy 2005:7). In June 2004 the BNP had recorded the highest vote, averaging 20.5 per cent in the Barking and Dagenham borough in the London Assembly elections. In September 2004 the BNP gained a local councillor with over 50 per cent of the vote.[2] Banal but meaningful representations of local belonging informed the public profile of extreme groups like the BNP. The BNP was marginal. But it was also achieving pockets of rising electoral success as it continued the 'modernisation' of its profile and addressed the sense of abandonment and disenfranchisement felt by some white citizens in impoverished local communities (Copsey 2007, Eatwell 2004).

In December 2004, the *Guardian* reported on a recent British Social Attitudes survey based on responses made by 3000 people in 1995 and 2003 to questions about immigration. The 'proportion agreeing that Britain should "take stronger measures" to exclude illegal immigrants

rose from 78% to 82% over this period.' The findings seemed to indicate that 'public "opposition to immigrants" had increased during Blair's
premiership' (Carvel 2004). It was New Labour's aim to be elected to
a third term of power. Throughout 2004 then British politicians of all
political hues were beginning to reposition themselves in anticipation of
the May 2005 General Election, and debates about immigration became
increasingly fraught. On 13 April 2005 competing parties' manifestos
were launched and continued the ongoing highly contentious debate
about immigration. Labour's manifesto, entitled *Britain Forward Not
Back*, addressed questions of immigration under an early chapter called
'Crime and security: safe communities, secure borders'. The Conservative opposition's manifesto was rhetorically entitled *Are You Thinking
What We're Thinking?* and listed its agenda items quite clearly on the
front page: 'more police, cleaner hospitals, lower taxes, school discipline, controlled immigration'. The implication here was that citizens
had views which they felt they could not express out loud about
disciplinarity, services, taxes and immigration. It also fiercely attacked
Labour's record on securing borders, pointing to the Government's loss
of 'effective control', the arrival each year of a new population the size
of Peterborough and 'an asylum system in chaos'.

In February 2005, Labour had published its five-year plan on asylum and immigration, which attracted some criticism from its own
party members. The tone responded to criticism from the media and
the opposition that the Government had lost control of the immigration system, especially worrying when issues of race relations and
immigration were linked to concerns over national security and terror-
ism. In response, Labour's emphasis was on a strict regime of controls
on benefits, policing access, tightened surveillance and removal proce-
dures. In his foreword to the policy document *Controlling Our Borders*
(Blair 2005a), Tony Blair set out Britain's rich tradition of immigrant
settlement and the ways in which the 'movement of people and labour
into the UK remains vital to our economy and our prosperity' and
highlighted the tradition of tolerance and hospitality held by the British
nation. However, he stated (Blair 2005a:5) that the British 'quiet success story' of race relations was 'under threat' and that there were
illegal immigrants who were 'abusing our hospitality'.[3] The government had to tackle these abuses or open the way to exploitation 'by
extremists to promote their perverted view of race' (Blair:ibid.). Abuse
and discipline were the watchwords that structured this political template on how 'we' deal with newcomers to the homeland. The first
principle on which the policy was claimed to be founded was, 'to

enforce strict controls to root out abuse' (Blair:ibid., see Charteris-Black 2006).

A balance had to be achieved between discipline and tolerance, limitations and openness to new people and new cultures, and this had to be enacted both operationally and discursively. In the run-up to the 2005 General Election, Tony Blair spoke out against the Conservative Party election campaign message in which opposition party leader Michael Howard had declared, 'It's not racist, as some people to claim, to talk about controlling immigration, far from it.' Indeed, the sub-slogan employed in the Conservative manifesto was 'it's not racist to impose limits on immigration.' Blair (2005b) asserted in his speech (22 April 2005) that his concern was 'not about racism'. It was 'about fairness'. He stated that his priority following a successful re-election would be to 'tighten the asylum system further' and restrict immigration, but that Labour would never use asylum and immigration 'as a political weapon, an instrument of division and discord'. Instead, it would acknowledge that 'diversity' was a 'strength, not weakness, a reflection of a modern country striving to be at ease with the modern world'.[4]

These and the many other debates about immigration from the first decade of the 2000s followed long-established, damaging patterns which tried to distinguish clearly between legitimate insiders and illegitimate outsiders. They aimed to mark out the boundaries of moral, social and individual worth in the context of competition for jobs, services and welfare resources (as well as within prevailing concerns about security and terrorist threats). As noted above, there were calls to keep 'race' out of politics even as (non-white especially) immigration continued to be highly politicised. All mainstream parties sought to find a language which could discuss immigration controls without attracting accusations that they were resorting to racism or pandering to racist constituencies (a strategy known as 'playing the race card').

The interesting question for us about these times is where and with whom racist attitudes were considered to reside. To whom did parties, newspapers and political pundits think they were speaking, and on whose behalf, with regard to concerns about immigration? When the Tories, for example, asked rhetorically: 'are you thinking what we're thinking?' who were the 'you' and the 'we'? Whose voice were they projecting, for whom did they presume to speak? Labour Home Secretary Charles Clarke implied that he, at any rate, knew the answer to these last questions when his Newcastle speech (14 February 2005) criticised the opposition's approach to immigration on the grounds that it played to 'saloon bar' racism. He maintained that the Tory suggestion of holding immigrants somewhere offshore pending the processing of their applications was a 'saloon bar response'; a phrase which hinted at the vociferous and uninformed expression of personal opinion after a few too many drinks.

In reply, the mid-market *Daily Mail*'s populist retort was to speak *on behalf* of the saloon bar Briton. In doing so, it sought to divide Britain's visitors into two morally defined groups: the productive, economically 'honest' and the 'bogus' immigrant. Speaking for a 'tolerant' Britain (as in the opening quotation), the *Mail* questioned Labour's current policy on immigration and asylum and raised the spectre of criminal subterfuge and the gang-master exploitation of immigrants on British turf. It claimed: 'They [Britons] are equally exasperated by the countless bogus asylum seekers who abuse an honourable system and by the even greater number of illegal migrants who slip into Britain in the back of lorries, pay no taxes and, even more worryingly, are probably exploited by gangmasters.'[5] Alongside these abuses, it also set the vision of a social system under strain from the 'influx' of newcomers demanding healthcare, education and housing. Whereas Clarke had summoned up the rather old-fashioned image of the saloon bar as the location of a casual racism, the *Mail* retrieved it as the proper talking-shop of the citizen concerned about both abuses of the immigration system and the depletion of resources.

In the same week, the *Mail* also published the response of think-tank/lobby group Migrationwatch UK's Chairman Sir Andrew Green. Here Green (2005) counterpointed 'racism' to 'commonsense' in his defence of the ordinary person and the 'vast majority' who, he contended, had been silenced by Labour and the politically correct. He observed, 'Working people may not be schooled in economics but they are certainly not short of common sense. They know that large scale immigration is against their interests and they are very tired of it.' In a new twist on the 'swamping' theme, Green claimed that London and the South East were 'choking' under the weight of the influx of people and their cars. He claimed to speak for the 'ordinary worker' for whom 'large-scale immigration' lowered wages and raised unemployment. And he spoke, too, for 'the white working class' whose local resources were under pressure but who could not afford the privileged escape route: 'a flight to the leafy suburbs' (Green 2005).

The following year the *Mail* cited Green again as he cautiously praised new Home Secretary John Reid's announcement of an annual quota limit to migrants (Slack 2006). Reid had declared that 'We have to get away from this daft so-called politically correct notion that anybody who wants to talk about immigration is somehow a racist. That isn't the case.' He called for a 'mature discussion' of how to reassure the country that 'our services' would be 'accessible, managed and preserved' and workers' own terms and conditions protected (Slack 2006). In these and many other debates, the white working class, the ordinary person, the 'saloon bar' Briton and the lower-paid worker became the mechanism by which a defence of the nation could be spoken. Through a string of roll-over associations and elisions, it was the protection of these groups which became the ground for claiming a principled rejection of immigration and the defence against the charge of racism at the same time. Not quite ventriloquism, more a performance of patronage, the nation could contemplate turning in on itself by defending those unable to escape to leafy suburbs or who are stranded in low-paid unskilled work or who would have to fight for their share of dwindling public services.

In response to the public debate and media coverage of the new disciplinary approaches to asylum by both Labour and the Conservatives (e.g. Michael Howard's call for health checks on immigrants wishing to spend more than six months in the UK), Labour MP Diane Abbott (2005) argued that the Government's strategy of responding to negative media coverage and opinion polls by adopting more repressive measures for immigrants was misdirected: 'the truth', she claimed, 'is that fear of asylum is really about fearing a stranger, "of inferior stock" in our midst.' She concluded that 'People do not really care whether these people are technically designated work-permit holders, legal immigrants or asylum seekers' but instead were preoccupied with the *imagined* amount of people in the country. In essence, she argued that mounting defensive structures and wielding bureaucratic labels only perpetuated the fear of annihilating numbers of immigrants. Abbott concluded that, as long as the government did not fundamentally challenge the *terms* of the debate, the public panic would not subside.

In the middle part of the first decade of the 2000s the long-established media narratives of the exploitation of 'our' welfare systems and of strangers abusing British hospitality continued unabated. Far from being changed, the terms of the debate became, if anything, further entrenched. It seemed, then, at that time (and well before the 2008 global financial meltdown which triggered a new age of austerity in Britain) that some of the anxieties levelled at asylum seekers and other incomers were linked to the then *imaginary* future of depleted resources and to an anticipated or projected event in which social support systems would collapse and/or be overwhelmed by needy or greedy strangers. These anxieties were, and continue to be, framed around economies – monetary, relational, psychic – which meshed fears about loss and abandonment to desires for social belonging and security, often fixed upon the physical and social spaces we inhabit. As Povinelli (2011:28–9) has indicated, it is precisely in such moments that politically inflected legitimations of both social abandonment and belonging appear. Underpinning these is an assumption that emotional economies – belonging, abandonment of others – are integrally and unquestionably linked to market economies – wealth, prosperity, wages, benefits. From this perspective the market is the normative achievement of aggressive social policies (Povinelli:22).

It was certainly the case that issues around space, resources and cultural identity were of notable concern to populations. Citizens were invited to voice their opinion through the usual mechanisms. For example, also in 2005 the Information Centre about Asylum and Refugees (ICAR) in the UK surveyed a range of media coverage and polls, large-scale surveys such as the British Social Attitudes Survey and the European Social Survey, and other polls conducted by organisations such as MORI and YouGov. First, it concluded from its aggregated results that the past decade had witnessed a rise in interest in public attitudes towards asylum issues among politicians, service providers, media and community groups, as well as ordinary citizens. It seemed that policy makers and special interest groups wanted to know people's views. ICAR noted that across data there was a consistently large majority of respondents who regarded immigration as a 'problem' and who questioned the genuineness of asylum seekers and refugees. So, too, there were associated fears expressed about threats to British values, ethnicity and health, increased competition for resources and the economic burden upon the British economy. One respondent declared: 'They [asylum seekers] are getting thousands of pounds for cars, they get mobiles, they get computers... they get everything. But like, you see, me and [friend] we're both single parents so if we go to get anything, we can't get it.... That's what gets a lot of people's backs up' (D'Onofrio and Munk in ICAR 2005, see also D'Onofrio and Munk 2003). There also appeared to be a broad set of anxieties about incomers who were imagined to be 'given preferential treatment' and were 'better off than the average *white* Briton' (ICAR 2005:1, our emphasis). Here it seemed that the final grounding upon which overall judgements were made by respondents about the unjust allocation of resources was based around a generic 'whiteness' as the touchstone of the success or failure of the system rather than through any more complex notions of inequalities between social classes, communities or cultures.

To understand the contemporary processes of constructing selves, groups and communities during this period and the way in which whiteness and class are articulated to a fear of dwindling public resources, we might also turn to the five-year research programme *Identities and Social Action* (2004–08). Here a diverse range of researchers focused on the 'attempts of people with very different trajectories and from very different contexts to build communities and "liveable lives"'.[6] One of the key questions that informed this research focused on what it was like to build an identity in situations of social exclusion. Drawing on psychosocial methods, researchers Clarke, Garner and Gilmour carried out 128 interviews with white people on large housing estates and middle-class residential areas in Bristol and Plymouth about their views on identity, community and the idea of home (see Clarke *et al.* 2007). The researchers noted that family and socialisation were central to most responses about community and that there was a sense of community-building as a duty. Social class continued to be a key factor in respondents' life narratives, with recognition of one's own difference from the norm in school, workplace or residential area as a source of anxiety or pride. Interestingly, grand narratives of 'nation, country and erstwhile empire' no longer seemed central as markers of identity and belonging for most respondents, and English respondents often relayed a desire to 'shrink' their British identity to a more 'localised English one like those of the Scots, Welsh and Irish' (Clarke and Garner undated:2). Tellingly, discourses on whiteness were often latched to those of *welfare*, with entitlement to the welfare system at the core of this discussion. Here, overlap between whiteness, black and minority ethnic citizens and ideas about belonging and otherness appear to have been 'complex, selective and sometimes contradictory', and entitlement to an identity which *fitted in* was rehearsed through notions of productive activity, integration and assimilation (Clarke and Garner:2).[7]

Hylton-Potts and the cabbies' manifesto

Paxman: 'If people are terrified, tortured, persecuted. Arrive on your doorstep, you say no!'

Hylton-Potts: 'I'm afraid so. We're closed for business. That's what people want in this country.'

(*Newsnight* BBC2 24 January 2005)

In January 2005 and with the General Election in its sights, ITV began its broadcast of a five-part reality series entitled *Vote for Me*. The theme was that hopeful candidates – ordinary people presenting themselves as a political package for the programme – would appeal to the public with their simple manifesto which could be tested by public vote. The show was overseen by the current affairs team and aimed to increase public interest in democracy. Would-be candidates were grilled by breakfast TV host Lorraine Kelly, former ITN political editor John Sargeant and former *Sun* editor Kelvin MacKenzie; public figures who, we would suggest, seemed representative of a range of constituencies, including those marked by social class. Candidates were filmed undertaking typical political tasks such as doorstep canvassing, meeting the British lobby press and participating in phone-ins.

One of the seven short-listed candidates was Rodney Hylton-Potts (a convicted fraudster and former solicitor), who promoted unalloyed anti-immigration views. He argued that Britain was 'swamped with immigrants and governed by faceless bankers in Brussels'. Hylton-Potts confidently rebutted MacKenzie's question of whether he had any sense of 'shame' and joked off Kelly's clear animosity to his extreme political views, which included total anti-immigration ('because Britain is full'), zero intake of asylum seekers, legalisation of hard drugs, more prisons and compulsory castration for paedophiles. His tag-line was that he had secured the 'cabbie's vote': the ordinary (implicitly white working-class) person's vote whose views he'd canvassed with the drivers who carried him to the TV studio. As a self-styled 'people's politician', Hylton-Potts was very clear that he was 'on a show trying to get votes', and he went on to comfortably win, albeit through a rather un-representational multiple voting system. When asked by Jeremy Paxman on *Newsnight* whether, if asked today, he would allow Jewish refugees in from Nazi Germany, Hylton-Potts replied in the negative; repeatedly declaring that we're closed for business on the grounds of 'that's what the people want.'[8]

As Mick Temple (2006:265) observed in his analysis of politics and the public sphere, despite ITV's promotion of the series, the suspicion remained that the channel itself regarded Hylton-Potts' selection as embarrassing and hence buried it in the late-night schedules; it is certainly the case, he added, 'that most broadsheet commentators saw it as an essentially risible exercise'.[9] As we have shown, *Vote for Me* aired the territorial, quite muddled and strongly contested views of Hylton-Potts in a period of heightened debate about immigration and in anticipation of the 2005 British General Election. Critics' responses to the series and to Hylton-Potts' victory varied from the incredulous to the disdainful, with some small, more subdued pockets of support or sympathy. But what's interesting from our perspective was the speculation about who exactly had voted for Hylton-Potts, and for whom was he speaking. Why exactly was this anti-liberal platform supposed to appeal to the London black cab driver? To answer this we need to touch on the classed folk mythology around cabbies and the way in which their views have been characterised as right wing or conservative and illiberal. The British media, always charged up when social class is in the air, conveyed these well. In a BBC online magazine article called 'Rank and bile', reporter Jonathan Duffy (2005) summed it up:

> In popular folklore, the cabbie's credo does not fit the profile of any one political party, but goes something like this: Europe – one big gravy train; criminals – lock 'em up and throw away the key; government – nannying overlords; business leaders – fat cats; single mothers – spongers; asylum seekers – foreign spongers, and so on and so forth.

Duffy himself went on to poll the views of a number of white male cab drivers, who were asked to speculate on why they'd been stereo-typed. Their suggestions included: 'We're capitalists, the smallest version of capitalists you can find,' that historically cabbies often came from white working-class backgrounds, and that they (or many of their colleagues) did indeed tend to vote to the right. The BBC's straw poll of cab drivers secured a mix of anti and pro responses to Hylton-Potts' proposals.

All the mainstream coverage suggested that a vote for Hylton-Potts was a vote for extremism and that those that voted for him were either ignorant or deluded. Martin Bell in the *Mail on Sunday* (16 January 2005) condemned him as a 'silver tongued extremist'. The anti-racism campaign group *Hope not Hate* (2005) revealed that he had made a pact with the British National Party, who had agreed to stand down their own candidate for Folkestone and Hythe in his favour on the grounds that it and Hylton-Potts 'share so much common ground'.[10] *The Economist* (20 January 2005) declared disdainfully, 'The people have spoken' and reassured readers that the media had 'reacted with horror', with tabloids, broadsheets and mid-market papers alike all denouncing Hylton-Potts as a 'racist'. The enormous gulf between the reality TV candidate, his noisily populist Cabby Manifesto policies and the more politically astute was exposed in David Aaronovitch's (2005) piece for the *Guardian*, which addressed mainstream party political policies on immigration and asylum with passing references to *Vote for Me*. He begins by suggesting quite credibly that recent Tory and Labour proposals on immigration and work rules had been governed by 'fear of the distant prejudice' of its electorate, what he refers to as the shadow of the elephant in the room. In other words, there's a somewhat unspoken sense that they do indeed know what the electorate is thinking and that its thinking is rooted in prejudice. He then goes on to argue that only racists, populists and xenophobes would lump together complex issues of immigration, asylum, identity and community into one 'amorphous question of race and demographics'. He then adds:

> And let's acknowledge another problem in the demographic debate, which is that the folks coming in are often more desirable than the ones already here. As New Zealander Craig told the BBC Your Say website, 'It isn't immigrants that are the problem in the UK – as a whole, people come here to work hard and contribute to society. It is the indigenous population festering on the dole and incapacity benefit, littering the streets and causing all the anti-social behaviour.' Think about Rodney Hilton-Potts [sic], the insurgent proto-populist who won that silly competition on ITV and will now stand for parliament at the next election.

This association of Hylton-Potts with the 'festering' indigenous population serves to disconnect him from the entrepreneurial, hard-grafting cabby and yokes him instead to stereotypes of the socially corrosive underclass discussed in Chapter 3. If there are resources to be battled for, and these references to unproductivity, unemployment and disability benefits suggest that there are, then there are others less deserving of support than the immigrant targets identified by Hylton-Potts. These more useless people form the counterweight to Aaronovitch's larger argument for the rich diversity of London, specifically, which is made dynamic by its immigrant life. Here, the capital itself becomes a symbol of difference and exceptionality, not only through its vibrancy but by virtue of its more progressive attitudes, which are opposed to those of the 'rest of Britain' which he presents stereotypically as 'so crabbed and provincial in its attitude towards newcomers'. He adds: 'However much swingeing restrictions might suit the sensibilities of the white suburbs, they don't do anything for those places where the immigrants actually go.'

Vote for Me, then, brought together popular media, high politics, questions of race and asylum, and threaded through this were publicly expressed assumptions about prejudice, whiteness, class, and lived spaces of the home, city and suburb. Hylton-Potts was styled as a cartoon character who expressed extreme views to glean support and to stay before the camera. His moment of fame was transient. What is interesting is that he provoked a range of noisy condemnations of his racism. Critics worked to disassociate themselves not only from Hylton-Potts himself but from the kinds of people who they imagined he might represent. This was a moment of performative disgust in which commentators, and indeed the judges in the programme itself, removed themselves from the scene.

Sara Ahmed (2004) writes powerfully of the embodied and discursive status of disgust. She links it to psychic notions of abjection, when something is transformed into a border object which provokes a sickened response. The border object can be material – the skin of milk, the decaying corpse – but it can also be linked to imaginary threats to the integrity of the self. That a subject is disgusting, then, relies on a history and also a sense of proximity: only that which is too close to us or that makes contact with us must be repelled with such embodied vehemence. Hylton-Potts' comments made commentators sick, outraged and disgusted, and rightly so. But, in pulling away from him and disassociating from him, the accusation of racism, parochialism, narrow-mindedness and social corrosiveness had to be made to stick elsewhere. This is the stickiness of certain emotions that Ahmed so clearly outlines in relation to hatred and fears of the asylum seeker and the racial other. We should add that, albeit perhaps less obviously, other fears also emerge, of small-minded middle-class parochialism located in the suburbs, of opinionated right wing entrepreneurial cabbies, tabloid readers, reality TV audiences and, above all, of the anti-social and ill-informed white working class. Fear and/or prejudice about the racialised other can be displaced or overly loaded onto these groups (sometimes with good cause but not always with *reason*). It seems to us that in public discourse racist attitudes, extremism and the rejection of the ethnic or racialised other are rarely to be found in London, in metropolitan middle-class homes or watering holes, or in mainstream party politics. But they are all too easily spied in the middle distance; residing with the white working class, in white suburbia and in extreme politics. These views are never 'here'; they are always 'elsewhere'.

The 'good woman' from Rochdale

> The three main things … were education, health service and looking after people who are vulnerable … but there's too many

people now who aren't vulnerable but they can claim [state support].... You can't say anything about the immigrants because if you say anything you're racist.

Lifelong Labour supporter Gillian Duffy confronts Gordon Brown during a campaigning visit to Rochdale.

On 28 April 2010, with only weeks to the General Election before him, incumbent Prime Minister Gordon Brown was on a campaigning visit to Rochdale when he stopped to talk with 66-year-old Gillian Duffy, who, he'd been reassured, was a long-term Labour supporter. During a conversation concerning the local community and her contribution, Brown observed, 'you're a very good woman, you've served the community all your life.' However, the conversation took a difficult turn when Duffy declared herself ashamed of Labour and vigorously challenged Brown on a diverse range of issues including his management of the then-collapsing economy, pensions and taxes, crime and community, access to services, and eastern European immigrants. Once off camera, and not realising he still had a microphone pinned to his shirt, he was heard to tell an aide as he climbed into his car: 'That was a disaster – they should never have put me with that woman.' Asked what she had said, he replied: 'Ugh everything! She's just a sort of bigoted woman that said she used to be Labour.'[11]

After Brown's comments were relayed to her, Duffy observed:

I'm very upset. He's an educated person. Why has he come out with words like that? He's supposed to be leading the country and he's calling an ordinary woman who's come up and asked questions that most people would ask him.... It's going to be tax, tax, tax for another 20 years to get out of this national debt, and he's calling me a bigot.

After the flurry of media coverage Brown apologised for his gaffe on the Jeremy Vine radio show (BBC Radio 2 28 April 2010) and visited Duffy in person. During the apology-round Brown's spokesman stated on his behalf that 'this is exactly the sort of conversation that is important in an election campaign and which he will continue to have with voters.' Some days later the *Daily Mail* drew on the story and an extensive interview with Duffy in support of its own poll of public opinion, which demonstrated that 'Bigot-gate' had damaged Labour's chances of re-election. Here the paper outlined, in heavily illustrated detail, Duffy's working-class and Labour credentials, including her strong family history of union-based politics and public service, further reinforcing, perhaps, Duffy's declared disappointment and unmet expectations: 'The thing is, I'm the sort of person he was meant to look after, not shoot down' (Collins *et al.* 2010).

In the *Mail* Duffy recalled in painstaking detail the second, far longer, conversation with the Prime Minister, in which they addressed not only detailed issues of political ideology and strategy but also personal topics about family and feeling. She recalled how she had first tidied the house pending his arrival but decided not to offer him a cup of tea (and certainly not a whiskey) and how the conversation had strayed from the political to the personal (at his behest) and then back again (at her insistence). According to Duffy, the PM talked about his wife and sons and Duffy addressed her hopes and concerns for her grandchildren. Duffy also bearded him on personal economics: 'I asked him, "If you and Sarah [Brown's wife] were to go out for a nice meal with a bottle of wine in London I bet it would cost you more than £60 wouldn't it? And if you live in London you might do that twice, maybe more, a week? Well, pensioners are living on £60 a week up here.' Towards the end of the article Duffy is quoted as saying: 'You know the thing that upset me the most wasn't the word bigot. It was the way he called me "that woman". I'm not "that woman". It's no way to talk of someone that is it? As if I'm to be brushed away.'

An accompanying piece by broadcaster Liz Kershaw, who also hailed from Rochdale (in Collins *et al.* 2010), argued that Duffy's views needed to be respected because of the ways she had called attention to how the town had become mired in post-industrial decline long before the economic crisis. Signalling her own working-class heritage and investment in Rochdale, Kershaw muses: 'I wonder what my grandparents, who lived in the town's Irish ghetto, operated cotton looms at the age of 12 and worked their way out of poverty with the help of the Labour movement, would make of the place now.' Here Kershaw discloses her own past naïve enthusiasm for the 'progress' which was achieved when factories made way for retail parks, when industry made way for the service sector. For Rochdale the promised brighter future never arrived. There was little point in having shops when no-one had any money to spend. Kershaw addressed Duffy directly: 'You are not a bigot. You are just like my Mum or my Grandma. You are struggling and worried for the future.'

In the Gillian Duffy media scandal, once again, as with 'bar room' Britons and the cabby vote, the voices and opinions of the ordinary person became the site of political and media negotiation, recognition, attempted co-optation and contestation. For Brown, Duffy was the wrong kind of Labour voter and she established the wrong kind of campaign conversation. Brown was certain, even before his private views were disclosed, that the media would run with the footage of their vigorous debate, which he presumed to be against him. Ironically, he didn't know at the time that Duffy had already declared to reporters on the scene that she had been perfectly satisfied with this public exchange of views – it was the overheard conversation that blew it for Brown, as audiences learned what he was really thinking. Finally, Brown travelled back to meet with Duffy in her own home, but left without managing to secure the hoped-for and requested doorstep hand-shake photo opportunity. And, as noted, only days before the election the *Mail* devoted substantial coverage to the story, and of Duffy's life history and views, with an emphasis on her redoubtable authenticity as a good woman of the family, the church and the town.

As Nick Couldry (2010:1) explains in his discussion of the 'value of voice', there is a growing crisis of voice being experienced across cultural, economic and political domains. In his words, one element of this crisis 'is a loss of the connecting narratives that would help us to grasp many specific break-downs as dimensions of the same problem'. The breakdowns he alludes to are those of the neoliberal project in which British Thatcherism and its aftermath played a part. Couldry (ibid.) contends: 'a particular discourse, neoliberalism, has come to dominate the contemporary world (formally, practically, culturally and imaginatively). That discourse operates with a view of economic life that does not value voice...' Couldry outlines a number of what we might call voice 'modes': the conventional ones of the speaking voice and the expression of (political) opinion, but also voice as process and voice as value. 'Process' refers to 'the act of giving an account of oneself', one's life and one's circumstances and the conditions of that process, the conditions, perhaps, of what makes that process possible. 'Value' refers to the act of valuing voice and of choosing to value frameworks which facilitate and validate the expression of voice. As Couldry (ibid.) sees it (and there is little doubt that he is right), currently 'offers of voice are increasingly unsustainable; voice is persistently offered, but in important respects denied or rendered illusory.'

The examples we have discussed thus far point to the horrendously difficult business of facilitating voice, of making space for public expression and political opinion in relation to class, inequality and immigration within extant media and political structures. The frames of debate about immigration, good citizenship, home and the competition for resources have become ossified, but they are also, finally, the only parameters in which people are enjoined to speak publicly. Reality TV, polls and surveys, journalistic comment and political campaigning all seem to grant value and give credibility to voice and to the voices of 'ordinary people', but too often this is merely lip service. Indeed, for various reasons and in different ways, the survival of media and political institutions crucially depends on accessing and sampling opinion, and it is their credibility which is at stake. It seems in some ways that there are more opportunities, more invitations than ever to give an account of one's self, to narrativise one's conditions, to contribute to public discourse, and so on. But, as Couldry suggests, the deployment of voice and its public recognition should mean far more than simply the canvassing of political opinion; rather, it should be enacted in a social world where the frameworks of debate can shift and in which voice actually matters. But not only are the voices of immigrants and black and minority ethnic citizens themselves startlingly, grotesquely absent from many of these public debates, but the voices of other Britons with views on immigration, inequality and resources are frequently ventriloquised, distorted, co-opted, fought over, misattributed and misread. Perhaps the problem here in terms of political communication is that opinion is mistaken for representation and the expression of opinion is mistaken as the expression of voice. Perhaps the 'ordinary' voice is the hardest thing to hear in the hubbub of a noisy public realm in which Hylton-Potts knows what people 'really' want, political parties know what voters are 'really' thinking, when papers respectively speak to and for the saloon bar Brit, the progressive metropolitan or the suburban home-owner, and when political culture articulates the commonsense view.

A recognition of the significance of home is also crucial here to an understanding of how social class and immigration are articulated in media debates. That Gillian Duffy allowed Gordon Brown into her home but did not offer him any hospitality was culturally significant. Brown entered her home ground to make amends and she made him welcome, but only to a limited degree and evidently on her own terms. This encounter is doubly resonant because in the national imaginary the private home is still the final boundary of demarcation between the personal and the public sphere. It is the resident in their own home who is entitled by right of occupancy to adopt a position of tolerance or to exclude others, and who is also able to accept and welcome strangers, outsiders and those with whom they might disagree. As Gibson (2006:695), glossing Borradori, notes: 'Tolerance is, for the host, a "wish to limit my welcome, to retain power over the limits of my "home". Tolerance is thus equated with conditional hospitality, charity and mastery over one's own home.'[12] Duffy may have been seriously displeased with Brown, she may have been wary of his intentions and she was certainly sceptical about the whole visit, but nonetheless she tidied her house and she invited him in to have that conversation. She scolded Brown for his mismanagement of the economy and of their earlier meeting, but she also declared her sympathy: 'I'm sorry for you, Gordon, because you have more to lose than me. I'm very sorry that this has happened but it's you who's going to lose out, not me' (Collins *et al.* 2010).

In contrast, then, to much that has gone before, the emphasis in the conclusion of this chapter is on the ways in which anxieties about immigration can become transformed into something else; how welcome, dialogue, reciprocity and an openness to others can be articulated. Home, to twist a cliché, is where the heart is supposed to be. But home is always both less and more than a space of intimacy, protection, neighbourliness and daily life. How can it be otherwise when, as Roger Silverstone (2007) indicates, home is a concept bound up with powerful emotions such as desire, longing, hope and insecurity? We might also add to these pride, resentment and shame. The question of what home, community and society might be and the interrelationship between these loaded concepts has preoccupied recent political discourse in the late twentieth and early twenty-first century. In imaginary terms at least, home invites a sense of grounded personal investment. As cultural critic Kathleen Stewart (2007:2) has observed, home is both an idea and an experience inextricable from material culture and market forces. The embodied experience of being in the physical space of the home is linked across to 'social expectations and values, status anxiety, financial (in)security and notions of futurity' (Nunn 2011:169). Across all of these fields tensions are experienced between proximity and distance, between oneself and others, between too near, too far and just right.

It is obviously the case that in Britain many of our local spaces undergo change in character and population; they are sometimes experienced as fractured, unsettled and reoriented by the company of strangers. Importantly, too, many people never or rarely move on from their local space; not everyone is equally mobile, not everyone has the desire or resources. As David Morley (2000:14) has pointed out, despite widespread notions of 'global connexity' many people are 'kept in place' by 'structures of oppression of various forms'; for many people the global experience is of the transformation of the local space. Many people are tied especially, in the long term and historically, to deeply impoverished areas, and in these conditions newcomers can be perceived as competitors for resources and services. But affective investments in the local community are also centrally important. As the Economic and Social Research Council (Clarke and Garner undated:2) research already cited above on 'mobility and unsettlement' in contemporary Britain suggested: 'People's concepts of home range from attachments to physical environment through to mobile ones, relating to security and family.' When asked about their sense of what community meant, 'the concepts advanced tend toward the affective rather than the instrumental. People often seemed to be trying to recreate what they imagine a better community to have resembled in the past'. The research also noted that there was also an emphasis amongst residents on 'a sense of community-building as a duty' and that this was linked to imagined values. Many of their respondents were 'attached to the idea of living in a small, almost village-sized unit, seeing themselves as members of "village" communities (sometimes subsections of larger estates)' (Clarke and Garner undated:2). How people make sense of their lives, hopes and aspirations, then, is often linked to the home and immediate locale, and it is in these spaces that the public discourses of social class, material resources, national identity and immigration become concretised through lived experience.

All White in Barking

> It's not us anymore.
> (local resident speaking in *All White in Barking* 2008)

To conclude, then, we will engage with the question of home, hospitality and tolerance and its mediated relationship to social class through a discussion of Mark Isaac's documentary *All White in Barking* (2008). The film charted the complex responses of the white working-class inhabitants of the East London borough of Barking and Dagenham to relatively high levels of local immigrant settlement. Its context was quite obviously the backdrop of the controversial and then still memorable 2006 Local Council Election in which the BNP became the main party of political opposition in the historically Labour-run council. The film opens with the observation that Barking and Dagenham has one of the 'highest levels of immigration' in the country and that 10,000 people had voted for the BNP there in the last election. Here Barking and Dagenham is presented as a 'testing ground' on which 'to confront our fear of foreigners'. Against this backdrop the documentary chose to focus on the older community of white working-class inhabitants and their encounters with the diverse range of immigrants moving into the area.[13]

All White in Barking (*AWIB*) was broadcast in March 2008 as part of BBC2's White Season. This series of five documentaries was commissioned by Richard Klein to address the perceived omission of the white working-class voice on public service television. As such, all of the films were concerned with the relationship between the white working class and immigrants, refugees or asylum seekers. In a piece published by the *Daily Mail* and illustrated with a black-and-white photograph of a working men's club dating from the 1970s, Klein (2008) positioned the films in the heart of the current 'noisy debate within the media, politics and academia' about Britain's status as one of the 'most culturally and racially diverse places in Europe'. In this sense, Klein's article and its presentation already epitomised criticisms which were to be levelled at the series, as it juxtaposed a 30-year-old photograph of white working-class people with an argument about the absence of their views in the current moment. He noted with irony that amid 'heated discussion . . . one voice has been largely absent: that of the white working class.' He argued that the values of 'community spirit', 'attachment to strong families' and 'respect for tradition', for which the working class were once celebrated in political discourse and popular culture, had been obscured by the frequent portrayal of them as 'reactionary or backward, with opinions so outdated they can easily be dismissed . . .'. Klein maintained that the season aimed to address the white working class's sense of abandonment by the political classes. He added: 'there can be few greater arenas for emotional conflict than the state of the white working class in modern Britain, struggling to embrace the modern, diverse, globalised, everchanging world.'

The trailer for the series caused some controversy. A white shaven-headed man in his middle years stares out of the frame – his pale face set against a black backdrop. Then, accompanied by the soundtrack of Billy Bragg singing the British anthem 'Jerusalem', disembodied black and brown-skinned hands enter the frame to scribble in black ink across his face and skull in different languages and scripts. Before his face is obliterated by script, the words 'Britain is changing' are legible to the English-speaking viewer. Swiftly the man's face is totally 'blacked out' by script. It disappears against the dark background so that only an uncanny pair of eyes look out as viewers hear the lyrics 'in England's green and pleasant land'. The careful use of Barking-born Bragg, a left-orientated musician with a long history of anti-racist activism, is overwhelmed by the affective connotations of the visuals, which suggest racial incorporation or even annihilation.

In a famous account of his humiliation and psychic transformation as a feared black man, Frantz Fanon (1952:86) recalled the moment when he was confronted by a white child clearly terrified of his black skin. The physical sign of difference, Fanon's black skin, is, as he recalls, read by the young boy as a sign of horror and he fears that the black man will 'eat' him up. Fanon (p. 86) recollected: 'My body was given back to me sprawled out, recolored, distorted, clad in mourning in that white winter day.... All this whiteness that burns me...'. Sara Ahmed (2004:62–3) uses Fanon's story to demonstrate the ways in which both the black and, indeed, the white body and their difference are over-determined and mediated, in this case through traces of Fanon's memories, but also through those he encounters who enclose his black body in fear. The White Season's trailer, while promoting a series designed to depict the complexity of classed, ethnic and racial encounters, arguably re-established both the distance and closeness between white and black body. The crude signifier of the white working class – a man with a shaven head staring fixedly ahead – is overwritten with other crude signifiers of racial and cultural difference. The scribbles across the white skin obliterate the man's features. Fear is established in such representations – the trailer works by opening up fantasies of white incorporation which are written onto the white working-class body: a kind of white skin, black mask.

BBC2 Controller Roly Keating refuted charges of racism and defended the trailer as 'arresting' and there to 'stimulate public debate' (*Guardian* 10 March 2008). In contrast, *Socialist Worker* writer Yuri Prasad (2008) likened the trailer to a BNP recruitment campaign. While Prasad had some praise for *All White in Barking* and the film *White Girl*, he bemoaned the series overall for its lack of complexity in representing working-class lives:

> It is true that the white working class in Britain has been profoundly changed by mass immigration. The music it listens to, the food it eats and its leisure pursuits have all been transformed in the last half-century. And there is a much wider range of ethnic groups making up the working class of today.

The BBC in-house magazine *Ariel* also published the criticisms of journalist Sarah Mukherjee, who had grown up on a predominantly white council estate in Essex. She accused the season of risking 'reinforcing the stereotype of the white working class as violent and racist alcoholics who live on benefits' (in Martin 2008). She recalled that the white working-class people she knew had the same concerns as the middle classes living in West London's Notting Hill: 'A good education for their kids, a good standard of living, enough left over for a nice holiday.' She added that listening to the patronising conversation in some newsrooms would make one think that 'white working class Britain is one step away from anarchy, drinking themselves senseless and pausing only to draw benefits and beat up a few Asian and black people' (in Martin 2008). Taken in its entirety, the White Season, and its promotion, revealed what was at stake in trying to access and amplify, in Klein's terms, the largely absent voice of the white working class. Even as it sought to make white working-class lives central to current debates, it styled them as outmoded. Even as it sought to understand new community relations, it set up white working-class culture as under threat of erosion by the cultures of immigrant communities.

As we shall see, *AWIB* works within this confining framework but it also, arguably, strives to challenge it. The themes of home, hospitality and the encounter with the stranger are central to *AWIB* and not all of the encounters are negative or predictable. The film begins by intercutting Barking's small town centre with scenes featuring the key characters as they meet and reflect upon the wide diversity of immigrants moving into the area. The filming shifts between several key interiors (domestic homes and gardens, the inside of the butcher's shop) and closely framed outside communal spaces (Dagenham Heathway station, East Street – the main shopping thoroughfare in Barking and its market). However, while specific characters are richly complex, the white working class in general are depicted in a strangely melancholic generic fashion. An early scene set on a grey and windy day focused on the demolition of the Liberal and Labour Club, lighting on a crumpled Union flag before picking out younger black faces in the busy market below. The mournful music and subjective point-of-view shots set up Barking as a town that had lost its way in the wake of dramatic social change. If Essex County has been figured as energetic, aspirational and classless, then former Essex London Boroughs such as Barking have been styled as embattled and backward. The contrast between the older white people and the new Barking is writ large and characterised quite poignantly as generational (the old and the young), temporal (the past and the present) and even sensory (familiar versus the unfamiliar sounds and foods and flavours). At times the filming recalls an almost anthropological mode, as though chronicling a slowly dwindling tribe and its struggle to adapt.

Barking itself is established through several long slow takes of the market and lingering close-ups of mainly older, weathered white-skinned faces; people gathering around a market auction-stall selling the cheapest cuts of meat. Mouths open, rarely smiling, watery-eyed, not speaking to each other, they seem to stand disconnected and alone, gaping at the off-screen trader as he sells his goods. These shots are strongly reminiscent of Lindsay Anderson's famous 1953 film of working-class leisure called *O Dreamland*, in which working-class people are figured *en masse* as voiceless, bemused onlookers. In *AWIB*, these images, accompanied by the plangent drift of violin music, convey its subjects as not quite the objects of nostalgia, perhaps more as objects of pathos. They seem to represent an older, defunct group, outmoded and cut off from the younger, vibrant and more colourful street market and community that surrounds them. Richard Hoggart's (1957) recollection of the 'settings' of his own working-class childhood and its 'landscape with figures' also comes to mind here. Speaking of the insularity and bounded nature of the working-class lives he had moved away from, and their close ties to home and neighbourhood, he conjured up the figure of the solitary old man. For Hoggart, it was the old men who were 'most pathetic' in their spatial and psychological entrapment; a condition which becomes ever more confining as families grow up, wives die, times change and young people move on. 'In these brick and concrete wastes' they became alienated figures, retreating to the haunt of communal spaces – the local public library, the railway station: 'this is the special refuge of the misfits and the left-overs, of the hollow-cheeked, watery-eyed, shabby, and furtively sad' (Hoggart 1957:69–70). He describes them in almost phobic terms; perhaps envisioning with some relief and also guilt a quite differently classed future for himself. Hoggart's reflection on these insular entropic lives could be applied to Isaacs' ciphers of old Barking in *AWIB* and, albeit a half century apart, they both offer up a troubling picture of working-class entropy: 'They exist on the periphery of life, seeing each other daily but with no contact. Reduced to a handful of clothes, a few primary needs and a persistent lack, they have been disconnected from the only kind of life in which they ever had a part ... ' (Hoggart:70).

Against this gloomy and unpromising backdrop *AWIB* introduced six white working-class characters who were long-term inhabitants of Barking and whose views and life experiences arguably contradict, in their quirky complexity, the gloomy social realism of its collective scenes. One of these is a Jewish market trader and holocaust survivor called Monty who has a complex friendship with the younger Betty, a recently arrived immigrant from Uganda. There is also East-End born Dave, who has two daughters, one of whom is the mother of a mixed-heritage child and a survivor of an abusive relationship with her Nigerian partner, and the other whose boyfriend describes himself as an 'ethnic mix' with an English father and a half-African mother. Also appearing are Valerie and her husband Steve, who run the local butcher's *Farmers Meat*, which closes during the filming because it is no longer sustainable. Finally, there are Sue and Jeff, a late middle-aged couple who have lost their adult son to cancer and who live next door to fairly newly resident Albanian neighbours, with whom, at the start of the film, they have barely spoken.

The business of the film seems to be respectful but persistent inquiry into the attitudes of its key protagonists. They, in turn, reply with mainly wary or guarded assessments of the changes they have experienced. For some subjects, such as Sue and Jeff, the concern seems to be with proximity and strangeness. For them, the cultural difference between people is marked by their discomfort at strange smells of cooking, unusual music and the loud voices which they associate with non-white neighbours; these differences make them nervous. In an equally tentative fashion, Valerie and Steve also express concerns about the new ethnic makeup of Barking. Their alienation is exemplified in a point-of-view shot of them looking out at multiracial shoppers beyond the window while serving customers. In a telling moment, when black shoppers peep into his shop window Steve mutters: 'black people looking in … Not used to it'. Dave, as a staunch member of the BNP, is the most assertive of these figures and seems the most sure of his views. Of all of those featured, he argues most vociferously that 'you prefer to live among your own' and struggles with his daughters' 'preference' for what he calls 'sunburnt people'.[14] He presents himself as the victim of strangers and alien cultures which he deems responsible for the evident decline of Barking and Dagenham, and, beyond that, the decline of the nation. Dave roundly refutes Isaacs' suggestion that, bearing in mind his love for his mixed-heritage grandson, his aversion to immigrants must be irrational. On the contrary, Dave declares that his grandson is his 'blood' and that 'this is England.'

Nearly all of these characters, then, express concerns about newcomers to their town which are crosshatched with the complexities of lived experience. But it is perhaps the story of widower Monty, and his relationship with Betty, which most richly reveals the complexity and promise of the classed and immigrant encounter. Betty cooks for Monty and he cares for her, and they both openly acknowledge and yet choose to override their cultural and racial differences. Monty jokingly expresses racist assumptions about Africans and 'cooking pots', while Betty mocks Monty's prejudices as she contemplates taking him home to meet her family in Africa. She mockingly confides to Isaacs that Monty thinks 'he will be killed or raped' when he visits Uganda. Monty shrugs this off, declaring that all he wants is 'love'. Later he is filmed taking Betty to his Auschwitz liberation anniversary dinner, where both have to face up to the consternation of his elderly relatives and friends. Here he laughs with evident approval at Betty's traditional dress worn for the occasion and calls her the 'Queen of Sheba'. Monty's friends have to learn to welcome his new companion into their midst. Scenes such as these (albeit perhaps contrived) convey the complexity of lived experience where friendship, love and reciprocal care cut across prejudice or fear of the unknown.

We want to conclude here by focusing on another moment of hospitality in *AWIB*, in which Sue and Jeff are asked by Isaacs to visit their Nigerian neighbour Dickson (with whom they have never conversed) and his family for dinner. To their credit, they agree to this unwarranted and demanding request, and the camera captures their discomfort and unease about going to a stranger's house and, as Sue puts it, to 'walk in stone cold'. The social etiquette complexities of this moment are partly overwritten by the film's emphasis on the cross-racial/cultural encounter, but they are there nonetheless. There is an understandable reticence on visiting the home of a stranger, anxiety about whether to take wine, and which one, and much deliberation on what the food will be and whether they will be able to eat it. Food throughout the documentary figures as a symbol of cultural difference and a point for almost abject reflection on what the stranger might consume: goat head, pig's ear, who knows? In a rare moment in the film when the camera goes into another butcher's filled with meats for the African consumer, one young woman laughs as she tells Isaacs that white people don't know what to do with what she considers good meat: the inside of the goat, the nose of a cow. Meanwhile, Valerie in *Farmers Meat* on the opposite side of the road tells Isaacs that her customers don't like the new butcher's: they 'don't like the way the chickens are hanging up. They don't like the smell'.[15]

On the other hand, both the Auschwitz dinner and Dickson's supper show shared food to be a source of communion and welcome. In the visit to Dickson's home the offering of a meal is crucial to the bonding of the two families as near neighbours. Jeff and Sue eat the carefully prepared food, including the braised cow heel and mashed yam. They joke with their hosts about their error in bringing wine to their tee-total neighbours. Jeff turns in pleasure to Dickson, calling him 'my friend' and praises the food as 'different, but enjoyable'. Back home viewers watch on as Sue and Jeff make tea and reflect warmly about the food and their pleasure in the visit. Sue recalls how she was once asked out by a young black man and Jeff discloses that has admired the beautiful black girls on screen and stage, although he never could make the leap to imagining a relationship. In these scenes, and at the subsequent barbecue to which both Dickson's family and the new Albanian neighbours are invited, cross-cultural differences in religion and diet, as well as shared moments of discomfort about strangers, are explored (albeit a little heavy-handedly). The significance of hospitality and reciprocity is made clear. As Sue reflects on her visit to Dickson's home: 'The hospitality and making you welcome...couldn't fault them'.

These obviously staged moments of encounter, in which traces of reality TV's influence on the documentary format are clear, at least offer up scenes of plurality and connection: of what Paul Gilroy (2008) has described as multicultural 'conviviality'. While *AWIB*, like many of the public discussions about race, ethnicity, immigration and class already discussed, is framed by unpromising binaries of black and white, old and new, Britishness and otherness, it ultimately strives to disrupt these. It paints a picture of Barking (and therefore of all formerly white working-class locales) as a rich environment in which lived experience, and especially white working-class experience, is far more diverse, more contingent, more fluid and more open than commonly depicted. White working-class experience is also more contradictory than the media would most often have us believe. Even Dave, who cannot forgive the 'foreigner's' apparent refusal to integrate, to dress or eat or to live 'Westernised' like him, can love his mixed-heritage grandchild.

In conclusion, *AWIB* was framed by the White Season's highly conventional parameters of the immigrant threat to an outmoded white working class: a framework also deployed more broadly in media discourses and political debate. It also reinforced this through its own treatment of the white working class and non-white immigrant as *generalities*, as collective victims and as collective threats. However, it also went some way towards offering a process for the facilitation of voice, allowing people to give an account of themselves and their lives and ascribing those voices a value (Couldry 2010 above). This film arguably goes some way towards the production of what Roger

Silverstone (2007) called a 'proper distance' with regard to the ideal functioning of the media:

> Proper distance refers to the importance of understanding the more or less precise degree of proximity required in our mediated relationships if we are to create and sustain a sense of the other sufficient not just for reciprocity but for a duty of care, obligation and responsibility as well as understanding. Proper distance preserves the other through difference as well as shared identity.
>
> (Silverstone 2007:47)

Here Silverstone specifically argues for morally aware and self-scrutinising media as they construct a sphere of potentially democratic global connection which he calls the 'mediapolis'. He (p. 34) argues that the media are duty-bound to *challenge* polarisation and to try to build ways in which human beings can connect and respect each other in the mediapolis. The mediapolis is democratic in intentions but 'less than the public sphere, in its modesty. There is no expectation that all the requirements for fully effective communication can be met by those responsible for its initiation, and those, in good faith, who contribute to it'. But what is required is the 'recognition of cultural difference' (Silverstone:ibid.). In this thesis he focuses on a range of spaces and modes of media representation which shift from the adversarial to the connective, most notably from our perspective on what he termed 'encountering the other' with reference to discussions of hospitality and justice mediated through home (Silverstone:136–61).

For Silverstone, proper distance is the *condition* of the media's responsible ethical 'trade in otherness'. Silverstone outlines a range of media characters and tropes which illustrate the failed capacity to properly represent and calibrate the spectrum and space of difference and sameness between individuals and groups. Embedded journalists in conflict zones, the exposure of the private lives of public figures, the use of the exotic in global advertising are all examples of the reduction of difference: 'too close' (Silverstone:48). The mediated representation of the other – a Muslim, an Iraqi, a Jew or an American – as 'beyond the pale of humanity' exemplifies 'the irresponsibility of distance': 'too far' (ibid.). The ideal for the media, then, as proposed by Silverstone in the quotation above, would be the adoption of that 'proper distance' which allows recognition of difference together with hospitality and reciprocity. As Silverstone (p. 48) makes clear, this is essentially a process rather than a product, and the responsibility for making it work falls on everyone:

> Proper distance... requires imagination, both from those who construct the narratives and images of the media, and those, the audiences and readers, who, more dependently, construct their own images and narratives based upon them.... There is a doubling of responsibility involved. Both actors and spectators are present in public space, and both actors and spectators must carry the burden of judgement. Both have choices.

8
Austerity Britain: Back to the Future

It would not be controversial to observe that the global financial downturn and its immediate impact in Britain inaugurated a shift in popular perceptions of personal (in)security and financial prospects. For many Britons, the hegemonic mantle of British economic prosperity which had shielded the nation for much of the previous decade became increasingly threadbare and finally shabby. From 2008 the recession and the threat of recession were a constant in news and current affairs as politicians, economists and pundits sought to explain fresh surges in unemployment, tighter squeezes to family budgets, government spending reviews, a crisis in the Eurozone and the mill-stone of negative equity for mortgage holders. Perhaps it is a truism to say that, in times of national adversity such as this, public culture turns to its own national history for guidance and for strength. We report that this was certainly the case in austerity Britain, and it is this turn to history which we wish to consider in some detail. In this concluding chapter we have chosen to highlight the ways in which historical lessons have been deployed in political and popular discourses to encourage citizens to rethink their strategic everyday acts and their political values in the light of this financial downturn and the public reassessment of citizens' current and future prospects. How should citizens make sense of the downturn from a relatively buoyant economy, and how should they conduct themselves? Should they support the public sector and defend its funding, or accept that cuts need to be made? Is it right that organised labour should strike over terms and conditions of employment, or should workers accept that sacrifices need to be made? Are Britons all really in this predicament together, as Chancellor George Osborne (2009) famously declared, or are they being conscripted to a myth of national unity which belies deep and deepening inequalities?

170

This chapter analyses the ways in which public political discourses have deployed historical resources, analogies and stories to provide certain *authorised* and *persuasive* answers to these questions: answers which, we will argue, are generally supportive of the continuance of neoliberal enterprise, its values and its current practices.

To pursue this analysis, we focus on the public referencing of two historical periods in the context of present austerity: the 1970s and the mid-twentieth century. Our approach is to examine how the political conscription of some historical events and periods such as the Winter of Discontent in 1978–79 and the years of industrial 'strife' of 1970–85 have been figured as largely dystopian, while others such as the Home Front and the austerity years of 1945–51 have been invoked far more positively. Here we make the case that the 1970s were invoked by the media and by politicians as a warning to citizens against undertaking industrial action and thereby further damaging the economy. We will also suggest that this message was dependent on depicting organised labour as an outmoded and dangerous form of class politics which belonged to an earlier, more divisive era. We then go on to argue that the more desired models of public conduct and the 'right kind' of values (e.g. stoicism, thrift, 'being all in this together') were promoted through the deployment of historical resources and myths of wartime British pluck. So, as the spectre of recession surfaced in broadsheets, broadcast news, current affairs and documentary, there was a distinct turn to myths of 'making do' and of thrift as one positive strategy for individuals to manage a growing insecurity around homes and jobs. From this perspective the chapter begins the work of unpacking how historical resources are deployed to formulate and underpin arguments not only about how responsible citizens should behave in current times but also about how these times should best be interpreted. We contend that in deft manoeuvres political opinion invoked the past to stall debates and counter-arguments about the present and to insist that there is only one viable option for future progress. During this process, already fragile and fractured class alliances became further weakened as certain political constituencies and certain counter-discourses and their classed associations became labelled as outmoded, retrograde or damaging.

It is surely a cause for concern when in hard times citizens are being asked to make do, to accept the rolling back of state provision and to modify their expectations of a civil society on the basis of historical myths as well as of current realities. We conclude, then, by considering what kinds of counter-myths, what kinds of alternative historical resources are available and what opportunities exist or might be found for citizens to actually participate in national historical storytelling. We conclude by enquiring where we might find more 'alternative' historical stories of the nation, its people and its social formation and how these might counter or challenge recent dominant messages about ideal economic strategies and individual conduct, morals and values in the age of austerity.

In times of strife: the myth of the 1970s now

'Sir, may I, writing by candlelight, express my total support for the government in their attempt to halt the unbelievably inflated wage claims now being made?' So wrote a correspondent to *The Times* newspaper in the midst of a national emergency caused by the Electrical Power Workers' strike in 1970; a bout of industrial action triggering a media commentary which was to set the tone for much of the 1970s and become mythologised in popular memory for decades to follow. This letter was quoted by the socialist historian E.P. Thompson (1981:280) in an article he wrote in 1970 for the *The New Statesman* magazine and which was reprinted in Stanley Cohen and Jock Young's landmark collection *The Manufacture of News*. Thompson cited it as part of his wider analysis of what he referred to as the 'epistolary levée' or surge of defensive letter-writing which breaks out during times of popular revolt or industrial action. In times of national emergency, he observed, correspondents claim to know to what common-sense actions 'honest folk' should subscribe, calling for the outlawing of strike action, the bringing out of troops and the formation of an emergency corps to put down and outwit public enemies such as 'communists, shop stewards or militant students', to quote from one of the *Times* correspondents. Thompson noted, with acerbic amusement and a little condescension perhaps, the moral outrage voiced by the middle classes of Surrey and Chelsea as they were forced to write by candlelight (thanks to power cuts caused by industrial action) to express their disgruntlement at the unreasonable demands and inconvenience caused by those withdrawing their labour. Thompson (p. 283) reflected that it is only in times of grave adversity that the British middle classes overcome their usual reticence to openly express their values and moral outlook; feeling suddenly 'their own value in the world' and the risks they bear as honest, law-abiding, prudent and industrious people. He (p. 283) wrote: 'It is not to be thought that in such national emergencies, the bourgeois is solely concerned with such paltry matters as money or comfort or class power. Not at all: the full moral idealism blazes out.'

Writing for a left-wing readership, Thompson maintained that these letters to the editor had, since the late 1880s at least, become a genre in their own right, marked by self-righteous indignation and conventional criticisms of greedy unions, unruly protestors and selfish strikers versus 'the long-suffering public'. He also observed that it is in times of strife and when labour is withdrawn that the middle classes are rather sharply reminded of who delivers their services, of their dependence on working-class labour for their comforts, and of the 'intricate reciprocity' of services and human needs which sustains the social whole (Thompson:286). He quotes (p. 284), as an example, a Lancashire woman who, in her words, condemns an 'exhibition of power surely grotesque in its selfishness': '... the radio is dead. The television is dead. The electric heaters are dead. The kettle is dead. The fridge is dead. My washing machine is dead. My iron is dead. All the street lights are dead... Goodness knows how many *tragic* deaths may result...' (ellipses and emphasis in the original).

Thompson's article makes plain the divisive and moralistic muddle which ensues when social protest and industrial action take place in times of austerity; a condition which arose once again when the British Government Coalition's 'Plan A' to manage the 'credit crunch' started to bite in 2010. Thompson pays no attention to the gendered profile of what we might call the 'offended citizen' and the inconvenienced consumer whose domestic appliances are rendered unusable and whose own domestic labour is then frustrated. However, he is incisive in his identification of the *overall* resentment underlying the more benign attributes of what has become referred to as 'middle England' when it finds its resources and services suspended.

We take Thompson's piece as a departure point for this chapter for two reasons: first, because it establishes elegantly and concisely the mythological backdrop of current public debates about work, entitlement, remuneration and public responsibility – which is the 1970s or, to stretch a point perhaps, the 'long decade' of industrial protest and embattlement which reached right up to the miners' disputes of the mid-1980s. Current debates about the rightness and purposes of industrial action by public sector workers, in particular, have been regularly cast against the backdrop of the 1970s. Cuts to services, the paring down and 'simplification' of welfare benefits, reduction of education allowances, the implementation of university fees and the threats to public service employment contracts in terms of pay, conditions and pensions have all contributed to public discord and divisive debate about who works hardest and who takes the biggest financial hits as the country struggles to find its way out of the financial mire. As will be seen, much of this debate has appeared within the framework of news-making in which the 1970s have loomed large, summoned up as a dire warning of the state of things to come. As in the era chronicled by Thompson, letters to online comments pages are once again criticising the socially irresponsible or fiscally naïve for their damaging anti-social behaviour (although there is space now in the mediasphere for the defenders of public sector strike action to have their say). The same tensions are present, too, between the publicly advocated need to all pull together, the individual adoption of virtues of restraint and 'just getting on with it' and a marked reluctance by some to capitulate to deep financial cuts and welfare restraint. The second cue we take from Thompson is his emphasis on the moral rhetoric and idealism which 'blazes out' when money, comfort, consumerism and class power come under threat. We consider how anxieties about a damaged social fabric and proposals to repair it are refracted through the lenses of a variety of historical references and recollections which reappropriate the past in order to understand the present. We wish to consider the wider public discourses about austerity and the ways in which a recourse to history has informed their articulation, development and circulation in moral terms.

E.P. Thompson's piece was published on the brink of the 1970s, a period now soldered into political rhetoric and right-wing journalism as a time of crisis marked by work-based political protests. This included a series of industrial actions by workers from both private and public industries and services, including building workers, miners, dockers, car manufacturers, workers in film-processing and typewriter factories, and so on, all culminating in the so-called Winter of Discontent of multiple industrial actions towards the end of the decade in 1978–79. This period, while memorialised by some as the last assertive expression of white male working-class collectivity, also witnessed an increase in middle-class or 'white collar' trades union membership and the growing participation of women and 'immigrant' workers, who were conspicuously active in some disputes and other socialist initiatives (see, for example, Dhondy 1974, Campbell 1984, Joyce 1995:69–72). Faced with dire global economic pressures, the two Labour periods of government from 1964–70 and 1974–79 were essentially engaged in the negotiation of voluntary agreements and then statutory policy which would, in theory, secure a viable 'social wage' alongside controls on prices and incomes. The term 'social wage', now never used in mainstream political discourse, denoted free or subsidised universal benefits such as education, libraries and healthcare funded wholly or partly by the state through taxation. Ultimately, the formulation of a Social Contract agreement between the government and the unions sought wage restrictions in exchange for measures to increase the social wage through increased government expenditure. As political economist Calum Paton (2000:21) remarked, the Tory victory and the abandonment of these initiatives has led to a 'conventional history...which makes it difficult to argue that the policy "nearly succeeded" rather than "finally failed".' Hence, despite the complexity of these times and the honourable sentiments and values which underpinned the actions of many of its left of centre protagonists, media coverage contemporaneously (see Philo *et al.* 1982a, 1982b) and in retrospect has largely figured the era as one of increasingly irresponsible and damaging (working-)class-based, socialist activity which 'inevitably' heralded in the tough but necessary 'solution' of Thatcherism.

It was in the 'first dark days of 1979', as she described them, that the then opposition leader Margaret Thatcher appealed to the electorate in a television broadcast to support Conservative proposals for wide-sweeping trades union reform. She proposed to eliminate 'the wreckers among us' in order to overcome the present crisis caused by industrial discord. The following day the *Daily Mail* reprinted the speech in full with the headline: 'Why we must be one nation, or no nation!' inviting a collective rejection of what is sometimes referred to as 'bully-boy' socialism.[1] Thatcher's subsequent election would mark the launch of 18 years of Conservative government and a growing raft of civil legislation aimed at curbing what critics would call 'union power' (see Joyce:81–2). Many decades later both Tory and New Labour politicians such as David Cameron and Tony Blair would also refer to the era as one of either tragic mismanagement or tragically missed opportunities (see Beckett 2009:1). As James Thomas (2007:268) indicates in his revealing analysis of right-wing Winter of Discontent myth-making in the national press, both at the time and in the years that followed, the 'abiding images of "what happened before Thatcherism" ' were of 'backwardness, anarchy and industrial militancy'. In the view of Colin Hay (2009) who has also critiqued the 'crisis' of the late 1970s as a highly constructed one which sustained various myths about the nature of the power of unions and the public sector, the Winter of Discontent was thus a significant landmark in contemporary British political history. This was because it marked the 'symbolic point of transition' which shifted Britain 'from then to now': 'from the postwar consensus to Thatcherism, from Keynesianism to monetarism, from corporatism to austerity' (Hay 2009:551, but see also Black and Pemberton 2009 and Hay 2010).

In fact, mediated memories of the 1970s are fairly polarised into those organised around the 'strife' of candlelit Britain blighted by power-cuts and three-day working weeks and the more nostalgic recollections of less complicated times epitomised in popular culture. It seems quite remarkable that as recently as 2007 historian Mark Garnett (2007:6) could write that Britons had a tendency, albeit a rather puzzling one, to look back on the 1970s with an unreflective nostalgic eye; as a pre-Thatcher era which was happier and when the quality of life was better. This apparently fond regard for the pre-Thatcher years was reinforced, in his view, by a spate of golden-hued television programming including superficial documentaries, situation comedy reruns and emotional rock band reunions, all of which added a flattering warmth to collective memories of the 1970s. But, despite these warmer reminiscences, some of them actually substantiated by quality of life surveys, polls and reports, the prevailing ideological message about the 1970s has always been, and continues to be, largely and consistently negative. Thomas (2007) suggests that this dominant interpretation of the past is far from accidental or innocent. For example, his own analysis of newspaper references to the late 1970s made during the 2000s revealed that during times of industrial discord, such as the fuel crisis of 2000 and the fire-fighters' strike of 2002, journalistic comment was once again framed by the Winter of Discontent and chose to selectively resurrect the most disturbing imagery from the period of rubbish uncollected, patients untreated and the dead unburied. Here he argued that the press's tendency to conspire with an overwhelmingly conservative history of the pre-Thatcher years 'helped to sustain and secure the neoliberal political settlement' (Thomas 2007:278). In other words, up to and during the New Labour administration it suited a right-wing press to paint recent industrial actions and unrest as the thin end of the wedge, as a potential return to dreadful socialist times.

Thomas (2007:278) considered that these selective references to the troubled 1970s and the Winter of Discontent 'had receded from everyday political use' and largely lost their potency. But, in fact, within only a few more years the British gaze once again turned towards the 1970s. For those born before the late 1960s it was perhaps inevitable that the prevailing political message of responsible frugality, together with rising discontent contained in an austerity project, would recall the industrial actions of that time. As noted, that decade experienced the power workers' strikes of 1970 (which triggered a national emergency) and also of 1974. The later winter of industrial action from 1978 to 1979 featured local authority trades unions claiming larger pay rises for their members in the face of the Labour government's attempt to freeze pay to counter and control inflation. For those born later, the media have naturally played their part in educating citizens about a time that had long since been mythologised as essentially socially damaging and mostly grim. In the last few years British journalism, current affairs and documentaries have continued to draw analogies, asking what lessons have been learned and what changes have occurred to class relations, social aspiration and citizens' expectations of the welfare state in the intervening years.

Towards the end of the first decade of the twenty-first century, new flare-ups of social unrest and worker-related protest in Europe and the UK triggered the resurrection of this media emphasis on the darker side of the 1970s. Moreover, by April 2012, England, already well engaged in an austerity project designed by the governing Coalition to tackle the fiscal crisis, had entered a long-anticipated and dreaded 'double-dip' recession, the first since 1975 and soon to be followed by its Scottish neighbour. It has seemed during the last several years, with public sector strikes looming or actually taking place and a return to recession, that no media outlet would miss an opportunity to name-check the ugly decade. In the two years up until July 2012 national newspaper references to the 1970s in the context of austerity were numerous, with many of them conjuring the spectre of social strife. The *Mirror* (29 May 2012) observed that economic circumstances were 'chillingly similar', the *Sun* (9 December 2010) pointed to the 'fresh wave of football hooliganism' in the context of austerity which recalled the 1970s, and Vernon Bogdanor, writing in the *Guardian* (28 June 2012), summoned up the 1970s 'abyss in which civic order and decency' broke down. An opinion piece in the *Express* (15 September 2010) by Kerry Gill headed 'Sorry Bob, civil disobedience is just too 1970s' deployed the era to emphasise just how tragi-comically outmoded industrial activism (and working-class masculinity) had now become:

> If central casting were looking for someone to play a fearsome, finger-stabbing trade union bombast, even they could never come up with anyone more suitable to play the part than Bob Crow, general secretary of the Rail Maritime and Transport union.

Mr Crow, with his shaven head and brawny arms, looks and sounds like a union leader from the distant past; no wonder he and his more militant colleagues have been widely, and inevitably, depicted as dinosaurs in the media over the past few days.

Comment by the BBC, other broadcast news outlets and all the national newspapers would reference the Winter of Discontent in particular in relation to public worker disputes. Of those that deployed the 1970s as a warning of things to come, the *Express* paper was far from unique in setting a bellicose tone. In an editorial praising Chancellor Osborne's frankness in spelling out the facts that 'it's going to hurt,' Patrick O'Flynn remarked in the *Express* on 30 November 2011:

The big message from the Chancellor was that the public sector must be cut down to size. Unions representing teachers, health workers, border control staff and the rest have thrown down a gauntlet with their strike and now Mr Osborne has picked it up.

He believes the 80 per cent of the working population that earns its living in the private sector and whose taxes fund public services will back his cost-cutting approach. Labour begs to differ. So let the winter of discontent begin.

In the months leading up to the strikes, the *Daily Mail* alone managed to reference the return of 1970s discontent in an impressive variety of contexts, including pieces about 'union bullies who live like kings', transport workers being 'bribed' to work overtime during the forthcoming London Olympics, workers insisting on striking despite a government 50 billion pound 'capitulation', a European Union 'out of touch' with struggling European Union members and British state workers who 'cannot lose' whether they go on strike or not. O'Flynn's piece appeared on the day of the public sector workers' strike against changing, far less favourable retirement pension arrangements. On 31 November 2011 the *Daily Mail* newspaper judged that the 'Union barons power to bring Britain to its knees' had turned out to be a flop: 'True, most children's education was disrupted, surgery was shamefully delayed and in a few areas, trains and buses didn't run. But for the most part, life carried on pretty much as normal.' The online *Daily Mail Comment* went on to concede more charitably, or perhaps just grudgingly, that, had these public servants truly understood that 'the cupboard is bare,' they would willingly have made the same 'sacrifice' as had their fellow private sector workers.[2]

On the online *Comment* page several reader contributions echoed the paper's anti-union views and its expression of offended citizenship, and in tones that recall the long-established conventions of the newspaper epistolary genre. 'Philip' from 'Bankrupted Britain' observed: 'This strike could be a defining moment in UK politics, for allowing people to see the real truth about the state of affairs in this country. More fool the Union leaders for allowing the public a clear view – I hope it brings them down.' Others, however, vigorously defended public sector workers by turning their criticism against the government or bankers. Susan from the Wirral mobilised offended citizenship (via taxpayers and the armed forces) into a trenchant critique of failing politicians and irresponsible elites:

> Something needs to change and fast when we are living in a country that looks after everyone but us with our money while we graft and our families are suffering. I think the only way to force government to take notice is refusal to pay tax and rethink the way democracy works. When i [sic] think of all those young men who have died for us [in recent conflicts] while we have pompous MPs spending £37,000 of taxpayers money on a coat of arms it sickens me to my stomach!

Overall, the strike further amplified the already noisy public conversation, triggered by government austerity measures, about the differences between private and public sector workers in terms of pay, financial expectations, job security and long-term 'reward'; especially in terms of the 'gold-plated' pensions 'enjoyed' by the latter. The issue of whether one could be both a responsible citizen *and* a striker was critical. For example, on the same *Comment* page 'Desperate Dan' from Derby made the following, not untypical, observation:

> The day the figures show that children are benefiting from education in this country, rather than the figures that show in fact we are turning out more youngsters with poor language, writing and mathematical skills, is the day you can rightly get on your high horse. As for this article my question would be why do you people in the public sector need to have this explained to you, especially the teachers among you who one would presume had at least a modicum of common sense and intelligence, when we in the private sector can see the problem as plain as the nose on our faces, THERE IS NO MONEY IN THE BANK AND WE ARE LIVING LONGER, wake up and accept these facts and join the rest of us in the real world.

Desperate Dan's frustration with 'you people', who, unlike 'the rest of us', refuse to understand that the shelves are empty and supplies are running low, says much about the hard times in which many people now find themselves: times marked by discord, division and a splintering of associations among people who have much in common but whose resources are meagre or felt to be under threat. Desperate Dan turns on the performance of teachers, who, through their failure to do their jobs properly, have forfeited their right to speak out against pension cuts and who are, in any case, dreaming if they believe that the contractual arrangements made in another age (the age of affluence, perhaps, or the age of irresponsibility) are still sustainable. This and other national newspaper discussion threads, which there is no space to reproduce here, are typical of much journalistic and reader comment in the national press, which had, for two years or more, already questioned the contemporary role of trades unions and the costliness of both the 'expanding' welfare state and the public sector in new, more straitened times. Calls to live in the 'real world' were often based in the genuine conviction or resignation that the state had to be 'rolled back' and, along with it, the anachronistic attitudes which were rooted in the stereotypically working-class politics that had been practised in the 1970s and resulted in the follow-up conflicts of the Thatcher years.

As with the *Daily Mail* article and its online discussion thread just noted, most often the message, as framed by the 1970s, seems to have been one of 'bite the bullet' or else be prepared to return to times of strife. For example, in a piece called 'Here we go again, another day of shame' written on 31 December 2010 in the shadow of oncoming strikes, controversialist Richard Littlejohn recalled:

> I've written stories by candlelight during the power cuts caused by the miners' strike which brought down [Tory Prime Minister] Grocer Heath. In the mid-to-late Seventies, I worked in Birmingham, documenting the destruction of the British motor industry by bloody-minded shop stewards and lame management.

> I was around when the starting gun was fired for the Winter of Discontent, culminating in the dead going unburied and the rubbish piling up in Leicester Square.

Again, in a *Daily Mail* (18 June 2011) piece called 'Déjà Vu', historian Dominic Sandbrook advocated 'tough choices' in the face of 'vested interests'. When faced with unions 'flexing their muscles' (another reference which both gendered and dated industrial action), he remarks that:

> nobody who recalls the miners' strikes of 1972 and 1974, which sent Britain into darkness and forced Heath to impose a three-day week, or the Winter of Discontent in 1978/79, when rubbish piled up in Leicester Square and supermarket shelves lay cold and empty, will dismiss their threats too casually.

Even where press comment was more instinctively suspicious of austerity measures and the erosion of public sector services and conditions of service, such as in the *Guardian* (1 December 2011), depressing and, we would suggest, unhelpful comparisons were still drawn with the years of doom and gloom: 'You think the 1970s were bad? This is shaping up to be a lot worse: Austerity and more austerity.'

As Alastair Bonnett (2010:169) has noted, 'radicalism has a particularly uncomfortable alliance with the past', more especially (and as we have seen) because the left has to work very hard to combat accusations of inhabiting an outmoded political tradition. This was evident in New Labour's debates around its 2010 leadership contest on the departure of outgoing Prime Minister Gordon Brown. The advice of New Labour's first Prime Minister Tony Blair to look to the future was widely read as an endorsement of the more 'centrist' David Miliband over his brother Edward, who had a stronger following among the trades unions. Blair remarked in interview with Andrew Marr: 'I mean I think that for me the thing with the Labour party is, always be at the cutting edge for the future. That means on public services and welfare, you cannot run them in 2010 as if you were still in 1950.' So, too, Blair's former political strategist favoured David as the more assertive leader at a sticky moment: 'There's a danger, that like the Winter of Discontent in 1979, Labour could be really saddled with a reputation which could damage it for a decade.'[3] Following Ed Miliband's election, the importance of avoiding retrogressive labels with regard to his relationship to organised labour continued to be paramount. The *Daily Mail* (14 July 2012) was one of many papers that subsequently kept a sharp eye on his conduct and highlighted any signs of New Labour slipping into old ways. For example, on 14 July 2012 the *Mail* anticipated Miliband's yet to be delivered 'tub-thumping' speech at an 'annual socialist jamboree' of the Durham Miners' Gala with undisguised glee and took the opportunity to include a disproportionately large black-and-white photograph of Arthur Scargill and Neil Kinnock (union leader and Labour leader respectively) marching with miners in the 1980s.

Broadcast news, current affairs and documentary also reached for the long decade of industrial conflict and the 1970s yardstick in particular. *Dispatches* (C4 2010) was trailed with a reference to the Winter of Discontent when asking 'what's the point of the unions?', although the programme itself focused rather obsessively on the Thatcher years. Sandbrook's four-part documentary *The 70s* (BBC2 2012) concluded that the 1970s are 'startlingly current'. A *Panorama* broadcast (BBC 2012) entitled 'Britain on the Brink: Back to the 1970s?' asked whether Britain would be able to cope with a new age of austerity. Made in the context of the 'longest peace time slump in decades', the latter explored how 'we've been here before' in similar conditions leading to social unrest and political upheaval. Focusing on the area of Clapham in South London and making much of the proverbial ordinary person on the Clapham omnibus as the embattled subject of austerity measures, it explored gentrification and class mobility, growing financial pressures on ordinary people and the 'English riots' of the previous summer, some of which took place in Clapham. While some of the examples cited here across formats, platforms and channels were genuinely interrogative in their orientation towards the 1970s as the obvious context and foil for current debates and disputes in the context of austerity, the majority were not and, taken in aggregate, they did little to illuminate current conditions.

The embattled citizen: keeping calm and carrying on

While 1970–85 was the dystopian past to which Britain must never return (indelibly marked by industrial action and working-class 'bully boy' socialism), other eras of national struggle and financial restriction have been deployed rather more approvingly. The Second World War, the actions of the Home Front and the austerity years of 1945–51 have all been more positively resurrected for the lessons they might teach twenty-first-century citizens. The Blitz spirit, 'digging for Britain' and the ubiquitous injunction to 'keep calm and carry on' (which first appeared well before 2008) provided an alternative discourse which, when deployed conservatively, chimed well with an era of protracted recession whose 'only' solution was the Coalition Government's Plan A: stringent austerity measures. As John Clarke (forthcoming) argues, debates about austerity and the struggle for consensus with which they are articulated have been framed within a moral discourse of 'virtuous necessity'. Thus, the Coalition Government promoted itself as making 'honest choices' and argued that 'we will get through this together' with bull-dog determination and noses to grindstones (Chancellor Osborne and PM Cameron, both cited in Clarke and Newman 2012:303). The Coalition administration has been most favourably depicted as embattled but determined. For example, in a *Sunday Telegraph* piece David Cameron's 'senior counsellor' William Hague was flatteringly profiled as someone for whom 'The wartime slogan – recently popular once again – "keep calm and carry on" could have been designed' (Hennessy 2012:4). In response to complaining bankers, and indeed to all who would complain, Hague chided:

> There's only one growth strategy – work hard! And do more with less – that's the 21st century. . . . We're trying to rescue the work ethic just in the nick of time. With the introduction of the universal benefit next year, with the cap on benefits that we are bringing in, this is part of making sure we are recreating the work ethic for everybody in Britain.

In Patrick Hennessy's account, Hague is described, reassuringly, as the son of a soft drinks manufacturer (i.e. with industry credibility), wearing shirtsleeves (i.e. a *working* politician) and projecting 'a businesslike air in his large, wood-panelled room'. As John Clarke and Janet Newman (2012:300) explain, the field of play in which the austerity project is taking place has shifted considerably, relocating the problem from the private to the public sector and from a financial sector problem to a fiscal problem. In this context the private sector – of business, industry, manufacture and enterprise – becomes valorised as the potential hero of the new economic revolution, and the politician is accorded gravitas by his or her association with these. Accompanying the rallying cry to the private sector as the vanguard of progress is a necessarily pragmatic expectation that everyone must work harder, work for longer and protest less – keeping calm and carrying on – an attitude which bears a moral and affective weight drawn from the Second World War and the post-war austerity years of the 1950s. For Clarke and Newman (ibid.:300), this move to shift the blame-laden centre of gravity for financial laxity from the private to the public sector, which we are tracking here specifically in relation to discursive historical returns, is 'intensely ideological' and its logical outcome, if successful, would be a 'new neo-liberal settlement'. We would argue that the drive towards this settlement is articulated in the double discourse of frugality and productivity employed by Hague and others, which both solicits consensus and cross-class cooperation and aims to head off resistance and complaint. The *practical* agenda (which supposedly supersedes all other agendas) becomes one of money, or rather the lack of it, and the repayment of the national debt. The short-term sacrifice is one of working hard, enduring discomfort and making do.

In the Hennessy profile readers encounter the conflation of two time periods: ration-book Britain and the new era of austerity. The first of these, as referenced in the slogan 'keep calm and carry on,' has entered into popular culture, alongside others from the modern mid-century such as 'dig for victory' and 'make do and mend.' The slogan and the iconography of the government information poster from which it originates are astonishingly ubiquitous. Even the BBC commentator introducing the London Olympic Games opening ceremony (itself a spectacular montage of historical references) on 27 July 2012 began by invoking 'the best British tradition' of keeping calm and carrying on. Unlike the recourse to the 1970s as a compass for understanding the present, which has emerged via journalism and political commentary, the 'keep calm' mantra circulated initially through merchandising and dialogued with other discourses and practices flowing round what we might call retro-leisure and life-change agendas: frugal living, vintage clothing, voluntary downsizing, lifestyle television, and so on. Home economics, home-making and cooking programmes such as *Superscrimpers* (C4 2011–), *Kirsty's Hand Made Britain* (C4 2011) and *Ration Book Britain* (Yesterday 2010) and recipe books such as Jane Fearnley-Whittingstall and Imperial War Museum's (2010) *Ministry of Food*, together with the new visibility of war-time domestic icons such as Marguerite Patten, helped set the tone of patient endurance and self-management. If the 1970s was painted as an essentially brutish era of masculine working-class power in the context of a divided society, then these mid-century austerity years connoted a more middle-class feminine ideal in the context of a nation unified in adversity.

The era was eulogised via 'simplistic portrayals of the successes of wartime sufficiency and governance' (Hinton and Redclift 2009:5). 'Keep calm and carry on' invoked both a dry British humour and a heads-down and let's gets through this posture. The *Daily Mail* declared in 2011:

> With the world in the grip of financial insecurity and political unrest, times certainly call for a bit of resolve. So it is good news that more than a quarter of Britons still possess a stiff upper lip. The finding

came in a study of personality traits, which found that 11 million adults adopt the 'Keep Calm and Carry On' approach that served the nation so well during the Second World War.

(Poulter 2011)

The success of this resolve lies partly in accepting an idealised cross-class return to frugality inspired by an earlier era and also necessarily in smothering any discontent around the present inequality of resources. This is epitomised in a *Times* newspaper Royal Jubilee special headed: 'Keep calm and carry on: what we can learn from the Britons of 1952; The frugal mindset at the start of the Queen's reign has lessons for us all.' Here mid-century thrift is the order of the day and acts as inclusive metaphorical bunting spanning both royalty and the *hoi polloi*:

> The current economic climate may seem tough, but the Queen's accession year of 1952 saw much more real hardship in the aftermath of the Second World War, with rationing ongoing and some Britons still living in slums. Nevertheless, it was a time of rebuilding and rising standards of living, and today we can take much inspiration from the grit of that generation's positive approach.
>
> (Bridge 2012)

Thus, reporter Mark Bridge commends Mass Observation diarist Nella Last (best known as the subject of the ITV 2006 drama *Housewife, 49*) for her resolution to make do.

> On the day of the Budget...Nella Last wrote: 'I felt slight dismay. It's not just food, it's coal, soon electricity too, and every tiny item that seems dearer.' But she reassured her husband: 'We will keep the car. Rising cost of living, petrol, etc, won't make us pinch. I'll economise and make do...' Her determination to keep the car could be a 21st century statement, after successive petrol price increases, but her 'make-do' resolution is typical of the wartime and postwar culture of thrift.

Crucially, Bridge praises Nella Last (and the era) for the cultivation of the privately useful virtue of thrift *and* the nationally useful virtue of aspiration. Yes, there was hardship, but there were also rising living standards; there was proscriptive rationing, but there was also a 'positive approach'. Even when she was harried by rising prices, Last demonstrated an admirable determination to keep the car. Here the 'housewife citizen' of the post-war period is revived as an exemplar for present times (see Giles 2004:132) and also fits well with wider discourses of domestic make do and mend.

As Owen Hatherley (2009:2) explains in his account of the plethora of commercial and political deployments of the keep calm slogan during the 2000s, this 'austerity nostalgia' more broadly revealed the 'contradictions produced by an economy of consumption attempting to adapt to thrift'. For many the phrase has become the 'unofficial motto of the recession', allegedly gracing the office wall of the Conservatives' Strategy Unit alongside those of struggling shopkeepers and restaurateurs. In 2009 its use seemed to signify a very British attitude of steadying one's nerves in the face of hardship and in the light of a quite spectacular mismanagement of the national purse, as well as the damage wrought by the financial sector, which was the recipient of 'bail out' investment. The political commentator Simon Heffer (2009), often looked to as someone well able to take accurately the temperature of middle England, concluded in a leading article for the *Daily Telegraph* that the attempt to 'keep calm' under the New Labour government as it dealt with the first phase of the financial meltdown was: ' … but the first phase in a justified, and dangerous, souring of the public mood. And if nothing improves … at some stage people will realise that they cannot KEEP CALM AND CARRY ON long enough to come out intact on the other side of the crisis'. Finally, however, Heffer doubted whether Britons had the temperament for a revolution.

While a very few, such as Heffer, speculated that keeping calm was actually the calm before the storm, on the whole it has been presented as a wholly benign, even admirable, attribute of British pluck. Some months later, Benedict Brogan (2009), writing in the same publication, maintained that then Shadow Chancellor George Osborne would be keeping calm and carrying on with his unpalatable but needful proposals for fiscal belt-tightening in the face of an uncertain electorate. Two years on and with the Conservatives now in power, Tory budgeting was still being yoked to the phrase: 'KEEP calm and carry on. I doubt George Osborne will sneak the Ministry of Information's wartime slogan into today's Budget speech – although it will, I suspect, neatly sum up the Chancellor's message' (Fletcher 2011).

As well as the Jubilee celebrations, other national events have also been deployed to conjure wartime fortitude, a sense of embattlement and the survival spirit of ordinary people living in a post-war threadbare, ration-book aftermath (see Kynaston 2007). This was especially true of the coverage running up to the London 2012 Olympic Games. These had last taken place in Britain in 1948 and were consequently known as the 'Austerity Games', so naturally they chimed with current exigencies and invited the airing of personal recollections of shoe-string sports and making do. While many reports rightly marvelled at the ingenuity of post-war domestic resilience and the telling contrast between that and the current lavish, thoroughly corporatised Olympic Games, some also found a way to link the Games to a more bellicose attitude. For example, in a hyperbolic *Times* newspaper piece entitled 'Keep calm and carry on: how the wartime spirit will help protect the London Games,' readers were reassured that:

> Not since 1940 has Britain erected such a mighty ring of steel around London – a vast, multilayered, armoured force that everyone hopes (just as they hoped in the Second World War) will shield the capital, and never have to be used.... But in some ways the threats, and the challenge, are similar: to prepare for any and every eventuality, deploy overwhelming defensive capability, try to second-guess the enemy, and hope that the aggressor will realise that an attack is bound to fail and never attempt it. Those tactics worked in 1940, and they will probably work in 2012.
>
> (MacIntyre 2012)

Patrick Wright's (1985:23) influential book on the deployment of the national past in the present explains the importance of 'remembered war' in a way which helps us to make sense of the *Times* piece above. He suggests that, although its use is both abject and manipulative, it can also be said to offer a real and energising counterpoint to the routinised and constrained experience of modern living. In his view, the condition of embattlement can be regarded as a more meaningful existence and the constraints of war can also invoke a kind of purification or cleansing. So, too, cultural critic Jeremy Gilbert (2011) has observed that the post-ironic, often-times nostalgic, sometimes slightly sinister exhortation to 'carry on' regardless is both an emotional comforter and a warding-off of perfectly logical oppositional affects and political actions such 'anger, retreat, retrenchment and counter-attack'. Gilbert maintains: 'Keeping calm and carrying on is exactly how the coalition wants us to behave: about to lose your public sector job? Stay calm, retrain, go to work in the private sector. About to lose the right to subsidised Higher Education? Never mind – it won't make any difference really.' We might add that it works to buffer and damp down wholly rational but not necessarily oppositional feelings of fear and anxiety: fears, for instance, about declining economic or environmental resources or of security threats or of social breakdown. The challenge here is perhaps not to smother, repress or condemn historical resources as merely nostalgic and thereby always conservative *per se*, but to ensure that space is made for their contestation or even reappropriation by other, more radical voices and for different, more progressive purposes.

Past times, present politics

As the critiques already cited above suggest, the mediated and politicised recourse to the past, especially through invocations of other eras of austerity, most often marshals a conservative articulation of both past and present. This is arguably done in order to appease opposition, to manage dissent and to blur inequalities of resources of all kinds. Its patterning, as outlined here with regard to the disinterment of the 1970s, can establish unwarranted divisions between what might be naturally affiliated social groups (e.g. workers in the private and public sectors) in the service of a greater national unity in which citizens all consent to austerity measures whatever their personal circumstances or political convictions. So, too, these mobilisations of the 1970s and mid-1980s often figure social class, and especially working-class alliances and the affiliations of organised labour, as old-fashioned or irrelevant or threatening. Meanwhile, the repetitious journalistic patterning of the 'keep calm' slogan, alongside other references to myths of the Home Front, may also work to muffle oppositional feelings and/or alternative actions and practices in the service of a kind of voluntaristic national unity which overrides all other considerations.

This last point is well made by Emma Hinton and Michael Redclift in their 2009 analysis of the austerity and sufficiency agenda. Here they chart how the part-government, part-business-funded UK Energy Saving Trust conflated past and present in its 'Wartime Spirit' campaign, which was launched in cooperation with the Imperial War Museum. Here citizens were encouraged to modify their consumption practices in response to the twinned issues of recession and climate change, including through the issuing of 'top tips' based on a 1943 pamphlet called 'How to Make Do and Mend.' The directive to 'keep calm' appeared alongside others such as 'holiday at home', 'don't waste water' and 'dig for victory' (Hinton and Redclift 2009:2). As the authors (2009:9) explain, this encouragement to adopt Home Front habits was rooted in a 'demand side' solution in which the responsibility for change is placed at the feet of the individual 'together with the benevolent state'. Framed in this way, they argue (2009:9–10) that 'sustainable consumption thus suggests new forms of political compliance, rather than political agency…' and all without troubling corporations to take responsibility themselves for husbanding resources.

It seems for oppositional voices, especially those from the left of the political spectrum, for those with anti-capitalist sympathies, and so on, that the historical past is difficult to accommodate to progressive projects. It is far easier to co-opt historical resources to critique or reflect on individual conduct or collective labour movements than it is to turn them against the interests of class power. So, what are the political implications of what Rebecca Bramall (2011:68) has described as the 'insistence upon historical solutions for today's problems'; solutions which seem to be monopolised mainly by conservative voices? Where are the public spaces for counter-discourses which may also wish to lay a claim to a national history, to tell national stories and even to contest the dismantling of the welfare state? How might they work to resist the prevalent criticism of public services, organised labour and popular protest and to defend the class (and other) politics and values with which these have been historically associated?

Rebecca Bramall's (2011) lucid article about the re-emergence of another slogan from the mid-century austerity era – 'dig for victory' – makes an ideal departure point for a consideration of these questions. Here Bramall charts the public articulation of the 'home front myth' to concerns about frugality, thrift and environmental sustainability, and how these in turn have become yoked to current economic anxieties. As we have done above with regard to the references to the Winter of Discontent and 'keep calm and carry on,' she charts the iteration of the Dig for Victory injunction across official culture (e.g. the 2007 Imperial War Museum allotment project with the Royal Parks), mainstream political culture and popular culture such as lifestyle television. In her article she highlights how the subject positions most readily interpolated by the mainstream conservative deployment of these discourses are those of white middle-class affluent female *consumers*, members of what Hinton and Redclift above referred to as the market 'demand side'. She also signals, through its chains of equivalence, the interconnection of this mid-century propaganda with the Coalition's political and economic austerity project and current trenchant critiques of the preceding Labour government's earlier economic practices. In this way, her work seeks to understand the 'persuasiveness' of these 'symbolic resources', their significant purchase in public culture and, more crucially, the spaces available for counter-narratives and transformative practices (such as anti-consumerism) within the same discursive field.

In her words, Bramall (2011:71) explores 'how we might theorise the function of historicity as a discursive element in processes of subject constitution' and what theorisations might reveal about the potential for a more radical co-option of the past in the present. Her approach is to map out why 'austerity discourses' are likely to be conservative and why they might be regarded as deeply unpromising for radical politics. As she explains, Marxist or left-political perspectives are bound to be sceptical because they would obviously condemn the deployment of historical resources which have been stripped of historical experience, of context and contingency and which are disconnected from memory and proper conceptions of struggle and oppression. In other words, we might say that they are condemned on the basis of a fully worked out political philosophy which adopts a particular, very clear position in relation to history and to lived experience. From this perspective, Bramall allows that the Dig for Victory narrative is seriously problematic; we might say that ultimately this is because it can be read as ideology-in-action. However, as she makes plain, this does not explain why these kinds of uses of the past continue to be regarded with suspicion by scholars working in the context of *post*-Marxist, post-structuralist models, whose dominance we signalled in our introduction to this book. These models tend to understand history, the historical and the constitution of the subject quite differently; for example, by rejecting the notion of experience as illuminating and explanatory, by problematising any mapping of continuity or identity across time, and by emphasising plurality, complexity, shifts and discontinuities. Bramall's (p. 73) contention is that, where scholars are engaged in theorising the past in the present, they nonetheless continue to 'find it difficult to think beyond certain highly thematized versions of the radical' and that this throws up many unresolved issues about the potential of progressive politics.

Bramall (p. 74) attempts to move beyond the impasse by deploying Laclau and Mouffe's well-known conceptualisations of discourse and hegemony in order to explore 'how subjects come – through discursive processes – to be persuaded of certain positions, and thus to be transformed *as* subjects, rather than to explain how subjects come to perform certain acts'. Having made a case study of Dig for Britain and related austerity and heritage discourses, she re-evaluates their 'hegemonising potential' and presents a more open interpretation of their potential invitations to subjects to intervene in the world 'in ways that would otherwise be closed down' (Bramall:79). She cites as exemplary a 2008 episode of the *River Cottage* (C4 1998–) series fronted by Hugh Fearnley-Whittingstall, which deployed Dig for Britain wartime footage to promote landshare or common land initiatives. While acknowledging the series' limitations in terms of the classed subject positions on offer, she also suggests that it successfully renders certain radical ideas palatable, possible and beneficial. From this perspective, she posits that the drive within history-telling should not be towards telling '*more truthful*, disclosive stories' but towards telling stories that resonate with those whom we would wish to *persuade* and with 'the ways that those constituencies construe their interests' (Bramall:81, emphasis in the original).

This chapter will conclude, then, with a consideration of the ways in which a significant national event – the 2012 London Olympics – deployed history and historical reference in its 27 July Opening Ceremony. In doing so, we will by-pass issues of truthfulness, revelation, authenticity and experience, and instead raise the possibility that it provided a space for a counter-austerity discourse which invited viewers to query prevailing political messages about money, comfort, consumerism, class power and morality. In other words, we wonder whether we might positively read the Olympic Games' re-enactment of Britain's history (its 'island story') in the context of a hugely commercialised, global media event as a retort to or refusal of 'the dominant articulation of austerity to an argument about morality and the necessity of welfare cuts' (Bramall 2011:82).

'The isle is full of noises': history answers back

> And if everything possible should be done to enable a more diversified public expression of social imagination, isn't this also to say that there should be a movement (both economic and cultural) towards a *democratic* (rather than merely spellbinding) re-enchantment of everyday life?
>
> (Wright 1985:255, emphasis in the original)

We noted above that the much anticipated London 2012 Olympic Games provided yet more opportunities for the media to advocate keeping calm and carrying on, including through references to the earlier Austerity Games, the ongoing preparations and security, and even in the opening sentences of the BBC commentary. Indeed, even several days into the Games the *Telegraph*'s (31 July 2012) eye-catching front page headline urged readers in *upper case* to KEEP CALM AND CARRY ON and not to 'panic' about Team GB's failure so far to secure a gold medal. So far, so unsurprising. However, the opening ceremony itself arguably fashioned a less predictable national story from commonly shared and widely recognised historical resources. The ceremony, entitled 'Isles of Wonder', was devised by film-maker Danny Boyle and scripted by Frank Cottrell Boyce. The two men's professional credentials were many and varied, although they also shared an Irish Catholic heritage, working-class sympathies and a collaborative professional relationship. Boyce is a film-writer, a former critic for *Living Marxism*, a novelist and quondam writer for several well-loved British soap operas. Boyle is best known for the 'post-class', post-realist films *Trainspotting* (1996) and *Slumdog Millionaire* (2008), which dealt innovatively with characters living severely impoverished lives at the edge of official culture. The show they devised for the Games arguably bore the hallmarks of their earlier works and the values with which these were invested, and we propose here that at the very least it offered audiences alternative historical resources with which to furnish an interpretation of current times. To pursue this, then, we begin with a necessarily selective synopsis of the dense, complex and diverse entertainment, which we would argue was comprised of a kind of *bricolage* of well-known historical elements recombined to create counter-discourses to those described above (with all quotations from the BBC commentary).

Following a two-minute film and an audience countdown, the live entertainment began several minutes after 9 pm on 27 July 2012. The first sequence encapsulated British economic and social development from a rural economy to the Industrial Revolution and then on to the 1960s. Scenes of a bucolic agrarian life were played out against Glastonbury Tor, counterpointed with the four 'unofficial anthems' of England, Northern Ireland, Scotland and Wales. As the performances progressed, horse-drawn coaches entered the stadium, carrying men in nineteenth-century dress led by the engineer Isambard Kingdom Brunel. After ascending the Tor, Brunel delivered verses from the outcast Caliban's 'Be not afeard' speech from Shakespeare's play *The Tempest*. Green fields disappeared as chimney stacks rose from the ground in a dark and dynamic *son et lumière* setting signifying a hellish 'pandaemonium'. Agricultural workers were banished from the land. Here industrial workers forged what was to become the linked golden Olympic rings 'against the backdrop of industrial turmoil' and with Brunel looking on approvingly. This part of the show also included a period of silence in remembrance of the two world wars, featuring ordinary British

'Tommies' and a field of poppies. A variety of historical subjects arrived on scene who had contributed towards changes in British social and political life, including members of the suffragette movement and the Jarrow Hunger March of the 1936, as well as Caribbean immigrants from the Windrush years and The Beatles. Real-life Chelsea Pensioners and Pearly Kings and Queens ('the other royal family') also featured. The sequence ended with the performers looking up, dazzled, at the interlocked Olympic rings.

The next sequence celebrated the National Health Service and children's literature with a choreographed show of nurses wearing vaguely mid-century uniforms and children on hospital beds. The scene segued into a story-book world featuring the child-catcher from the film *Chitty Chitty Bang Bang* (1968) and in which *Harry Potter*'s Voldemort (Rowling 1997) is defeated by a host of Mary Poppins figures, the fictional English nanny from the much-loved film. Here children were rescued, perhaps by a metaphorical nanny-state, to be returned to the safety of their beds. The sequence ended with the appearance of a giant new-born baby. These happenings were accompanied by a roughly chronological musical sampling of British popular culture and ended with an appearance by World Wide Web inventor Sir Tim Berners-Lee. The conclusion was a memorial to the victims of the July 2005 London bombings. Throughout the show, synchronised performers, viewed from above, formed shapes and symbols including the moon and the Campaign for Nuclear Disarmament (CND) logo. There were also filmed sequences, live music of all kinds and comedy sketches. This was both a pageant and a party and a depiction of history, mostly from the perspective of ordinary people; it was, to borrow a phrase from Patrick Wright (1985:5), a fair attempt at 'a vernacular and informal history'.

Evidently, the sequences fused fiction, fantasy, historical references and historical story-telling. More than 7000 non-professionals took part, including 600 real-life hospital staff, health workers and patients. It was also a conspicuously multicultural event, with no concession made towards the historical realism often seen in British costume drama, which routinely excludes black actors. This participation of numerous volunteers signalled, too, the status of the show as a kind of grand-scale historical re-enactment. This inclusion naturally framed it quite differently from the earlier examples of redeployed historical resources discussed above. As Jerome de Groot (2009) explains in his book *Consuming History*, historical re-enactment, at the very least, suggests a democratising or progressive relationship to history; perhaps because it operates at the production as well as the consumption end of the process of historical story-telling. In de Groot's words (2009:103, emphasis in the original), re-enactment offers 'a range of *experience* within history and a complexity of consumption'; it can be an appealing combination of play, sociality, self-improvement and educational enrichment harnessed to entertainment, art or politics. 'Isles of Wonder' fitted the bill, performing cultural work which could also be political work through a meshing of popular culture, social historical and social commentary.

It seemed that as an entertainment the show was received with great pleasure and some bemusement (especially by non-Brits, for whom some of the jokes were obscure or who failed to understand why the Health Service should be quite so prominent). Early reports suggested that the show would also be read politically. Conservative MP Aidan Burley tweeted his disgruntlement about 'The most leftie opening ceremony I have ever seen', while a Labour MP blogged his delight as the 'Trojan Horse' smuggled 'progressive socialist sentiments' into the arena by conspicuously featuring the working class, a multicultural cast, and so on (in Murray 2012). A reading of opinion in the left-leaning *Observer* (29 July 2012:6–7) underlined its generally positive but multifaceted reception, with historian and MP Tristram Hunt remarking that it could be said that 'while the right has won the economic arguments, the left took victory in the "culture wars" ' (in Ai *et al.* 2012).

Others variously praised its 'collective vision', its 'brave' celebration of the welfare state, its affirmation of the Act of Union and the monarchy, its creation of a 'new myth' of social diversity, and so on (Ai *et al.* 2012). This suggested a contradictory but open and optimistic text which offered audiences multiple points of engagement. The perceived optimism of the show also chimed with Boyle's (2012) own programme notes (also in the *Observer* of that date), which maintained that running through the spectacle would be a glimpse of 'a single golden thread of purpose – the idea of Jerusalem – of the better world'. Boyle's (2012) personal statement fused past and present, the radical and the conservative, an idea and a dream into his depiction of 'a world that can be built through the prosperity of industry, through the caring nation that built the welfare state, through the joyous energy of popular culture, through the dream of universal communication.' Boyle's references to Jerusalem also, of course, conjured up a memory and reinterpretation of the post-war austerity years which were quite different from those invoked by the 'keep calm' mantra. The utopian golden thread, the 'better world', clearly recalled and valorised the political impulses, principles and philosophy which had underpinned the pursuit of the 'New Jerusalem' under the Labour Government of 1945–51. That government, which presided over the austerity years so frequently referenced in current public discourse and popular culture, had initiated a radical project of social and economic reorganisation which included the founding of 'cradle to grave' state care and the nationalisation of industries and the Bank of England. It thereby implemented a programme of Keynesian economics which advocated a mixed economy, including a significant role for the public sector: an economic model which was increasingly maligned and rejected until the recent financial crisis prompted an urgent reassessment of its value. This, then, is a quite different view of both the past and the present age of austerity, and offers an alternative reading of then Shadow Chancellor George Osborne's (2009) proposal that 'we are all in this together'.

In these and other ways which we have no space to address here, 'Isles of Wonder' arguably offered a counter-history to those we have already considered: one which reminded audiences as *citizens* and social actors why the public sector (the arts, welfare, health) should be valued and defended and why social enfranchisement mattered. In contrast to the political and media references to the 1970s which were employed to ward off radicalism and public sector rebellion, and to those of the modern mid-century which advocated stoicism and compliance, this living historical patchwork invoked a more dynamic and assertive interpretation of the past and its application to the present crisis. There is much to criticise in a historical performance such as 'Isles of Wonder' which took place in a thoroughly corporatised, securitised commercial environment. But, in Patrick Wright's (1985) terms above, it could also be argued that the ceremony attempted a kind of 're-enchantment' of everyday life worked through as a 'history from below' rather than simply a spell-binding diversion. A plethora of class and political protestors, soldiers and health service workers, factory hands and rural labourers overwhelmingly possessed the historical field.

This enchantment was effected most importantly, perhaps, through the ceremony's *embodied performance* of the past in the present and its energetic co-option of historical resources, which allowed the kinds of open, more progressive readings and reception that Bramall (2011) advocated above. We discern in 'Isles of Wonder' traces of other historical reconstructions, pageants, protests and marches that have undertaken the complex cultural work of sociality, solidarity, education and entertainment. Those with a political–critical inflection might arguably include the annual Durham Miners' Galas, artist Jeremy Deller's 2001 re-enactment of the 'Battle of Orgreave' which restaged the miners' strike of 1984–85, the Port Talbot immersive theatre *Passion Play* (2011) and even the recent adoption of Guy Fawkes masks by global political activists.[4] Happenings such as these placed non-professional performers, protestors and political actors at their centre to sample and reuse history and to retell national or local stories of classed collective life, of social history and of political activism. Above all, they made space or took space to pursue a qualitatively and politically different kind of public remembering from those examples which we scrutinised earlier in this chapter: a remembering which answers back to official history and the ways it is deployed to understand and manage the inequalities, economic strategies and constraints of the social present.

Afterword: 'We Are All in This Together'

'We are all in this together.'

(Conservative Chancellor George Osborne 2009)

'Work harder, those on benefits rely on you!'

(2012 bumper sticker)

On reflection, we have found that this book, which was intended to be about the ways in which culture articulates, frames, organises and produces stories about social class, class difference and its various attachments, is also a book about the accumulation, defence, distribution and usage of resources, both material and immaterial, during periods of pronounced inequality. We stated at the outset that we understood social class as being formed through material conditions and economic (in)securities and as being shaped by early disadvantage or privileges of birth and the uneven distribution of life chances which these conditions create. We also acknowledged that throughout our lives we are buffeted by changing socio-economic circumstances which hammer at and refashion our classed identity, sense of self and individual status within social and civil society. But our emphasis was intended to be on how class categories continue to be commonly used in culture and how these are ideologically loaded in popular and political discourses; used as shorthand to dispense judgement, criticism or praise, to evoke pride, fearfulness, nostalgia, disgust or shame. What we have come to appreciate as we have worked through different *cultural* accounts of classed relations and their positioning of social groups is that the moralistic and emotional values articulated in culture are strongly attached to submerged, messy, contradictory and sometimes aggressive collective and individual struggles for financial resources and resources-in-kind: education, housing, healthcare, and so on. As we write this afterword, these struggles have been encapsulated in a slogan which has been circulating on T shirts, posters and bumper stickers, which urges readers rather facetiously to 'Work harder, those on benefits rely on you!' Sometimes this statement is accompanied by a pointing index finger reminiscent of wartime conscription campaigns. The slogan expresses the perceived and real 'battle' for resources in austerity times and a profound resentment on the part of those who still have something to lose or to preserve. Its offensiveness is, in fact, deeply defensive and highlights the divisive undercurrents beneath the unified flow of everyone pulling together.

Every report we have offered here of the cultural articulation of classed identities and social difference has also been an account of the haves and the have-nots and the ways in which the possibilities and resources for social mobility and for the maintenance of social position have been pursued, patrolled or protected. We have seen, for example, how during the 1990s and beyond Essex Man and Essex Girl became objects of admiration, envy or disgust because they seemed to overturn the rules of social class: of class fixity, affiliation, politics and consumption. Here a 'post-working-class' constituency appeared to possess not only an *aspiration* towards social advancement but also the *capacity* to earn, to attract credit and to spend. Money and prospects had broken out of their normal class-bound confines and attached themselves to different kinds of social subjects. We have also seen how underclass debates were not only about morals and conduct and a lack of aspiration, but also concerned a seemingly unfair allocation of public resources. We have argued that the underclass is symbolically central to political debate even though it is figured as a socially marginal, albeit growing, minority; this is precisely because the few are perceived to be a drain on the collective assets of the many. We also showed that, while debates about educational values and access to education have been rooted in meritocractic models of individual social progress based on ability, hard work and intelligence, resources of every kind are at the heart of the uncertain journey to become educated, skilled and ready for work.

So powerful is the myth that social advancement is achieved through individual merit (rather than via the supportive structures of birth, inheritance and the deployment of capital of all kinds) that celebrities especially become trapped in an ethical double-bind. They are clearly exceptional figures in culture because of their *conspicuous* rise to prominence, but many appear to their critics to have achieved success without real merit. Hence, we have shown how celebrities must endeavour to show that they have worked hard to earn their fame, their money and their lifestyle. So, too, their individual self-told stories of a rise to fame from humble origins help to reassure audiences that their success is deserved and that they have not been given wealth on a plate. Often, too, these stories also convey the reassuring message that wealth in itself cannot guarantee happiness. We have also suggested that, while the assets of celebrities are often conspicuously on display because they form part of the branding of the celebrity persona, those of the upper classes and the aristocracy have to be managed quite differently. This is because the very existence of the upper class, which is often based in inherited class privilege, is all too easily read as an offence to the ideal model of a meritocractic society, and more lately to neoliberal notions of the self-made subject. So, rather like celebrities, rich elites, especially those with inherited wealth, titles and power, also take care to advertise their labour and their social, cultural and even financial contribution to the national good. From this perspective we have argued that the ability of the British aristocracy, in particular, to adapt and to at least appear to change and to promote itself as the guardian of national heritage or as an advocate of social entrepreneurism has been impressive. Perhaps these strategies have helped deflect public criticism and academic scrutiny away from an examination of the state resources (tax breaks and other benefits) which enable them to continue in the manner to which they have become accustomed.

If the aristocracy and other class elites have been the consummate social insiders, quietly benefiting from material wealth and family connections across the generations, then the immigrant has been figured as the very opposite, as an all-too-visible outsider and an interloper on the national scene. In our penultimate chapter we showed how public discourses sought to differentiate between legitimate insiders and illegitimate outsiders and to mark out the boundaries of moral, social and individual worth in the context of competitions for jobs, services and welfare resources. Here we suggested that a collective, referred to as the 'white working class', had become the container for broader social unease about national identity, cultural difference and also the allocation of increasingly scarce social benefits. Public and political discourses amplify cultural differences and economic competition between mostly poor working-class people from all ethnic backgrounds, while offering very few opportunities for those people to speak for themselves.

It was in our final chapter that issues of resources (both national and individual) were highlighted specifically in the context of the new age of austerity and in the light of the 2008 financial downturn. We noted here that the cloak of British economic prosperity which had shielded the nation for much of the previous decade has become increasingly tattered and threadbare. We chose to highlight the ways in which historical lessons have been deployed in political and popular discourses to head off dissent and to encourage compliance with the sometimes unpalatable policies and economic strategies advocated by the UK Coalition. The contention here was that a recourse to history was being mobilised to persuade citizens of how best to make sense of the downturn and to accept austerity measures such as the cutting of public services and the further dismantling of the welfare state. Our suspicion has grown throughout the research and writing of this book that citizens are very far indeed from being all in this together, and that ultimately it will be the struggle for resources which throws into stark relief the sharper contours of the ongoing neoliberal project and its implications for class relations and a progressive politics of class. The fair allocation of resources, the opportunity to make a dignified living and the sustenance and social support of those who are struggling must remain central to the politics of hope.

Notes

1 Introduction: Beginning the Work of Class and Culture

1. There are different versions of this speech. The version published in Cooke as cited includes material removed from the text after the speech press release had been distributed.
2. This is not to say that there were no outbursts of social disorder during the mid-1980s. In addition to industrial disputes, there were also riots arising from the ongoing fraught relationships between minorities and the police, such as the Broadwater Farm incident in Tottenham, North London, which took place in 1985.
3. See Palmer (2003), Biressi and Nunn (2008), Tyler (2008), Nunn and Biressi (2009 and forthcoming), Doyle and Karl (2010), Ferguson (2010), Nunn and Biressi (2010b), Wood and Skeggs (2010) and Biressi (2011).

2 Essex: Class, Aspiration and Social Mobility

1. Stuart Hall was a key theorist of a perceived crisis in British social democracy and its relationship to Thatcherism. In a series of papers throughout the 1980s, Hall described how Thatcherism was a distinct articulation of economic policies and cultural and racial discourses and how these helped sustain its hegemonic authority across three successive general elections. On authoritarian populism, see Hall (1983).
2. This interview with Tory blogger Iain Dale took place on 20 December 2010 at http://iaindale.blogspot.com/2010/12/simon-heffer-interview-full-length.html, accessed on 12 December 2011.
3. As Joe Moran (2005:144–6) explains, Barratt homes were associated with the rise of cul-de-sac edge of town estates which offered detached and 'starter' homes, fully furnished and with easy to access financial packages which eased the process of home-buying, presenting it as accessible to all.
4. This sketch was viewed at http://www.youtube.com/watch?v=L4r_a5adehs, accessed on 3 March 2012.
5. Loadsamoney first appeared in *Saturday Live* (C4 1984–87). Although Loadsamoney was fundamentally a South Londoner, he was consistently read as an Essex Man. Enfield eventually devised the Geordie 'Buggerall-money' who openly loathed his Southern counterpart.
6. See the music video (1988) 'Loadsamoney: doin' up the house' at http://www.youtube.com/watch?v=ON-7v4qnHP8, accessed on 14 December 2012.
7. For an alternative view of the Essex barrow boy and the entrepreneurialism of the 1980s, see David Eldridge's (2006) partly biographical play *Market Boy*,

which is set in Romford, Essex. His 2011 play *In Basildon* further explored the mythology of Essex via a family drama about money, inheritance and home ownership (Eldridge 2012).

8. Yuppies was an acronym for 'young urban' or 'young upwardly mobile' professionals.

9. Speech available on the BUFVC website http://radio.bufvc.ac.uk/lbc/index .php/segment/0004200265013, accessed on 18 December 2012.

10. Speech available at the Margaret Thatcher Foundation at http:// www.margarettthatcher.org/document/107352, accessed on 16 December 2012.

11. Even as recently as 2007 Essex County had a 'non-white' ethnic population of about 8 per cent as opposed to 11.8 per cent across England. See Essex JSNA (2010:12). While the notion of a black Essex Girl is rarely entertained in the media, there is an example of three white *The Only Way Is Essex* stars featuring in a fashion shoot for the magazine *Asian Woman* (Winter 2011 Issue 49). This appeared to cause controversy, but it is hard to evaluate how much of this was deliberately generated publicity.

12. The purported ignorance of Essex people, and especially of the Essex Girl, continues to fuel journalism, television and popular culture more generally and to be deployed to hook in audiences. Headlines such as 'Essex Girl goes for PhD' (Goddard 2002) and reality series such as *Educating Essex* (C4 2011), while often dealing with complex topics, help reproduce an overall picture of clever (working-class) Essex people as a rare exception. *Educating Essex* is a good example, in which the title and trailers smack of a classed exploitation of Essex people as stupid and ill-disciplined, although the series itself is more sophisticated than this suggests. The filming follows one group of students at Passmores School in Harlow, Essex, 'a successful school in a challenging area', according to the Channel 4 website. In one TV trailer, already popular on youtube.com, a girl wearing comically heavy eye makeup sighs mournfully: 'what is pi, where did it come from?' TV reviewer Tom Sutcliffe wryly observed: 'if they could have found an excuse…they would probably have called it My Big Fat Gypsy School', with reference to the popular TV series featuring the gypsy and traveller brides getting ready for their big day. http://www.independent.co.uk/arts-entertainment/tv/reviews/last-nights-tv-educating-essex-channel-4-bryoung-soldiers-bbc3-2359417.html, accessed on 15 December 2012.

3 The Revolting Underclass: 'You Know Them When You See Them'

1. Underclass is frequently used in popular discourses as a pejorative term and normally we would use the word in inverted commas to signal the problems inherent in using it, but for ease of reading we have dispensed with these throughout this book except where we are drawing attention to underclass as a form of terminology.

2. See, for example, Neil Lawson's (Chair of left-orientated group Compass) talk on the riots on 16 September 2011, 'The London Riots and the Rise of Consumerism: what are the implications for social democracy?'

http://www.sorsafoundation.fi/tpl_actual_01.asp?sua=1&lang=1&s=401, accessed on 14 August 2012.

3. See the findings of the interim report on the English riots *5 Days in August*, Riots, Communities and Victims panel at http://riotspanel.independent .gov.uk/wp-content/uploads/2012/04/Interim-report-5-Days-in-August.pdf, accessed on 12 December 2012.

4. For an analysis of the 2001 British riots and underclass references to South Asian communities see Bagguley and Hussain (2008:33).

5. This account of the discursive construction of the underclass is an extended and modified version of an account featured in Nunn and Biressi (2010b).

6. A rare example of a self-identified member of the underclass replying to 'underclass debates' appears in an article called 'Job dole-claimers aren't fools – you are' in *The Sunday Times* 17 December 1989:7. Even here the writer is only known as 'Jake'.

7. There are a few British press references to the underclass in the late 1960s, which tend to refer to the impoverished circumstances of the working poor rather than the criminal or the welfare dependent (e.g. Chester 1967).

8. Thatcher (1992) recalled in later years: 'Class is a Communist concept . . . . . I remember practically exploding when I heard some Americans talking about "the underclass," as if they weren't individuals with feelings. Each one is entitled to his own dignity, to develop his talents and abilities.'

9. Prideux (2010:296) notes that by 1987 representatives of Thatcher's Policy Unit, the Treasury and the Department of Health and Social Security were meeting with Charles Murray, the key promoter of the underclass thesis.

10. There are competing, less dominant, definitions, for example Labour MP Frank Field's (1989) view that the underclass is the product of growing inequalities and consists of impoverished pensioners, single parents confined to welfare and the long-term unemployed – he attributed these inequalities in part to the individualist ethos of Thatcherism, a suggestion with which Murray did not concur. In a later book Field (1995) advocated a reorganisation of welfare on the basis of a particular understanding of human nature as primarily self-interested.

11. Other scandalous cases involving children during 2008 also inspired extensive underclass debate by both the press and politicians (see Garratt 2009). Aside from those already cited, examples from the *Sunday Times* alone include: Insight Bloody Britain Supplement (1990:13–16), Murray (1992), and Himmelfarb (1994).

12. For a detailed and illuminating analysis of the social exclusion thesis and its relationship to crime and the underclass see Jock Young (2007:17ff and 22ff).

13. In consumer research terms the aberrant consumer is someone who vandalises, thieves, defrauds or intimidates others in 'exchange settings' such as shops. As Ronald Fullerton (1993:570) explains, this is behaviour which 'violates the generally accepted norms of consumer behaviour . . . . It has financial, psychological, and social costs for both consumers and marketers.'

4 Top of the Class: Education, Capital and Choice

1. For an assessment of the philosophy and practical applications to education of New Labour's commitment to both encouraging individualism and enterprise together with principles of citizenship and cultural and moral regeneration, see Deuchar (2007).
2. Hannan said this in response to a question about married couple tax breaks in the debate show *Any Questions*, Radio 4, 8 January 2010.
3. For a landmark study on middle-class strategies within the education system, see Ball (2003). For a response to Ball which warns against moralistic critiques of middle-class behaviour, also see Beck (2007). For considerations of the ways in which middle-class families exercise choice in ways that undercut self-interest in the educational field, see Wilkins (2010).
4. The sharp-elbowed debate was picked up later by Nick Clegg with regard to debates about unpaid internships (see Groves 2011).
5. Mumsnet.com was set up in 2000 and at the time of writing attracted 1.3 million unique visitors each month, mainly from the UK, and 35 million monthly hits (Google Analytics 2011), accessed on 10 November 2011.
6. Reay's article appeared in a special edition of *Oxford Review of Education*, 34 (6): December 2008, dedicated to considering education policy under the Blair administration.
7. This choice is also negative in the sense that it is often expressed as the choice to move to a school which has fewer 'ethnic' children or fewer children who have English as a second language. Although there's no space to discuss this further, it should be noted that this avoidance of the poor and of the ethnic poor is evident in some middle-class strategies around choice and education (see Tomlinson 2005:11).
8. A theory of education-based meritocracy was developed in the 1960s and 1970s by Daniel Bell. 'What is envisaged,' explains John Goldthorpe (2003:235), 'is that as we get closer to the ideal of education-based meritocracy, social mobility steadily increases and, where it doesn't it will be for legitimate "meritocractic" reasons.' For an exploration of the argument that meritocratic factors (ability plus effort) do in fact outweigh social dis/advantage, see Saunders (1995 and 1997).
9. http://www.education.gov.uk/schools/leadership/typesofschools/freeschools, accessed on 10 October 2011.
10. Michael Gove Free School video at http://www.education.gov.uk/schools/leadership/typesofschools/freeschools/b0061428/free-schools, accessed on 10 November 2011.
11. See the Coalition's Open Public Services White Paper 2011 and the HM Government document Open Public Services 2012 at http://files.openpublicservices.cabinetoffice.gov.uk/HMG_OpenPublicServices_web.pdf, accessed on 1 December 2011.

5 The Ones Who Got Away: Celebrity Life Stories of Upward Social Mobility

1. For an extensive and informative analysis of the varieties of authorised and unauthorised celebrity, see Coombe (2006).

2. Successful ghost writer Hunter Davies observed: 'you're not necessarily trying to get their real voice, but rather the voice that the public believes belongs to them' (in Preston 2006).
3. It should be noted that, in the case of reality show contestants, they may well have signed contracts in which they ceded any rights over their own life stories to the production company (see Collins 2008:98).
4. 'Entertainment' can be defined as being both 'not art' and as part of leisure and in opposition to paid work and domestic labour (Dyer 2002/1992:6–8).
5. See, for example, the photographs included in Katie Price's (2010) autobiography, which show her having fun while shooting for her calendar. The production team and their equipment are invisible, so that the collaborative labour-intensive work of glamour modelling remains unseen.
6. It's interesting to note that Paul Willis's book *Learning to Labour* (1977), which recorded his observations and interviews with working-class boys soon to leave school, makes no mention of celebrity culture or of talent shows as routes out of the dead-end jobs for which they seemed to be destined. It's possible that he didn't choose to ask about these kinds of aspirations, but also valid to note that the boys don't seem to have raised the topic either. In his later book *Common Culture* (1990) Willis celebrates the ways in which young people, far from aping celebrities and the products of the entertainment industry, actually subvert and rework dominant culture.
7. At http://www.ollymurs.com/about/, accessed on 22 December 2011.
8. For an extensive discussion of celebrities as role models, the values they bear and the judgements levelled against them when they subvert established social protocols, see Gorin and Dubied (2011).
9. Read more: http://www.dailymail.co.uk/tvshowbiz/article-1234069/X-Factor-Cheryl-Cole-takes-Joe-McElderry-South-Shields-homecoming-gig.html#ixzz 1aUCHixBK, accessed on 21 December 2011.
10. According to Elena Egawhari (2010), between 2004 and 2010 four out of the five top-selling autobiographies in the UK were by entertainment celebrities, including Paul O'Grady's first book, which is discussed later in this chapter. The exception was *Dreams of My Father* by Barack Obama. Although there has been ongoing discussion in trade journals such as the *Bookseller* of a falling off from the peak sales of 2008–09, it has also been noted that publishers are continuing to publish them (see, for example, Gallagher 2010, Neilan 2010, Neill 2011).
11. For UK sales figures for Pelzer's novels in 2001 and an overview of 'dark memoirs' from a British perspective, see Sutherland (2002:166–9).
12. Katie Price's (2004) first autobiography has also been credited as the first notable breakthrough publication which demonstrated a public appetite for British (as opposed to American) celebrity autobiographies (see Preston 2006).
13. Reviews cited at http://www.amazon.co.uk/How-Did-Get-Here-There/dp/product-description/1844080501/ref=dp_proddesc_0?ie=UTF8&n=266239& s=books, accessed on 20 October 2011.

6   The Upper Classes: Visibility, Adaptability and Change

1. Mass coverage of the royal family is evidenced across the 16 national UK papers listed in the Nexis database for one year (26 November 2010–26 November 2011), which revealed more than 3000 major references.

2. Those working in cultural and media studies tend to address media representation of the monarchy alone rather than the rich upper classes across the board (e.g. Williamson 1986, Dayan and Katz 1992, Hartley 1992:76–83, Mallory Wober 2001, Blain and O'Donnell 2003).

3. The issue of the visibility of the upper classes, both historically and now, is rather complex. As late as the 1960s, for example, sociological research showed that it was precisely the visibility of the rich and the titled which confirmed working-class people's perception that there was indeed a class system. Here high status was equated with public visibility, and indeed there was 'far more certainty' about the existence of the upper classes than of the other two (Savage 2000:218). This chapter does not maintain that the upper class is now no longer visible, but rather that its visibility is differently configured and somewhat altered by celebrity culture and a culture of media intimacy. In these and other ways the power and privilege of the upper class are obscured.

4. See the BBC Class project at http://www.bbc.co.uk/labuk/articles/class/. The videoed interviews are available at http://www.youtube.com/watch?v= E9mHzOI9g_0&list=PL7CC9219365D319FD&index=11&feature=plpp_ video, accessed on 10 July 2012.

5. A Privilege Insurance advert from 2008 featuring Nigel Havers and using the slogan 'you don't have to be posh to be privileged' also mocked the upper classes in similar stereotypical fashion as eccentric and anachronistic. Complaints were subsequently made to the Advertising Standards Authority. These parallel, in some ways, the depiction of the underclass, who are also often styled as un-modern and unproductive (although urban rather than rural). This is humorously highlighted in the so-called underclass drama *Shameless*, in which the characters live on the Chatsworth Estate, equating them with upper-class freeloaders. But the aristocratic upper class is not regarded as a social problem, so it does not suffer the same level of scrutiny or criticism for its (lack of) contribution to society.

6. 'Heritage, localism and the big society', 11 October 2011, at http://www .english-heritage.org.uk/about/news/heritage-counts-2011/, accessed on 27 November 2011.

7. See 'Heritage Key to Local Economies and Economic Resilience' at http://www.helm.org.uk/server/show/ConWebDoc.17987, accessed on 27 November 2011.

8. Data of viewing figures at http://news.bbc.co.uk/onthisday/hi/dates/stories/ july/29/newsid_2494000/2494949.stm.

9. The series was very successful in terms of audience figures, but statistics do not, of course, tell us how viewers actually received the series and from which positioning in terms of class. For a discussion of the experiential aspects of viewing *WNTW* and other series, see Wood and Skeggs (2010).

10. http://www.rdftelevision.com/categories.aspx?programmeid=203&cid=2& type=factual entertainment, accessed on 30 November 2011.

11. http://www.gutenberg.org/files/3825/3825-h/3825-h.htm

7 'Are You Thinking What We're Thinking?': Class, Immigration and Belonging

1. The new countries were Cyprus, the Czech Republic, Estonia, Hungary, Latvia, Lithuania, Malta, Poland, Slovakia and Slovenia.

2. In November 2006, following media coverage of the BNP's success in gaining votes in Barking and Dagenham, the Unite Against Fascism campaign group held a rally in Central Park, Dagenham. Their concern was fuelled by figures from the Barking and Dagenham Race Equality Council which showed that there appeared to be a correspondence between BNP activity in the area and the rise in racist violence in the borough between 2004 and 2006, with racist incidents increasing by 30 per cent (see UAF 2006).

3. As Gibson (2006) has noted, there is a longstanding British mythology of offering 'hospitality' to those fleeing from political and religious persecution. She observes that 'Tolerance' and 'hospitality' are 'central tropes' in clarifying Britain's attitude towards perceived outsiders such as immigrants and more so asylum seekers and refugees.

4. BBC News (2005) 'Howard unveils asylum plans', 24 January 2005, http://news.bbc.co.uk/1/hi/uk_politics/4200761.stm, accessed on 26 July 2012.

5. This reference to the abuse of immigrant workers probably recalls the deaths of 23 Chinese cockle pickers who drowned in Lancashire's Morecambe Bay in February 2004.

6. This document is available at http://www.open.ac.uk/socialsciences/identities/aboutus.html, accessed on 3 August 2012.

7. For contemporaneous fieldwork which considered issues of status, inequality and social class from the perspective of migrant groups, in this case black Zimbabweans, see McGregor (2008).

8. Newsnight (2005) 'Jeremy Paxman interview with Rodney Hylton-Potts', http://www.youtube.com/watch?v=Fm216gsYHso, accessed on 3 August 2012.

9. At the May 2005 elections, Hylton-Potts roundly lost his subsequent bid for the Folkestone and Hythe seat under the party banner of 'Get Britain Back' to Conservative Shadow Home Secretary Michael Howard. See YouTube clips of *Vote For Me* on http://www.youtube.com/watch?v=aIhrUK3Fhwg&feature=relmfu and http://www.youtube.com/watch?feature=endscreen&NR=1&v=3D-7YBfHgbY. For the May 2005 voting results for Folkestone and Hythe, see BBC Election News on http://news.bbc.co.uk/1/shared/vote2005/html/256.stm, accessed on 3 August 2012.

10. Hope not hate website, 2005, 'Rodney Hylton-Potts', 18 April 2005, http://www.hopenothate.org.uk/news/article/225/rodney-hylton-potts, accessed on 3 August 2012.

11. The video of the exchange and transcripts were all accessed from http://news.bbc.co.uk/1/hi/8649012.stm, accessed on 3 August 2012.

12. This conditionality and mastery are signalled in scenarios or imaginary fantasies of hospitality featuring a welcoming Britain styled as inclusive, tolerant and implicitly white. Imogen Tyler (2006) illustrates this clearly in her analysis of the branding of the British government's official *Visit Britain* tourist website, in which the fantasies of a diverse multicultural inclusive Britain are undercut by the implied exclusion of *some* tourists. Tyler (2006:186) claims: 'it is a very particular kind of foreigner that is entreated to visit Britain. For not only are all the foreign visitors featured from countries with strong colonial ties to the UK, Australia, New Zealand and South Africa, they are all white..., it is evident that the British Government is not extending its hospitality to all foreigners'.

13. In 2010 a Channel 4 film called *The Battle for Barking* also presented the area as the testing ground for working-class race relations. It aimed to give an insight into the inner workings of the 'BNP family' and the working-class disillusionment with the Labour party that fuelled the BNP campaign, and to offer 'an honest, moving and humorous portrait of a white working class community forced to face the changes brought by new immigrant populations'. http://www.channel4.com/programmes/the-battle-for-barking/episode-guide/series-1/episode-1, accessed on 3 August 2012.

14. The film also follows Dave and his colleagues while campaigning for the BNP and illustrates the ways in which the BNP sought to embed itself in local communities by reference to local issues such as protecting children and defending local amenities. As Rhodes (2009:148) notes of similar strategies by BNP candidates in Burnley in this period, 'statements of entitlement and belonging' are 'articulated in a discourse embedded in the everyday and the proximate'.

15. Identification with someone or some group involves misalignment with another. 'I love or hate them *because* they are like me, or not like me,' observes Ahmed (2004:52). Importantly, there is an attitude of defensiveness, but also of respectability and shame, embedded in such responses. There is also, of course, an evaluative dimension. For example, Andrew Sayer (2005) takes this movement of emotional ebbs and flows – like me, not like me – and settles them on the complexities of class. Importantly, he argues for the moral implications of *class as a process* as each of us, individually and collectively, assesses our own and other people's worth.

8 Austerity Britain: Back to the Future

1. The Conservative Party Political Broadcast featuring Thatcher was broadcast on 17 January 1979 and is available at http://www.margaretthatcher.org/speeches/displaydocument.asp?docid=103926, accessed on 16 August 2012

2. *Daily Mail* Comment (2011) 'Public sector pension walkout' at http://www.dailymail.co.uk/debate/article-2068346/Public-sector-pensions-walkout-Strikers-told-simple-truth.html, 1 December, accessed on 14 July 2012.

3. At http://www.channel4.com/news/tony-blair-endorses-david-miliband-nearly, accessed on 1 August 2012.

4. Lyn Gardner (2011) in the *Guardian* observed of the *Passion* that it 'was like watching a town discovering its voice through a shared act of creation. Fact and fiction, myth and memory, rumour and reality, even the living and the dead stalk side by side'.

References

Aaronovitch, D. (2005) 'It's the Brits who need the points system', the *Guardian*, 8 February, http://www.guardian.co.uk/society/2005/feb/08/asylum .politics. Accessed 3 August 2012.

Abercrombie, N. and Warde, A. with Deem, R., Penna, S., Soothill, K., Urry, J., Sayers, A., and Walby, S. (2000) *Contemporary British Society*, 3rd edition, Cambridge: Polity Press.

Abbott, D. (2005) 'This racist appetite will never be sated: the political bidding war on immigration is unwinnable. Instead, the government should challenge the terms of the debate', the *Guardian*, 18 February 2005.

Adkins, L. and Skeggs, B. (2004) 'Feminism after Bourdieu', in Special Issue of *The Sociological Review*, 52:Issue Supplement s2, October.

Adonis, A. and Pollard, S. (1998/1997) *A Class Act: The Myth of Britain's Classless Society*, London: Penguin.

Agamben, G. (1998) *Homo Sacer: Sovereign Power and Bare Life*, Stanford, CA: Stanford University Press.

Ahmed, S. (2004) *The Cultural Politics of Emotion*, Edinburgh: Edinburgh University Press.

Ai, W. W., Stenham, P. Hunt,T., Phillips, T., Emmy the Great, Sawyer, M., Kay, J., Durkin, M., Goldsmith, H., and Charles, A. (2012) ' "Every part of our culture was woven into a dazzling tapestry" ': Writers, artists, historians and other leading figures from the arts world give their view of Danny Boyle's show – and almost all praise its quirky inventiveness' in the *Observer* (Home News) 29 July 2012: 6–7.

Alberoni, F. (2006/1962) 'The powerless "elite": theory and sociological research on the phenomenon of the stars', in P. D. Marshall (ed.) *The Celebrity Culture Reader*, Oxon: Routledge:108–23.

Allen, K. (2011) 'Ebury buys Sue Johnston memoir', in *The Bookseller*, 23 March, http://www.thebookseller.com/news/ebury-buys-sue-johnston-memoir.html. Accessed 7 July 2012.

Anderson, P. (1992, revised from 1964) 'Origins of the present crisis', in P. Anderson *English Questions*, London: Verso:15–47.

Anthony, A. (2011) 'Rewind TV', in the *Guardian*, 6 March, http://www.guardian .co.uk/tv-and-radio/2011/mar/06/jamie-oliver-attenborough-andrew-anthony-review. Accessed 12 March 2011.

Armstrong, S. (2010) 'Middle Class Quiz', http://www.telegraph.co.uk/news/ politics/7939549/Middle-Class-Quiz.html. Accessed 1 November 2011.

Auletta, K. (1982) *The Underclass*, New York: Random House.

Babcock, B. (1978) *The Reversible World: Symbolic Inversion in Art and Society*, Ithaca, NY: Cornell University Press.

Bagguley, P. and Hussain, Y. (2008) *Riotous Citizens: Ethnic Conflict in Multicultural Britain*, Farnham: Ashgate.

208

Bagguley, P. and Mann, K. (1992) 'Idle thieving bastards: scholarly representations of the "underclass" ', in *Work, Employment and Society*, 6:1:113–26.

Balibar, E. (1991) 'Class racism', in E. Balibar and I. Wallerstein (1991, orig. 1988) *Race Nation Class: Ambiguous Identities*, London: Verso:204–16.

Ball, S. (2003) *Class Strategies and the Education Market: The Middle Classes and Social Advantage*, London: Routledge Falmer.

Barker, P. (2006) 'A tract for the times', in *The Political Quarterly*, 77:Issue Supplement s1, June:36–44.

Barker, P. (2009) *The Freedoms of Suburbia*, London: Frances Lincoln.

Barkham, P. (2007) 'I'm famous, buy me', in the *Guardian*, 15 January, http://www.guardian.co.uk/books/2007/jan/15/biography.patrickbarkham. Accessed 14 July 2008.

Barnett, A. and Bourne Taylor, J. (1999) 'Diana and the constitution: a conversation', in *New Formations: Diana and Democracy*, 36:47–58.

Barr, A. and York, P. (1982) *The Official Sloane Ranger Handbook*, London: Ebury Press.

Barry, E. (2008) 'Celebrity, cultural production and public life', in *International Journal of Cultural Studies*, 11:251–58.

Bastin, G. (2009) 'Filming the ineffable: biopics of the British Royal family', in *Auto/biography Studies* 24:1:34–52.

Batmanghelidjh, C. (2011) 'Caring costs but so do riots', in *Independent*, 9 August, http://www.independent.co.uk/opinion/commentators/camila-batmanghelidjh-caring-costs-ndash-but-so-do-riots-2333991.html. Accessed 1 September 2011.

Bauman, Z. (1982) *Memories of Class: The Prehistory and After Life of Class*, London: Routledge and Kegan Paul.

Bauman, Z. (1997) *Postmodernity and Its Discontents*, Cambridge: Polity Press.

Bauman, Z. (2007) *Consuming Life*, Cambridge: Polity Press.

Bauman, Z. (2011) *Collateral Damage: Social Inequalities in a Global Age*, Cambridge: Polity Press.

BBC (2011) 'Cameron promises "people power" in public services plan', http://www.bbc.co.uk/news/uk-politics-14101481. Accessed 15 July 2011.

Beaven, D. (2001) 'The Essex clearances', in *Prospect*, 25 October, retrieved through Lexis UK Database.

Beck, J. (2007) 'Education and the middle class? Against reductionism in educational theory and research', in *The British Journal of Educational Studies*, 55:1, March:37–55.

Beck, U. (1992) *The Risk Society*, London: Sage.

Beck, U., Giddens, A., and Lash, S. (1994) *Reflexive Modernisation: Politics, Tradition and Aesthetics in the Modern Social Order*, Cambridge: Polity Press.

Becker, R. (2006) ' "Help is on the way!": *Supernanny*, *Nanny 911*, and the neoliberal politics of the family', in D. Heller (ed.) *Great American Makeover: Television, History, Nation*, London: Palgrave:175–91.

Beckett, A. (2009) *When the Lights Went Out: Britain in the Seventies*, London: Faber and Faber.

Bell, C. (2010) *American Idolatry: Celebrity, Commodity and Reality Television*, Jefferson, NC: McFarland.

Bell, E. (2008) 'From Bad Girl to Mad Girl: British female celebrity, reality products, and the pathologization of pop-feminism', in *Genders Online Journal*, Issue 48, http://www.genders.org/g48/g48_bell.html. Accessed 12 July 2012.

Bennett, P. (2006) *Pete: My Story*, London: HarperCollins.

Bennett, T., Savage, M., Silva, E., et al. (2009) *Culture, Class, Distinction*, Oxon: Routledge.

Benson, R. and Armstrong, S. (2010) *The Middle Class Handbook: An Illustrated Field Guide to the Changing Behaviour and Tastes of Britain's New Middle-Class Tribes*, London: Not Actual Size.

Best, G. (2001) *Blessed: The Autobiography*, London: Ebury Press.

Bidinger, E. (2006) *The Ethics of Working Class Autobiography: Representation of Family by Four American Authors*, Jefferson, NC: McFarland.

Billig, M. (1992) *Talking of the Royal Family*, London: Routledge.

Billig, M. (1995) *Banal Nationalism*, London: Sage.

Biressi, A. (2011) ' "The virtuous circle of social capital" or helping people to help themselves in British lifestyle programming', in H. Wood and B. Skeggs (eds.) *Reality Television and Class*, London: Palgrave/BFI:144–55.

Biressi, A. and Nunn, H. (2008) 'Bad citizens: the class politics of lifestyle television', in G. Palmer (ed.) *Exposing Lifestyle Television: The Big Reveal*. Hampshire and Burlington: Ashgate:15–24.

Black, L. and Pemberton, H. (eds.) (2009) 'The winter of discontent in British politics', in *The Political Quarterly*, 80:4:553–61.

Blain, N. and O'Donnell, H. (2003) *Media, Monarchy and Power*, Oregon: Intellect.

Blair, T. (1996) 'Ruskin Speech 16 December at Education-Line', http://www.leeds.ac.uk/educol/documents/000000084.htm. Accessed 10 October 2011.

Blair, T. (2005a) 'Foreword', *Controlling Our Borders: Making Migration Work*, Norwich: H.M. Government/Home Office.

Blair, T. (2005b) 'Full text: Tony Blair's speech on asylum and immigration', 22 April, http://www.guardian.co.uk/politics/2005/apr/22/election2005.immigrationandpublicservices. Accessed 26 July 2012.

Blair, T. (2006a) 'Our nation's future: social exclusion', http://www.britishpoliticalspeech.org/speech-archive.htm?speech=283. Accessed 26 July 2012.

Blair, T. (2006b) 'Respect agenda', http://www.britishpoliticalspeech.org/speech-archive.htm?speech=290. Accessed 26 July 2012.

Bloom, C. (2011) 'Economics not racism riles the Nando's generation', in *Financial Times*, 8 August, http://www.ft.com/cms/s/0/c6feac6c-c1b9-11e0-acb3-00144feabdc0.html#axzz1ruduL5NN. Accessed 10 August 2012.

Boyle, D. (2012), 'Daring. Genius. Creativity. Our special gifts', in the *Observer* 29 July:9.

Bonner, F. (2008) 'Fixing relationships in 2-4-1 transformations', in *Continuum: Journal of Media and Cultural Studies*, 22:4:547–57.

Bonnett, A. (2010) *Left in the Past: Radicalism and the Politics of Nostalgia*, London: Continuum.

Boorstin, D. (2006/1961) 'From hero to celebrity: the human pseudo-event', in P. David Marshall (ed.) *The Celebrity Culture Reader*, Oxon: Routledge: 72–90.

Bourdieu, P. (1984) *Distinction: A Social Critique of the Judgement of Taste*, Harvard: Harvard University Press.

Bourdieu, P. and Wacquant, L. (1992) *An Invitation to Reflexive Sociology*, Chicago: University of Chicago Press.

Bourne, J.M. (1991) 'The decline and fall of the British aristocracy', in *Twentieth Century British History*, 2:3:380–86.

Boyle, S. (2010) *The Woman I Was Born to Be: My Story*, London: Bantam Press.

Brake, M. and Hale, C. (1992) *Public Order and Private Lives: The Politics of Law and Order*, London: Routledge.

Bramall, R. (2011) 'Dig for victory: anti-consumerism, austerity and new historical subjectivities', in *Subjectivity*, 4:1:68–86.

Bridge, M. (2012) 'Keep calm and carry on: what we can learn from the Britons of 1952; Jubilee Special The frugal mindset at the start of the Queen's reign has lessons for us all', in the *Times*, 2 June, Business Section:63.

Bridges, L. (2012) '4 days in August: the UK riots', in *Race and Class*, 54:1:1–12.

Brogan, B. (2009) 'We say we're prepared for pain, but are we ready to vote for it?' in *The Daily Telegraph*, 8 October:22.

Bromley, R. (1988) *Lost Narratives: Popular Fiction, Politics and Recent History*, London: Routledge.

Brooker, C. (2011) 'Jamie's Dream School', 14 March, http://www.guardian.co .uk/commentisfree/2011/mar/14/jamie-olivers-dream-school/print. Accessed 16 March 2011.

Brunt, R. (1987) 'Thatcher uses her woman's touch', in *Marxism Today*, June:22–24.

Bryan, B., Dadzie, S., and Scafe, S. (1986) *The Heart of the Race: Black Women's Lives in Britain*, London: Virago.

Buckingham, A. (1999) 'Is there an underclass in Britain?' in *British Journal of Sociology*, 50:1:49–75.

Burns, K. (2009) *Celeb 2.0: How Social Media Foster Our Fascination with Popular Culture*, California: ABC Clio.

Bury, L. (2007) 'Tugging at the heart strings', in the *Bookseller*, 22 February, http://www.thebookseller.com/feature/tugging-heart-strings.html. Accessed 22 March 2011.

Byrne, D. (2005) *Social Exclusion*, 2nd edition, Maidenhead: Open University Press.

Cahill, K. (2010) 'Who really owns Britain?' in *Country Life*, 16 November, http:// www.countrylife.co.uk/property_news/article/506200/Who-really-owns-Britain-.html. Accessed 16 February 2011.

Campbell, B. (1984) *Wigan Pier Revisited: Poverty and Politics in the 80s*, London: Virago.

Campbell, B. (1993) *Goliath: Britain's Dangerous Places*, London: Methuen.

Cannadine, D. (1990) *The Decline and Fall of the British Aristocracy*, New Haven, CT: Yale University Press.

Cannadine, D. (1994) *Aspects of Aristocracy: Grandeur and Decline in Modern Britain*, New Haven, CT: Yale University Press.

Cannadine, D. (1998) *Class in Britain*, New Haven, CT: Yale University Press.

Canoville, P. (2008) *Black and Blue: How Racism, Drugs and Cancer Almost Destroyed Me*, London: Headline.

Carvel, J. (2004) 'Opposition to immigrants hardens under Blair', the *Guardian*, 2 December, http://www.guardian.co.uk/uk/2004/dec/07/immigration .immigrationandpublicservices. Accessed 20 July 2012.

Cassidy, M.F. (2005) *What Women Watched: Daytime Television in the 1950s*, Austin, TX: University of Texas Press.

Charlesworth, D. (2011) 'Journeying with Jamie Oliver: Masculinity, Social Entrepreneurialism and the Politics of C4', at Gender Politics and Reality Television Conference, 25–27 August 2011, University College, Dublin. (Unpublished.)

Charteris-Black, J. (2006) 'Britain as a container: immigration metaphors in the 2005 election campaign', in *Discourse and Society*, 17:5:563–81.

Chester, L. (1967) 'The people the budget forgot', in the *Sunday Times*, 16 April:11.

Church Gibson, P. (2010) 'Celebrities', in V. Steele (ed.) *The Berg Companion to Fashion*, New York: Berg:127–30.

Church Gibson, P. (2011) 'New patterns of emulation: Kate, Pippa and Cheryl', in *Celebrity Studies*, 2:3:358–60.

Churchill, C. (2002) *Serious Money: A City Comedy*, London: Methuen Drama.

Clarke, J. (forthcoming) 'Austerity and authoritarianism: the paradox of unpopular populism in the UK', in *La Revista della Politicia Sociale*, in press.

Clarke, J. and Newman, J. (2012) 'The Alchemy of Austerity', in *Critical Social Policy*, 32:3:299–319.

Clarke, P. (1996) *Hope and Glory: Britain 1900–1990*, London: Penguin.

Clarke, S. and Garner, S. (undated) 'Mobility and unsettlement: new identity construction in contemporary Britain', summary, http://www.open.ac.uk/socialsciences/identities/findings.html. Accessed 31 July 2012.

Clarke, S., Gilmour, R., and Garner, S (2007) 'Home, identity and community cohesion', in M. Wetherell, M. Lafleche, and R. Berkeley (eds.) *Identity, Ethnic Diversity and Community Cohesion*, London: Sage:87–101.

Cockburn, C. (1991) *Brothers: Male Dominance and Technological Change*, London: Pluto.

Collins, A., Chapman, A., and Walters, S. (2010) 'Gordon won't be getting my vote', in the *Daily Mail*, 2 May, http://www.dailymail.co.uk/news/article-1270337/Gordon-wont-getting-vote-Gillian-Duffy-reveals-REALLY-upset-devastating-exchange-PM.html#ixzz24058t5ff. Accessed 12 March 2011.

Collins, M. (2004) *The Likes of Us: A Biography of the White Working Class*, London: Granta Books.

Collins, S. (2008) 'Making the most of 15 minutes: reality TV's dispensable celebrity', in *Television and New Media*, 9:2:87–110.

Conley, D. (2008) 'Reading between the lines (of this volume): a reflection on why we should stick to folk concepts of social class', in D. Conley and A. Lareau (eds.) *Social Class: How Does It Work?*, New York: Russell Sage Foundation:366–73.

Conway, E. (2010) 'Poor cows or dangerous beasts: the representation of "underclass" women in broadsheet newspapers', http://www.social-policy.org.uk/lincoln/Conway.pdf. Accessed 10 August 2012.

Coombe, R. (2006/1998) 'Author(iz)ing the celebrity: engendering alternative identities', in P. David Marshall (ed.) *The Celebrity Culture Reader*, Oxon: Routledge:721–69.

Copsey, N. (2007) 'Changing course or changing clothes? Reflections on the ideological evolution of the British National Party 1999–2006', *Patterns of Prejudice*, 41:1:61–82.

Couldry, N. (2010) *Why Voice Matters: Culture and Politics After Neoliberalism*, London: Sage.

Coward, R. (2011) 'Kate Middleton and Charlene Wittstock: a tale of two princesses', in the *Guardian*, 9 July, http://www.guardian.co.uk/uk/2011/jul/09/princess-charlene-kate-fairytale-wedding. Accessed 15 July 2011.

Crosland, R. (2011) 'Jamie's Dream School changed my life', in *G2*, 6 March:2.

Cross, S. and Littler, J. (2010) 'Celebrity and *Schadenfreude*', in *Cultural Studies* Special Issue: The Economic Crisis and After, 24:3:395–417.

Dahrendorf, R. (1987) 'The erosion of citizenship and its consequences for us all', in *New Statesman*, 12 June:13.

Davies, C. (2011) *Jokes and Targets*, Indiana, IN: Indiana University Press.

Davies, J. (1999) '*Princess*: Diana, femininity and the royal', in *New Formations: Diana and Democracy*, 36:141–54.

Dayan, D. and Katz, E. (1992) *Media Events: The Live Broadcasting of History*, Cambridge: Harvard University Press.

Deacon, M. (2011) 'Jamie's Dream School', in the *Telegraph*, 3 March, http://www.telegraph.co.uk/culture/tvandradio/8357418/Jamies-Dream-School-Channel-4-review.html. Accessed 5 March 2011.

De Groot, J. (2009) *Consuming History: Historians and Heritage in Contemporary Popular Culture*, Oxon: Routledge.

Dench, G. (2006) 'Reviewing meritocracy', in G. Dench (ed.) *The Rise and Rise of Meritocracy*, Oxford: Blackwell:1–14.

Deuchar, R. (2007) *Citizenship, Enterprise and Learning: Harmonising Competing Educational Agendas*, Trent: Trentham Books.

Devine, F. (1997) *Social Class in America and Britain*, Edinburgh: Edinburgh University Press.

Devine, F. (2004) *Class Practices: How Parents Help Their Children Get Good Jobs*. Cambridge: Cambridge University Press.

Devine, F., Savage, M., Scott, J., and R. Crompton (eds.) (2005) *Rethinking Class: Cultures, Identities and Lifestyles*, London: Palgrave.

Dhondy, F. (1974) 'The Asian underclass revolts', in *Economic and Political Weekly*, 9:26:1007–9.

Dimbleby, J. (1995) *The Prince of Wales*, London: Little, Brown and Co.

Dodd, K. and Dodd, P. (1992) 'From the east end to east enders: representations of the working class 1890-1990', in D. Strinati and S. Wagg (eds.) *Come on Down: Popular Media in Post-war Britain*, London: Routledge: 116–32.

Doepke, M. and Zilibotti, F. (2005) 'Social class and the spirit of capitalism', in *Journal of the European Economic Association*, 3:2/3:516–24.

Donald, J. (1992) *Sentimental Education: Schooling, Popular Culture and the Regulation of Liberty*, London: Verso.

D'Onofrio, L. and Munk, K. (2003) 'Understanding the stranger: interim case study findings', The Information Centre about Asylum and Refugees in the UK (ICAR), http://www.icar.org.uk/utsinterimreport.pdf. Accessed 12 September 2012.

Dorling, D. (2010) *Injustice: Why Social Inequality Persists*, Bristol: Policy Press.

Doyle, J. and Karl, I. (2010) 'Shame on you: cosmetic surgery and class transformation in *10 Years Younger*,' in G. Palmer (ed.) *Exposing Lifestyle Television*, Aldershot: Ashgate:83–99.

Doyle, W. (2011) *Aristocracy: A Very Short History*, Oxford: Oxford University Press.

Duffett, M. (2011) 'Elvis Presley and Susan Boyle: bodies of controversy', in *Journal of Popular Music Studies*, 23:2:166–89.

Duffy, J. (2005) 'Rank and Bile', 18 January, http://news.bbc.co.uk/1/hi/magazine/4182093.stm. Accessed 7 July 2012.

Duncan, S., Edwards, R., and Song, M. (1999) 'Social threat or social problem? Media representations of lone mothers and policy implications', in B. Franklin (ed.) *Social Policy, the Media and Misrepresentation*, London: Routledge:238–52.

Dunleavy, P. (2005) 'Facing up to multi-party politics: how partisan dealignment and PR voting have fundamentally changed Britain's party systems' [online]. London: LSE Research Online August 2007, http://eprints.lse.ac.uk/2673. Accessed 26 July 2012.

Dyer, R. (2002) *Only Entertainment*, 2nd edition, London: Routledge.

Easton, M. (2011) 'England riots: the return of the underclass', 11 August, http://www.bbc.co.uk/news/uk-14488486. Accessed 14 August 2011.

Eatwell, R. (2004) 'The extreme right in Britain: the long road to "modernization"', in R. Eatwell and C. Mudde (eds.) *Western Democracies and the New Extreme Right Challenge*, London: Routledge:62–79.

Edgell, S. (1993) *Class*, London: Routledge.

Egawhari, E. (2010) 'Autobiographies of the rich and famous', 3 September, http://www.bbc.co.uk/news/magazine-11169914. Accessed 26 October 2011.

Ehrenreich, B. (2009) *Smile or Die: How Positive Thinking Fooled America and the World*, London: Granta.

Eldridge, D. (2006) *Market Boy*, London: Methuen Drama.

Eldridge, D. (2012) *In Basildon*, London: Methuen Drama.

Engel, M. (1996) 'Basildon Bondage', in the *Observer*, 8 December. Accessed through Lexis UK Database.

Engelen, E., Ertürk, I., Froud, J., et al. (2011) *The Great Complacence: Financial Crisis and the Politics of Reform*, Oxford: Oxford University Press.

Essex JSNA (2010) 'Geography and Demographics' at http://www.essexpartnershipportal.org/pages/uploads/JSNA/Demography%20refresh%20chapter%20-%20update%20v1.4.pdf. Accessed 27 February 2012.

Evans, B. (2002) 'Thatcherism and the British people', in S. Ball and I. Holliday (eds.) *Mass Conservatism: The Conservatives and the Public since the 1880s*, London: Frank Cass:218–41.

Evans, E. (1997) *Thatcher and Thatcherism*, London: Routledge.

Evans, G. (1993) 'The decline of class divisions in Britain? Class and ideological preferences in the 1960s and the 1980s', in *The British Journal of Sociology*, 44:3, September:449–71.

Fabian Review (2008) *Grown Up Guide to the Politics of Class*, Fabian Review Summer, http://www.fabians.org.uk/wp-content/uploads/2012/04/FabianReview2008Summer.pdf. Accessed 20 December 2012.

Fairclough, N. (2000) *New Labour, New Language?* London: Routledge.

Fanon, F. (1952/1986) *Black Skin, White Masks*, trans. C.L. Markmann, London: Pluto Press, http://melodypanosian.info/wp-content/uploads/2011/05/Frantz-Fanon-Black-skin-White-masks.pdf. Accessed 4 August 2012.

Fearnley-Whittingstall, J. and Imperial War Museum (2010) *Ministry of Food*, London: Hodder and Stoughton.

Feather, J. and Woodbridge, H. (2007) 'Bestsellers and the British book industry', in *Publishing Research Quarterly*, 23:3:210–23.

Featherstone, M. (1987) 'Lifestyle and consumer culture', in *Theory, Culture and Society*, 4:55–70.

Ferguson, G. (2010) 'The family on reality television: who's shaming who?' in *Television and New Media*, 11:2:87–104.

Field, F. (1989) *Losing Out? The Emergence of Britain's Underclass*, Oxford: Blackwell.

Field, F. (1995) *Making Welfare Work: Reconstructing Welfare for the Millennium*, London: Institute of Community Studies.

Fletcher, R. (2011) 'Little Red Book of Calm sums up Osborne's Budget aim', the *Daily Telegraph*, 23 March:5.

Foster, G. (2005) *Class-Passing: Social Mobility in Film and Popular Culture*, Carbondale, IL: Southern Illinois Press.

Frost, B. (1991) 'Mud-slinging and lager feed the progress of Essex man', in the *Times*, 1 August. Accessed through Lexis UK Database.

Fukuyama, F. (1992) *The End of History and the Last Man*, New York: The Free Press.

Fullerton, R. (1993) 'Choosing to misbehave: a structural model of aberrant consumer behaviour', in *Advances in Consumer Research*, 20:570–74.

Furlong, A. (2007) *Young People and Social Change*, Buckingham: Open University Press.

Gallagher, V. (2010) 'Celeb memoirs "here to stay" ', in the *Bookseller*, 31 January, http://www.thebookseller.com/news/celeb-memoirs-here-stay.html. Accessed 10 August 2012.

Gambles, R. (2010) 'Supernanny parenting and a pedagogical state', in *Citizenship Studies*, 14:6:697–709.

Gans, H. (1995) *The War Against the Poor: The Underclass and Antipoverty Policy*, New York: Basic Books.

Gardner, L. (2011) 'The Passion – review', http://www.guardian.co.uk/stage/2011/apr/24/the-passion-port-talbot-review. Accessed 1 September 2012.

Garner, R. (2011) 'Toby Young: "Free school movement should be all about mavericks like me" ', 7 September in the *Independent*, http://www.independent.co.uk/news/people/profiles/toby-young-free-school-movement-should-be-all-about-mavericks-like-me-2350355.html. Accessed 12 September 2011.

Garnett, M. (2007) *From Anger to Apathy: The British Experience since 1975*, London: Jonathan Cape.

Garratt, P. (2009) 'The case of "Baby P": Opening up spaces for debate', in *Critical Social Policy*, 29:533–47.

Gascoigne, P., McKeown, J., and Davies, H. (2006) *Being Gazza: My Journey to Hell and Back Again*, London: Headline.

Gaunt, J. (2007) *Undaunted: The Shocking True Story Behind the Popular Shock-Jock*, London: Virgin Books.

Gibson, S. (2006) ' "The hotel business is about strangers": border politics and hospitable spaces in Stephen Frears's *Dirty Pretty Things*', in *Third Text*, 20:6, November:693–701.

Giddens, A. (1991) *Modernity and Self-Identity*, Cambridge: Polity Press.

Giddens, A. (1994) *Beyond Left and Right*, Cambridge: Polity Press.

Giddens, A. and Griffiths, S. (2006) 'Poverty social exclusion and welfare', in A. Giddens and S. Griffiths (2006) *Sociology*, 5th edition, Cambridge: Polity Press:338–81.

Gidley, B. and Rook, A. (2010) 'Asdatown the intersections of classed places and identities', in Y. Taylor (ed.) *Classed Intersections: Spaces, Selves, Knowledges*, Aldershot: Ashgate:95–116.

Gilbert, J. (2011) 'Sharing the pain: the emotional politics of austerity', in *Our Kingdom*, 28 January, http://www.opendemocracy.net/ourkingdom/jeremy-gilbert/sharing-pain-emotional-politics-of-austerity. Accessed 29 July 2012.

Giles, J. (2004) *The Parlour and the Suburb: Domestic Identities, Class, Femininity and Modernity*, Oxford: Berg.

Gillies, V. (2005) 'Raising the "meritocracy": parenting and the individualisation of social class', in *Sociology*, 39:835–53.

Gilroy, P. (1987) *There Ain't No Black in the Union Jack: The Cultural Politics of Race and Nation*, 2nd edition 2002, London: Routledge.

Gilroy, P. (2008) 'Melancholia or conviviality: the politics of belonging in Britain', in S. Davison and J. Rutherford (eds.) *Race, Identity and Belonging: A Soundings Collection*, London: Lawrence and Wishart:45–56.

Goddard, A. (2002) 'Essex girl goes for PhD', *THES*, 30 August, http://www.timeshighereducation.co.uk/story.asp?storyCode=171323&sectioncode=26. Accessed 20 October 2011.

Goldthorpe, J. (2003) 'The myth of education-based meritocracy', in *New Economy*, 10:4, December:234–9.

Goldthorpe, J. and Marshall, G. (1992) 'The promising future of class analysis', in *Sociology*, 26:381–400.

Goldthorpe, J. with Llewellyn, C. and Payne, C. (1987) *Social Mobility and Class Structure in Modern Britain*, 2nd edition, Oxford: Clarendon.

Goodhart, D. (2011) 'The riots, the rappers and the Anglo-Jamaican tragedy', in *Prospect*, 17 August, http://www.prospectmagazine.co.uk/magazine/riots-goodhart/. Accessed 20 August 2011.

Gooley, D. (2010) 'From the top: Liszt's aristocratic airs', in E. Berenson and E. Giloi (eds.) *Constructing Charisma: Celebrity, Fame, and Power in Nineteenth-Century Europe*, Oxford: Berghahn Books:69–85.

Gorin, V. and Dubied, A. (2011) 'Desirable people: identifying social values through celebrity news', in *Media, Culture & Society*, 33:4:599–618.

Granter, E. (2009) *Critical Social Theory and the End of Work*, Farnham: Ashgate.

Green, A. (2005) 'It's not racism but pure common sense', *Daily Mail* article republished on Migrant Watch website: http://www.migrationwatchuk.org/pressArticle/48. Accessed 2 August 2012.

Greenwood, W. (1933) *Love on the Dole*, London: Jonathan Cape.

Greer, G. (2001) 'Long live the Essex girl', in the *Guardian*, 5 March:8.

Greer, G. (2006) 'Essex girls: we're the best', in the *Observer*, 5 February:26.

Groves, J. (2011) 'Nick Cleggs attacks sharp-elbowed', 4 April, http://www.dailymail.co.uk/news/article-1373410/Nick-Clegg-attacks-sharp-elbowed-middle-classes-internships.html. Accessed 20 April 2011.

Hall, P. (1992) *Royal Fortune: Tax Money and the Monarchy*, London: Bloomsbury.

Hall, S. (1983) 'The great moving right show', in S. Hall and M. Jacques (eds.) *The Politics of Thatcherism*, London: Lawrence and Wishart:19–39.

Hall, S. (1988) 'Blue election, election blues', in S. Hall *The Hard Road to Renewal Thatcherism and the Crisis of the Left*, London: Verso:259–67.

Hall, S. (1992) 'No new vision, no new votes', in *New Statesman and Society*, 17 April:14–15.

Hall, S. (1997) 'The spectacle of the other', in M. Wetherell, S. Yates, and S. Taylor (eds.) (2001) *Discourse Theory and Practice: A Reader*, London: Sage:324–44.

Hall, S. (1999/2005) 'Whose heritage? Un-settling "The Heritage", re-imagining the past-nation', in J. Littler and R. Naidoo (eds.) *The Politics of Heritage: The Legacy of Race*, London: Routledge:23–35.

Hall, S. and Jefferson, T. (2006, orig. 1975) *Resistance Through Rituals: Youth Subcultures in Postwar Britain*, Revised edition, Oxon: Routledge.

Hall, S., Critcher, C., Jefferson, T., et al. (1978) *Policing the Crisis: Mugging, the State and Law and Order*, London: Macmillan.

Halpern, D. (2005) *Social Capital*, Cambridge: Polity Press.

Hanley, L. (2007) *Estates: An Intimate History*, London: Granta.

Hardman, R. (2007) *Monarchy: The Royal Family at Work*, London: Ebury.

Hartley, J. (1992) *The Politics of Pictures*, London: Routledge.

Harvey, D. (2005) *A Brief History of Neoliberalism*, Oxford: Oxford University Press.

Hasan, R. (2000) 'Riots and urban unrest in Britain in the 1980s and 1990s: a critique of dominant explanations', in M. Lavalette and G. Mooney (eds.) *Class Struggle and Social Welfare*, London: Routledge:173–98.

Hatherley, O. (2009) 'Lash out and cover up: austerity nostalgia and ironic authoritarianism in recession Britain', *Radical Philosophy*, 157, September/October:2–7, http://www.radicalphilosophy.com/commentary/lash-out-and-cover-up. Accessed 22 August 2012.

Hay, C. (2009) 'The winter of discontent 30 years on', in *The Political Quarterly*, 80:4:545–52.

Hay, C. (2010) 'Chronicles of a death foretold: the winter of discontent and construction of the crisis of British Keynesianism', in *Parliamentary Affairs*, 63:3:446–70.

Hayes, D. and Hudson, A. (2001a) *Basildon: Mood of a Nation*, London: Demos.

Hayes, D. and Hudson, A. (2001b) 'Basildon: beyond the shell-suits', 5 April, http://www.spiked-online.com/site/article/11735/. Accessed 1 November 2011.

Hayward, K. and Yar, M. (2006) 'The "chav" phenomenon: consumption, media and construction of a new underclass', in *Crime, Media and Culture*, 2:1: 9–28.

Heffer, S. (1990) 'Maggie's mauler: profile of Essex Man', in the *Sunday Telegraph*, Sunday Comment Section, 7 October:23.

Heffer, S. (2009) 'The people say they'll keep calm and carry on…but for how long?' in the *Daily Telegraph*, 25 February:20.

Hennessy, P. (2012) 'William Hague: David Cameron is the sanest person to lead the Conservative Party in a long time', in the *Telegraph*, 12 May, http://www.telegraph.co.uk/news/politics/william-hague/9262295/William-Hague-David-Cameron-is-the-sanest-person-to-lead-the-Conservative-Party-in-a-long-time.html. Accessed 14 May 2012.

Hewison, R. (1987) *The Heritage Industry: Britain in a Climate of Decline*, London: Methuen.

Higgins, J. (1999) *Raymond Williams: Literature, Marxism and Cultural Materialism*, Oxon: Routledge.

Higham, W. (2009) *The Next Big Thing: Spotting and Forecasting Consumer Trends for Profit*, Philadelphia, PA: Kogan Page.

Higson, A. (2003) *English Heritage, English Cinema: The Costume Drama since 1980*, Oxford: Oxford University Press.

Himmelfarb, G. (1994) 'Will America's shame become Britain's fate?' in the *Sunday Times*, 11 September, Supplement:2.

Hinton, E. and Redclift, M. (2009) 'Austerity and sufficiency: the changing politics of sustainable consumption', Environment, Politics and Development Working Paper Series, Department of Geography, King's College London.

Hobsbawm, E. (1995, orig. 1994) *Age of Extremes: The Short Twentieth Century, 1914–1991*, London: Abacus.

Hodge, R. (2008) 'Holding up a mirror to a classless society', in A. Lareau and D. Conley (eds.) *Social Class: How Does It Work?* New York: Russell Sage Foundation:359–65.

Hoggart, R. (1957/1958) *The Uses of Literacy*, Harmondsworth: Pelican.

Hoggart, R. (1995) *The Way We Live Now*, London: Chatto and Windus.

Holland, P. (1992) *What Is a Child? Popular Images of Childhood*, London: Virago.

Hollows, J. and Jones, S. (2010) 'At least he's doing something: moral entrepreneurship and individual responsibility in Jamie's *Ministry of Food*', in *European Journal of Cultural Studies*, 13:3, August:307–22.

Holmes, S. (2010) 'Dreaming a dream: Susan Boyle and celebrity culture', in *The Velvet Light Trap*, 65:Spring:74–6.

Homans, M. (1998) *Representations: Queen Victoria and British Culture, 1837–1876*, Chicago: Chicago University Press.

Hope, C. (2010) 'Middle classes told to stop using Sure Start', in the *Telegraph*, 11 August, http://www.telegraph.co.uk/news/politics/david-cameron/7937248/Middle-classes-told-to-stop-using-Sure-Start.html. Accessed 7 December 2010.

Horgan-Wallace, A. (2009) *Aisleyne: Surviving Guns, Gangs and Glamour*, London: Mainstream Publishing.

Howker, E. and Malik, S. (2010) *Jilted Generation: How Britain Has Bankrupted Its Youth*, London: Icon Books.

Hunt, T. (2011) 'Monarchy in the UK', in *Public Policy Research*, December/February 17:4:167–74.

Hutton, W. (1996) *The State We're In*, Revised edition, London: Vintage.

Hutton, W. (2011) *Them and Us: Changing Britain – Why We Need a Fairer Society*, London: Little Brown.

ICAR (2005) 'Key issues: public opinion on asylum and refugee issues', June 2005, http://www.icar.org.uk/briefing_attitudes.pdf. Accessed 27 July 2012.

Insight (1990) 'Bloody Britain supplement', in the *Sunday Times*, 8 April: 13–16.

Ivens, S. (2004) 'The mother of all Essex girls', in the *Observer*, Review Section, 3 October. Accessed at Lexis UK Database.

Jacobs, M. (1988) 'Margaret Thatcher and the inner cities', in *Economic and Political Weekly*, 23:38:1942–4.

Jay, A. (1992) *Elizabeth R: The Role of the Monarchy Today*, London: BBC.

Jenkins, S. (2007) 'Thatcher's legacy', in *Political Studies Review*, 5:161–71.

Jones, C. and Novak, T. (1999) *Poverty, Welfare and the Disciplinary State*, London: Routledge.

Jones, O. (2011) *Chavs: The Demonization of the Working Class*, London: Verso.

Joseph, K. (1974) Speech 'Our human stock is threatened', 19 October, http://www.margaretthatcher.org/document/101830. Accessed 7 September 2011.

Joyce, P. (ed.) (1995) *Class*, Oxford: Oxford University Press.

Kaplan, C. (2004) 'The death of the working class hero', in *New Formations*, 52:94–110.

Karl, I. (2007) 'Class observations: "intimate" technologies and the poetics of reality TV', http://www.uta.edu/huma/agger/fastcapitalism/2_2/karl.html. Accessed 14 February 2009.

Katona, K. (2006) *Too Much, Too Young: My Story of Love, Survival and Celebrity*, London: Ebury Press.

Kay, P. (2006) *The Sound of Laughter*, London: Arrow Books.

Kelly, P. and Harrison, L. (2006) ' "Don't be a smart arse": young workers, individualisation and an ethic of enterprise in Jamie's Kitchen' at TASA Conference, 4–7 December, University of Western Australia and Murdoch University. http://www.tasa.org.au/conferences/conferencepapers06/papers/Education, %20Work,%20Stratification%20and%20Class/Kelly.pdf. Accessed 12 July 2012.

Kim, N.-K. (2010) 'Revisiting New Right citizenship discourse in Thatcher's Britain', in *Ethnicities*, 10:2:208–35.

Kinnock, N. (1988) 'Leader's speech, Blackpool', http://www.british political-speech.org/speech-archive.htm?speech=194. Accessed 12 August 2011.

Klein, N. (2011) 'Daylight robbery, meet night time robbery', in the *Nation*, 12 September, http://www.thenation.com/article/162809/daylight-robbery-meet-nighttime-robbery. Accessed 20 June 2012.

Klein, R. (2008) 'White and working class . . . the one ethnic group the BBC has ignored', *Mail online*, 28 February, http://www.dailymail.co.uk/news/article-523351/White-working-class—ethnic-group-BBC-ignored.html#. Accessed 4 August 2012.

Kleinman, M. (1998) *Include Me Out: The New Politics of Place and Poverty*, London: LSE.

Kramer, A.-M. (2011) 'Mediatizing memory: history, affect and identity in *Who Do You Think You Are?*' in *European Journal of Cultural Studies*, 14:4:428–45.

Kurzman, C., Anderson, C., Key, C., Lee, Y., Moloney, M., Silver, A., and Van Ryn, M.W. (2007) 'Celebrity status', in *Sociological Theory*, 25:4:347–67.

Kynaston, D. (2007) *Austerity Britain, 1945–51*, London: Bloomsbury.

Laclau, E. and Mouffe, C. (1985) *Hegemony and Socialist Strategy*, London: Verso.

Lahr, J. (2002) *Show and Tell: New Yorker Profiles*, California: University of California Press.

Lansley, S. (2006) *Rich Britain: The Rise and Rise of the New Super-Wealthy*, London: Politico's.

Lash, S. and Urry, J. (1994) *Economies of Signs and Space*, London: Sage.

Lawler, S. (2005) 'Disgusted subjects: the making of middle class identities', *The Sociological Review*, 53:3:429–46.

Lawler, S. (2008) 'The middle classes and their aristocratic others', in *Journal of Cultural Economy*, 1:3:245–61.

Lawson, M. (2008) 'Read all about me', in the *Guardian*, 18 December, http://www.guardian.co.uk/books/2008/dec/18/bestseller-biography-celebrity. Accessed 12 September 2011.

Lea, J. and Young, J. (1982) 'The riots in Britain 1981: urban violence and political marginalisation', in D. Cowell, T. Jones, and J. Young (eds.) *Policing the Riots*, London: Junction Books:5–20.

Leadbeater, C. (1989) 'Thatcherism and progress', in S. Hall and M Jacques (eds.) *New Times: The Changing Face of Politics in New Times*, London: Lawrence and Wishart:395–411.

Leadbeater, C. (1997) *The Rise of the Social Entrepreneur*, London: Demos.

Lehain, M. (2011) 'For free schools, the real work begins now', in the *Guardian*, 31 August, http://www.guardian.co.uk/commentisfree/2011/aug/31/free-schools. Accessed 2 September 2011.

Levitas, R. (1998) *The Inclusive Society? Social Exclusion and New Labour*, London: Macmillan.

Levy, A. (2010) 'It's hardly Hollywood. Basildon gets its own sign', 30 March, http://www.dailymail.co.uk/news/article-1261756/Its-hardly-Hollywood-Basildon-gets-sign-welcome-drivers-wonders-er-Essex.html. Accessed 10 April 2011.

Lewis, L. (2009) *Dreams*, London: Hodder and Stoughton.

Lewis, O. (1971) 'The culture of poverty', in M. Pilisuk and P. Pilisuk (eds.) *Poor Americans: How the White Poor Live*, New York: Transaction Publishers: 20–6.

Lister, R. (1996) 'In search of the "underclass"', in R. Lister (ed.) *Charles Murray and the Underclass: The Developing Debate*, London: IEA Health and Welfare Unit/the *Sunday Times*:1–13.

Littler, J. (2003) 'Making fame ordinary: intimacy, reflexivity and "keeping it real"', in J. Littler (ed.) *Mediactive: Ideas, Knowledge, Culture, Celebrity Issue 2*, London: Barefoot Publications:8–25.

Littler, J. (2008) '"I feel your pain": cosmopolitan charity and the public fashioning of the celebrity soul', in *Social Semiotics*, 18:2, June:237–51.

Littler, J. and Naidoo, R. (2004) 'White past, multicultural present: heritage and national stories', in H. Brocklehurst and R. Phillips (eds.) *History, Nationhood and the Question of Britain*, Basingstoke: Palgrave:330–41.

Lockyer, S. (2010) 'Dynamics of social class contempt in contemporary British television comedy', in *Social Semiotics*, 20:2:121–38.

Lowenthal, D. (2004) 'The Island Garden: English landscape and British identity', in H. Brocklehurst and R. Phillips (eds.) *History, Nationhood and the Question of Britain*, Basingstoke: Palgrave:137–50.

Lowenthal, L. (2006/1944) 'The triumph of mass idols', in P.D. Marshall (ed.) *The Celebrity Culture Reader*, Oxon: Routledge:124–52.

Lund, B. (2008) 'Major, Blair and the third way in social policy', in *Social Policy and Administration*, 42:1, February:43–58.

MacDonald, K. (2006) 'England: educating for the twenty-first century', in E. Kassem, E. Mufti, and J. Robinson (eds.) *Education Studies: Issues and Critical Perspectives*, Maidenhead: Open University Press:87–98.

Macintyre, B. (2012) 'Keep calm and carry on', in the *Times*, 7 May, http://www.thetimes.co.uk/tto/sport/olympics/article3406767.ece. Accessed 10 May 2012.

Mahoney, P. and Zmroczek, C. (eds.) (1997) *Class Matters: Working Class Women's Perspectives on Social Class*, London: Taylor and Francis.

Malik, S. (2011) 'The generation gap not rap is to blame for the riots', in *Prospect*, 22 August, http://www.prospectmagazine.co.uk/blog/the-generation-gap-not-rap-is-to-blame-for-the-riots/. Accessed 7 September 2011.

Mallory Wober, J. (2001) *Media and Monarchy*, Ann Arbor, MI: University of Michigan/Nova Science Publishers.

Mann, K. and Roseneil, S. (1994) 'Some mothers do 'av 'em: backlash and the gender politics of the underclass debate', in *Journal of Gender Studies*, 3:3: 317–31.

Mann, K. and Roseneil, S. (1996) 'Unpalatable choices and inadequate families: lone mothers and the underclass debate', in E. Silva (ed.) *Good Enough Mothering: Feminist Perspectives on Lone Motherhood*, Abingdon: Routledge:191–210.

Mansell, W. (2011) 'A permanent revolution', in *Phi Delta Kappan*, 92:8, May:91–2.

Marr, A. (2011) *The Diamond Queen: Elizabeth II and Her People*, Basingstoke: MacMillan.

Marshall, G., Roberts, S., and Burgoyne, C. (1996) 'Social class and underclass in Britain and the USA', in *The British Journal of Sociology*, 47:1, March:22–44.

Marshall, P. D. (1997) *Celebrity and Power: Fame in Contemporary Culture*, Minneapolis, MN: University of Minnesota Press.

Martin, N. (2008) 'BBC series "labels white working class racist"', the *Telegraph*, 12 March, http://www.telegraph.co.uk/news/uknews/1581438/BBC-series-labels-white-working-class-racist.html. Accessed 3 August 2012.

May, P. (2010) 'Essex Man: the Bonds of Basildon', in the *Independent*, 6 October, http://www.independent.co.uk/life-style/health-and-families/features/essex-man-the-bonds-of-basildon-2098663.html. Accessed 6 December 2010.

McAuley, R. (2007) *Out of Sight: Crime, Youth and Exclusion in Modern Britain*, Devon: Willan Publishing.

McCabe, C. (2007) 'An interview with Stuart Hall, Dec 2007', in *Critical Quarterly*, 50:12–42.

McCarthy, A. (2007) 'Reality television: a neoliberal theater of suffering', in *Social Text*, 93:25:417–42.

McClintock, A. (1995) *Imperial Leather: Race, Gender, and Sexuality in the Colonial Contest*, London: Routledge.

McCourt, F. (1998) *Angela's Ashes*, New York: Scribner.

McDowell, L. (1997) *Capital Culture: Gender at Work in the City*, Oxford: Blackwell.

McGlone, F. (1990) 'Away from the dependency culture? Social security policy', in S. Savage and L. Robins (eds.) *Public Policy under Thatcher*, Basingstoke: Macmillan Education:159–70.

McGregor, J. (2008) 'Abject spaces, transnational calculations: Zimbabweans in Britain navigating work, class and the law', in *Transactions of the Institute of British Geographers*, 33:4, October:466–82.

McGregor, P. (2011) 'This is what happens when underclass values triumph', in the *Independent Letters*, 12 August, http://www.independent.co.uk/opinion/letters/letters-this-is-what-happens-when-underclass-values-triumph-2336170.html. Accessed 14 August 2011.

McGuigan, J. (1996) *Culture and the Public Sphere*, London: Routledge.

McMurria, J. (2008) 'Desperate citizens and good samaritans: neoliberalism and makeover reality television', in *Television and New Media*, 9:4:305–32.

McRobbie, A. (2004) 'Notes on what not to wear and post-feminist symbolic violence', in *The Sociological Review*, 52:S2:97–109.

McRobbie, A. (2009) *The Aftermath of Feminism: Gender, Culture and Social Change*, London: Sage.

Medhurst, A. (2007) *A National Joke: Popular Comedy and English Cultural Identities*, London: Routledge.

Miles, A. (2011) 'Why Kate Middleton brings out the worst in us', in *The New Statesman*, 6 January, http://www.newstatesman.com/society/2011/01/kate-middleton-family-social. Accessed 25 February 2011.

Milner, A. (1999) *Class*, London: Sage.

Mooney, G. (2009) 'The "broken society" election: class hatred and the politics of poverty and place in Glasgow East', in *Social Policy and Society*, 8:4:437–50.

Moore, A. and Moore, J. (2004) *The Streetwise Investor*, Chichester: Capstone.

Moran, J. (2005) *Reading the Everyday*, Abingdon: Routledge.

Morley, D. (2000) *Home Territories: Media, Mobility and Identity*, London: Routledge.

Morreale, J. (2007) 'Faking it and the transformation of personal identity', in D. Heller (ed.) *Makeover Television: Realities Remodelled*, London: I.B. Tauris:95–106.

Morton, J. (1998) *Prince Charles: Breaking the Cycle*, London: Ebury.

Mulholland, H. (2011) 'Duncan Smith blames riots on family breakdown and benefits system', 3 October, http://www.guardian.co.uk/politics/2011/oct/03/duncan-smith-riots-benefits-system. Accessed 20 August 2012.

Mullard, M. (2004) *The Politics of Globalisation and Polarisation*, Cheltenham: Edward Elgar Publishing.

Munt, S. (2007) *Queer Attachments: The Cultural Politics of Shame*, Burlington, VT: Ashgate.

Murie, A. (2000) 'How can we end inequalities in housing?' in C. Pantazis and D. Gordon (eds.) *Tackling Inequalities: Where Are We Now and What Can Be Done?* Bristol: Policy Press:101–16.

Murray, C. (1984) *Losing Ground*, New York: Basic Books.

Murray, C. (1989) 'The emerging British underclass', in R. Lister (ed.) (1996) *Charles Murray and the Underclass: The Developing Debate*. IEA Health and Welfare Unit/the *Sunday Times*:23–53.

Murray, C. (1992) 'Underclass: from liberal guilt to awkward questions', in the *Sunday Times*, 3 May:1.

Murray, C. (1994a) 'Underclass: the crisis deepens', in the *Sunday Times*, 22 May:10.

Murray, C. (1994b) 'The New Victorians', in the *Sunday Times*, 29 May:12.

Murray, C. (2001) 'Underclass + 10', in ISCS (ed.) *Charles Murray and the British Underclass*, London: *Sunday Times*/ISCS:1–18.

Murray, D. (2012) 'Disliking the Olympics opening ceremony does not make one a Nazi', 30 July, http://blogs.spectator.co.uk/douglas-murray/2012/07/disliking-the-olympics-opening-ceremony-does-not-make-one-a-nazi/. Accessed 16 December 2012.

Murray, J. (2011) 'Is Jamie's Dream School a success?' in the *Guardian*, 7 March, http://www.guardian.co.uk/education/2011/mar/07/jamies-dream-school-teacher-verdicts. Accessed 9 March 2011.

Myrdal, G. (1963) *Challenge to Affluence*, New York: Random House.

Naik, A. (2008) 'Did Jamie Oliver really put school dinners on the agenda? An examination of the role of the media in policy making', in *Political Quarterly*, 79:3:426–33.

Nairn, T. (1988/1994) *The Enchanted Glass: Britain and its Monarchy*, London: Vintage.

Neilan, C. (2010) 'Celebrity memoir still viable, says Hachette head', 6 July, http://www.thebookseller.com/news/celebrity-memoir-still-viable-says-hachette-head.html. Accessed 7 July 2011.

Neill, G. (2011) 'Publishers battle for Townshend and Walliams books', 13 May, http://www.thebookseller.com/news/publishers-battle-townshend-and-walliams-books.html. Accessed 18 May 2011.

Ngai, S. (2005) *Ugly Feelings*, Cambridge, MA: Harvard University Press.

Nichol, M. (1990) 'Shades of blue', in J. Scanlon (ed.) *Surviving the Blues: Growing Up in the Thatcher Decade*, London: Virago:45–54.

Nicolson, N. (2003) *The Queen and Us: The Second Elizabethan Age*, London: Weidenfeld and Nicolson.

Norris, C. (1993) 'Old themes for new times: Basildon revisited', in *The Socialist Register*, 29, http://socialistregister.com/index.php/srv/issue/view/427. Accessed 17 September 2011.

Nunn, H. (1999) 'Violence and the sacred: the iron lady, the princess and the people's PM', in *New Formations: Diana and Democracy*, 36:92–110.

Nunn, H. (2002) *Thatcher, Politics and Fantasy: The Political Culture of Gender and Nation*, London: Lawrence and Wishart.

Nunn, H. (2011) 'Investing in the "forever home": from property programming to "retreat TV"', in H. Wood and B. Skeggs (eds.) *Reality TV and Class*, London: Palgrave/BFI:69–182.

Nunn, H. and Biressi, A. (2009) 'The undeserving poor', *Soundings: A Journal of Politics and Culture*, Recession *Blues*, 41:Winter:107–16.

Nunn, H. and Biressi, A. (2010a) '"A trust betrayed": celebrity and the work of emotion', in *Celebrity Studies*, Spring 1:1:49–64.

Nunn, H. and Biressi, A. (2010b) 'Shameless?: picturing the "underclass" after Thatcherism', in L. Hadley and E. Ho (eds.) *Thatcher and After*, Basingstoke: Palgrave:137–57.

Nunn, H. and Biressi, A. (forthcoming) '"Walking in another's shoes": sentimentality and philanthropy on reality TV', in L. Ouellette (ed.) *A Companion to Reality Television*, Oxford: Blackwell.

Oakland, J. (2001) *Contemporary Britain: A Survey with Texts*, London: Routledge.

O'Connor, A. (2001) *Poverty Knowledge Social Science: Social Policy, and the Poor in Twentieth-Century US History*, Princeton, NJ: Princeton University Press.

O'Flynn, P. (2011) 'Stop moaning and work harder', in the *Express*, 30 November:4.

O'Grady, P. (2008) *At My Mother's Knee ... and Other Low Joints*, London: Bantam Press.

O'Kane, J. (2001) 'Class, liberal pluralism and counterhegemony', in *Cultural Studies*, 15:2:295–325.

Olechnowicz, A. (2007) '"A jealous hatred": royal popularity and social inequality', in A. Olechnowicz (ed.) *The Monarchy and the British Nation, 1780 to the Present*, Cambridge: Cambridge University Press:280–314.

Oring, E. (2003) *Engaging Humour*, Chicago: Illinois University Press.

Osborne, G. (2009) 'We will lead the economy out of crisis', speech on 6 October 2009 at the Conservative Party Conference, http://www.conservatives.com/News/Speeches/2009/10/George_Osborne_We_will_lead_the_economy_out_of_crisis.aspx. Accessed 20 March 2010.

O'Shea, A. (1984) 'Trusting the people: how does Thatcherism work?' in T. Bennett (ed.) *Formations of Nation and People*, London: Routledge and Kegan Paul:19–41.

Ouellette, L. and Hay, J. (2008) *Better Living through Reality TV: Television and Post-Welfare Citizenship*, Oxford: Blackwell.

Pakulski, J. and Waters, M. (1996) *The Death of Class*, London: Sage.

Palmer, G. (2003) *Discipline and Liberty: Television and Governance*, Manchester: Manchester University Press.

Palmer, P. (2007) *All of Me*, London: Hodder and Stoughton.

Parkinson, M. (2008) *Parky: My Autobiography*, London: Hodder and Stoughton.

Parris, M. (2011) 'After a sunny spring, where did Britain get it so wrong?' in the *Times*, 11 August, Lexis UK Database.

Parsons, T. (2001) 'Dashed stupid tactics', in the *Mirror*, 5 February, Features Section:10.

Pascale, C.-M. (2007) *Making Sense of Race, Class, and Gender: Commonsense, Power, and Privilege in the United States*, Oxon: Routledge.

Paton, C. (2000) *World, Class, Britain: Political Economy, Political Theory and British Politics*, Houndmills: Macmillan.

Paton, G. (2010) 'Working class boys let down by 'lack of male role models', 31 March, http://www.telegraph.co.uk/education/educationnews/7538872/Working-class-boys-let-down-by-lack-of-male-role-models.html. Accessed July 2011.

Pelzer, D. (2001) *Child Called It: One Child's Courage to Survive*, London: Orion Books.

Phillips, C. (2009) *My Story: Building beyond Big Brother*, London: Bantam Press.

Philips, D. (2008) 'Noblesse Oblige: lifestyle training and femininity in reality television', at Media, Gender and Representation Symposium, 10 December, WMSN, Brunel University.

Philo, G., Hewitt, J., and Beharrell, P. (1982a) ' "And now they're out again": industrial news', in G. Philo (ed.) *Glasgow Media Group Reader*, Vol. 2, London: Routledge:3–20.

Philo, G., Hewitt, J., and Beharrell, P. (1982b) ' "Reasonable men and responsible citizens": economic news', in G. Philo (ed.) *Glasgow Media Group Reader*, Vol. 2, London: Routledge:21–36.

Pile, S. (2008) 'The duchess of calculation', in the *Telegraph*, 24 May, http://www.telegraph.co.uk/culture/tvandradio/3673643/The-Duchess-of-calculation.html. Accessed 20 July 2010.

Pimlott, B. (1998) 'Monarchy and the message', *Political Quarterly*, 69:B: 91–107.

Porter, A. (2011) 'UK riots: Michael Give pledges to tackle the underclass', 2 September, http://www.telegraph.co.uk/news/politics/8736640/UK-riots-Michael-Gove-pledges-to-tackle-underclass.html. Accessed 7 September 2011.

Poulter, S. (2011) 'Alive and well the stiff upper lip', in the *Daily Mail*, 8 April, http://www.dailymail.co.uk/news/article-1374696/Alive-stiff-upper-lip–just-British-personality-types.html. Accessed 10 April 2011.

Povinelli, E. (2011) *Economies of Abandonment: Social Belonging and Endurance in Late Liberalism*, Durham: Duke University Press.

Prasad, Y. (2008) 'BBC's White Season is founded on racist lies', in *Socialist Worker online*, http://www.socialistworker.co.uk/art.php?id=14303. Accessed 4 August 2012.

Preston, J. (2006) 'Ghost stories', in the *Telegraph*, 3 September, http://www.telegraph.co.uk/culture/3655062/Ghost-stories.html. Accessed 22 November 2011.

Price, K. (2004) *Being Jordan: My Autobiography*, London: Blake Publishing.

Price, K. (2010) *You Only Live Once*, London: Arrow Books.

Prideux, S. (2010) 'The welfare politics of Charles Murray are alive and well in the UK', in *International Journal of Social Welfare*, 19:293–302.

Prochaska, F. (1995) *Royal Bounty*, New Haven, CT: Yale University Press.

Putnam, R. (1995) 'Tuning in, turning out: the strange disappearance of social capital in America', in *Political Science and Politics*, 28:4:664–83.

Putnam, R. (2000) *Bowling Alone: The Collapse and Revival of American Community*, New York: Simon and Schuster.

Quinn, B. (2011) 'Shock as Starkey claims: the whites have become black', in the *Guardian*, 13 August, front page.

Ramsaran, C. (1990) 'So who's next in the firing line?' in J. Scanlon (ed.) *Surviving the Blues: Growing Up in the Thatcher Decade*, London: Virago:172–83.

Rayner, C. (2003) *How Did I Get Here from There?* London: Virago.

Reay, D. (1998) *Class Work: Mothers' Involvement in Their Children's Primary Schooling*, London: Taylor and Francis.

Reay, D. (2008) 'Tony Blair, the promotion of the "active" educational citizen, and middle class hegemony', in *Oxford Review of Education*, 34:6:638–50.

Redmond, S. and Holmes, S. (2007) 'Introduction: producing fame', in S. Redmond and S. Holmes (eds.) *Stardom and Celebrity: A Reader*, London: Sage:189–92.

Rees, J. (2003) 'Stars whose stories sell', in the *Telegraph*, 28 December, http://www.telegraph.co.uk/culture/books/3609153/Stars-whose-stories-sell.html. Accessed 17 August 2011.

Reitan, E. (2003) *The Thatcher Revolution*, London: Rowman and Littlefield.

Rhodes, C. and Westwood, R. (2008) *Critical Representations of Work and Organization in Popular Culture*, London: Routledge.

Rhodes, J. (2009) 'The Banal National Party: the routine nature of legitimacy', *Patterns of Prejudice*, 43:2:142–60.

Richie, S. and Crawford, S. (2003) *From Rags to Richie: The Story So Far*, London: Contender Books.

Ridell, M. (2011) 'London riots: the underclass lashes out', in the *Telegraph*, 8 August, http://www.telegraph.co.uk/news/uknews/law-and-order/8630533/Riots-the-underclass-lashes-out.html. Accessed 9 August 2011.

Roberts, K. (2011) *Class in Contemporary Britain*, 2nd edition, Basingstoke: Palgrave.

Rojek, C. (2001) *Celebrity*, London: Reaktion Books.

Rose, N. (1989) *Governing the Soul: The Shaping of the Private Self*, London: Routledge.

Rosen, A. (2003) *The Transformation of British Life 1950–2000: A Social History*, Manchester: Manchester University Press.

Rosenthal, A. (1972) '*Royal Family*: Richard Cawston', in A. Rosenthal (ed.) *The New Documentary in Action*, California: University of California Press:199–214.

Rowbotham, S. and Beynon, H. (2001) 'Handing on histories', in S. Rowbotham and H. Beynon (eds.) *Looking at Class: Film, Television and the Working Class in Britain*, London: Rivers Oram Press:2–24.

Rowbottom, A. (2002) 'Subject positions and "real royalists": monarchy and vernacular civil religion in Great Britain', in N. Rapport (ed.) *British Subjects: An Anthropology of Britain*, Oxford: Berg:32–47.

Rowling, J.K. (1997), *Harry Potter and the Philosopher's Stone*, London: Bloomsbury.

Rutherford, J. (2005) 'Ghosts: heritage and the shape of things to come', in J. Littler and R. Naidoo (eds.) *The Politics of Heritage: The Legacy of Race*, London: Routledge:82–93.

Salecl, R. (2010) *Choice*, London: Profile Books.

Sanghera, S. (2008) *If You Don't Know Me By Now*, London: Viking.

Särlvik, B. and Crewe, I. (1983) *Decade of Dealignment: The Conservative Victory of 1979 and Electoral Trends in the 1970s*, Cambridge: Cambridge University Press.

Saunders, P. (1990) *Social Class and Stratification*, London: Routledge.

Saunders, P. (1995) 'Might Britain be a meritocracy?' in *Sociology*, 29:1:23–41.

Saunders, P. (1997) 'Social mobility in Britain: an empirical evaluation of two competing explanations', in *Sociology*, 31:2:261–88.

Savage, M. (2000) *Class Analysis and Social Transformation*, Buckingham: Open University Press.

Savage, M., Barlow, J., Dickens, P., and Fielding, T. (1992) *Property, Bureaucracy and Culture*, London: Routledge.

Sayer, A. (2005) *The Moral Significance of Class*, Cambridge: Cambridge University Press.

Scheiner, G. (2003) 'Would you like to be Queen for a day?: finding a working class voice in American television of the 1950s', in *Historical Journal of Film, Radio and Television* 23:4:375–86.

Schumpeter, J. (2012, orig. 1942) *Capitalism, Socialism and Democracy*, London: Routledge.

Schwarz, B. (2011) *The White Man's World*, Oxford: Oxford University Press.

Shirley, J. (1981) 'Brixton: how a minicab check turned into a riot', in the *Sunday Times*, 12 April:2.

Silverstone, R. (1999) *Why Study the Media?* London: Sage.

Silverstone, R. (2007) *Media and Morality: On the Rise of the Mediapolis*, Cambridge: Polity Press.

Skeggs, B. (1997) *Formations of Class and Gender: Becoming Respectable*, London: Sage.

Skeggs, B. (2004) 'The re-branding of class: propertising culture', in F. Devine, M. Savage, J. Scott, and R. Crompton (eds.) *Rethinking Class: Cultures, Identities and Lifestyles*, London: Palgrave:46–68.

Skeggs, B. (2005) 'The making of class and gender through visualizing moral subject formation' in *Sociology*, 39:5:965–82.

Slack, J. (2006) 'Talking about immigration is not racist', *Mail online*, 6 August 2006, http://www.dailymail.co.uk/news/article-399334/Reid-Talking-immigration-racist.html. Accessed 2 August 2012.

Smith, A.M. (1994) *New Right Discourse on Race and Sexuality: Britain 1968–1990*, Cambridge: Cambridge University Press.

Smith, A.M. (1998) *Laclau and Mouffe: The Radical Democratic Imaginary*, London: Routledge.

Smith, L. (2006) *Uses of Heritage*, Oxon: Routledge.

Smith, L. (2009) 'Deference and humility: the social values of the country house', in L. Gibson and J. Pendlebury (eds.) *Valuing Historic Environments*, London: Ashgate:33–50.

Smith, R. (2010) 'Masculinity, doxa and institutionalisation of entrepreneurial identity in the novel *Cityboy*', at OpenAIR@rgu.[online] http://openair.rgu.ac.uk. Accessed 28 August 2012.

Solomon, S. (2011) *My Story So Far*, London: Michael Joseph.

Solomos, J. (2003) *Race and Racism in Britain*, 3rd edition, London: Palgrave.

Spanier, G. (2011) 'London's powerful come to our party', in *London Evening Standard*:3.

Spencer, C. (2010) 'Perfect manors: enemies of the state', in *Vanity Fair*, January, http://www.vanityfair.com/style/features/2010/01/english-aristocracy-201001. Accessed 7 August 2011.

Standing, G. (2011a) 'Who will be a voice for the emerging precariat?' in the *Guardian* 1 June, http://www.guardian.co.uk/commentisfree/2011/jun/01/voice-for-emerging-precariat. Accessed 1 September 2012.

Standing, G. (2011b) *The Precariat: The New Dangerous Class*, London: Bloomsbury Academic.

Steedman, C. (1986) *Landscape for a Good Woman*, London: Virago.

Steel, D. (1985) 'Leader's speech at Dundee', http://www.britishpoliticalspeech .org/speech-archive.htm?speech=47. Accessed 7 August 2012.

Steele, T. (2006) *Bermondsey Boy*, London: Michael Joseph.

Stephenson, D. (2011) 'School is not a dream', in *Sunday Express*, 6 March, http://www.express.co.uk/posts/view/232899/Jamie-s-Dream-school-is-not-a-dream. Accessed 9 March 2011.

Stephenson, P. (2001) *Billy*, London: HarperCollins.

Sternheimer, K. (2011) *Celebrity Culture and the American Dream*, London: Routledge.

Stevenson, N. (2010) 'Education, neoliberalism and cultural citizenship: living in X Factor Britain', *European Journal of Cultural Studies*, 13:3:341–58.

Stewart, K. (2007) *Ordinary Affects*, Durham: Duke University Press.

Stewart, S. (2010) *Culture and the Middle Classes*, Farnham: Ashgate.

Sutherland, J. (2002) *Reading the Decades: Fifty Years of the Nation's Bestselling Books*, London: BBC.

Taylor, C. (2012) 'How we can turn the underclass round', in the *Telegraph*, 7 March, http://www.telegraph.co.uk/education/9128779/How-we-can-turn-the-underclass-around.html. Accessed 8 March 2012.

Taylor-Gooby, P. (1988) 'The future of the British welfare state: public attitudes, citizenship, welfare and social policy under the Conservative governments of the 1980s', in *European Sociological Review*, 4:1:1–19.

Temple, M. (2006) 'Dumbing down is good for you', in *British Politics*, 1:257–73.

Thatcher, M. (1975) 'Let the children grow tall', in A. Cooke (ed.) *Margaret Thatcher: The Revival of Britain Speeches on Home and European Affairs 1975–1988*, London: Aurum Press:1–17.

Thatcher, M. (1992) 'Don't undo my work', in *Newsweek*, 27 April, http://www .margaretthatcher.org/document/111359. Accessed 12 April 2009.

Thatcher, M. (1995) *The Path to Power*, London: HarperCollins.

Thomas, D. (2007) 'So who is the most POINTLESS celebrity?' in the *Daily Mail*, 15 November, http://www.dailymail.co.uk/tvshowbiz/article-494372/So-POINTLESS-celebrity.html. Accessed 13 October 2011.

Thomas, J. (2007) ' "Bound in by history": the Winter of Discontent in British Politics, 1979-2004', in *Media, Culture and Society*, 29:263–83.

Thompson, E.P. (1981, orig. 1970) 'Sir, writing by candlelight', in S. Cohen and J. Young (eds.) *The Manufacture of News: Social Problems, Deviance and the Mass Media*, Revised edition, London: Constable:280–87.

Thomson, A. (2011) 'We've disabled a generation through kindness', in the *Times*, 2 March, Lexis UK Database.

Tomlinson, M. (1998) 'Lifestyle and social classes', CRIC Discussion paper no. 9, Manchester: Centre for Research on Innovation and Competition/University Manchester.

Tomlinson, S. (2005) *Education in a Post Welfare Society*, Berkshire: McGraw-Hill Education.

Tomlinson, S. (2008) 'Gifted, talented and high ability: selection for education in a one-dimensional world', *Oxford Review of Education*, 34:1, February: 59–74.

Townsend, P. (1979) *Poverty in the United Kingdom: A Survey of Household Resources and Standards of Living*, Harmondsworth: Penguin.

Tucker, I. (2011) 'Can Jamie Oliver revolutionise the nation's schools?' in the *Observer*, 13 February, http://www.guardian.co.uk/lifeandstyle/2011/feb/13/jamie-oliver-dream-school-interview. Accessed 15 February 2011.

Turner, G. (2004) *Understanding Celebrity*, London: Sage.

Tyler, I. (2006) ' "Welcome to Britain" ': the cultural politics of asylum', in *European Journal of Cultural Studies*, 9:2, May:185–202.

Tyler, I. (2008) ' "Chav Mum, Chav Scum": class disgust in contemporary Britain', in *Feminist Media Studies*, 8:1:17–34.

Tyler, I. and Bennett, B. (2010) ' "Celebrity Chav": fame, femininity and social class', in *European Journal of Cultural Studies*, 13:3:375–93.

Unite Against Fascism (2006) 'Rally against the BNP in Barking and Dagenham', 28 November, http://uaf.org.uk/2006/11/rally-against-the-bnp-in-barking-and-dagenham/. Accessed 26 July 2012.

Urry, J. (1995) 'A middle-class countryside?' in T. Butler and M. Savage (eds.) *Change and the Middle Classes*, London: Routledge:205–19.

Van Outen, D. (2010) 'Why my Basildon beats Hollywood', in the *Sun*, 31 March, http://www.thesun.co.uk/sol/homepage/features/2914277/Denise-Van-Outen-Why-my-Basildon-beats-Hollywood.html. Accessed 7 September 2011.

Vasey, R. [aka Roy 'Chubby' Brown] (2006) *Common as Muck! Roy 'Chubby' Brown My Autobiography*, GB: Time Warner Books.

Wacquant, L. (2008) *Urban Outcasts: A Comparative Sociology of Advanced Marginality*, Cambridge: Polity Press.

Walker, A. and Walker, C. (1997) *Britain Divided: The Growth of Social Exclusion in the 1980s and 1990s*, London: CPAG.

Walters, J. (2008) *That's Another Story*, London: Weidenfeld.

Ward, P. (2004) *Britishness Since 1870*, London: Routledge.

Webber, R. (1993) 'The 1992 General election: constituency results and local patterns of national newspaper readership', in *British Election and Parties Yearbook*, 3:1:205–15.

Welshman, J. (2006) *Underclass: A History of the Excluded, 1880–2000*, London: Hambledon Continuum.

Wiggan, J. (2012) 'Telling stories of 21st century welfare: the UK Coalition government and the neoliberal discourse of worklessness and dependency', in *Critical Social Policy*, 32:3:383–405.

Wilkes, D. (2007) 'Mother buys school to give her son a proper education', in the *Daily Mail*, 28 January, http://www.dailymail.co.uk/news/article-432085/Mother-buys-school-son-proper-education.html#. Accessed 8 June 2011.

Wilkins, W. (2010) 'School choice, social class and distinction: The realization of social advantage in education', *Journal of Education Policy*, 11:89–112.

Wilkinson, R. and Pickett, K. (2009) *The Spirit Level: Why Equality Is Better for Everyone*, London: Allen Lane.

Willetts, D. (2010) *The Pinch: How the Baby Boomers Took Their Children's Future*, London: Atlantic Books.

Williams, R. (1958) *Culture and Society*, London: The Hogarth Press.

Williams, R. (1961) *The Long Revolution*, London: Chatto.

Williams, R. (1977) *Marxism and Literature*, Oxford: Oxford University Press.

Williams, R. (1983) *Keywords: A Vocabulary of Culture and Society*, Revised edition, London: Fontana Press.

Williams, S. (2011) 'The kids have done alright: The teachers in *Jamie's Dream School* have had their say, but what do the teenagers who took part make of it?' in the *Sunday Telegraph*, 6 March:23.

Williams, Z. (2011) 'The UK Riots: the psychology of looting', in the *Guardian*, 9 August, http://www.guardian.co.uk/commentisfree/2011/aug/09/uk-riots-psychology-of-looting. Accessed 10 August 2011.

Williamson, J. (1986) *Consuming Passions the Dynamics of Popular Culture*, London: Marion Boyars.

Willis, P. (1977) *Learning to Labour: How Working Class Kids Get Working Class Jobs*, Farnborough: Saxon House.

Willis, P. (1990) *Common Culture: Symbolic Work at Play in the Everyday Cultures of the Young*, Milton Keynes: Open University Press.

Wilson, G. (2011) 'I predict a rioter', in the *Sun*, 25 October, http://www.thesun.co.uk/sol/homepage/news/politics/3891972/August-riot-yobs-and-thugs-revealed.html. Accessed 27 October 2011.

Wood, H. and Skeggs, B. (2010) 'Reacting to reality TV: the affective economy of an "extended social/public realm" ', in M. Kraidy and K. Sender (eds.) *The Politics of Reality Television: Global Perspectives*, London: Routledge: 93–112.

Woodburn, K. (2006) *Unbeaten: The Story of My Brutal Childhood*, London: Hodder and Stoughton.

Woods, M. (2004) 'Politics and protest in the contemporary countryside', in L. Holloway and M. Kneafsey (eds.) *Geographies of Rural Cultures and Societies*, Aldershot: Ashgate:103–25.

Worsley, G. (2005) 'Beyond the powerhouse: understanding the country house in the twenty-first century', in *Historical Research*, 78:201:423–35.

Wright, P. (1985) *On Living in an Old Country*, London: Verso.

Wynne, D. (1998) *Leisure, Lifestyle and the New Middle Class: A Case Study*, London: Routledge.

York, P. and Stewart-Liberty, O. (2007) *Cooler, Faster, More Expensive: The Return of the Sloane Ranger*, London: Atlantic Books.

Young, A. (1996) *Imagining Crime: Textual Outlaws and Criminal Conversations*, London: Sage.

Young, H. (1989/1990) *One of Us*, Revised edition, London: Pan Books.

Young, J. (1999) *The Exclusive Society: Social Exclusion, Crime and Difference in Late Modernity*, London: Sage.

Young, J. (2007) *The Vertigo of Late Modernity*, London: Sage.

Young, M. (1958) *Rise of the Meritocracy; 1870-2033*, Harmondsworth: Pelican.

Young, T. (2009) 'Why I will set up a new school to give my children the best chance in life', in the *Observer*, 23 August, http://www.guardian.co.uk/education/2009/aug/23/toby-young-grammar-school-michael-gove. Accessed 7 October 2011.

Young, T. (2011) 'Free schools – now the real hard work begins', in the *Telegraph*, 29 August, http://www.telegraph.co.uk/education/8729326/Free-schools-now-the-really-hard-work-begins.html. Accessed 7 October 2011.

Zaloom, C. (2006) *Out of the Pits: Traders and Technology from Chicago to London*, Chicago: University of Chicago Press.

Author Index

Aaronovitch, D., 152–3
Abbott, D., 148
Abercrombie, N., 118, 122, 126
Adkins, L., 16
Adonis, A., 122
Agamben, G., 68
Ahmed, S., 16, 154, 162, 207
Ai, W. W., 194
Alberoni, F., 100
Allen, K., 107
Anderson, P., 119, 123, 124
Anthony, A., 70, 75
Armstrong, S., 79
Auletta, K., 53–4

Babcock, B., 51
Bagguley, P., 54, 57, 202
Balibar, E., 143
Ball, S., 77, 203
Barker, P., 26, 87
Barkham, P., 107
Barnett, A., 134
Barr, A., 3, 120
Barry, E., 69
Bastin, G., 132
Batmanghelidjh, C., 46, 120
Bauman, Z., 17–18, 44, 50, 63–5, 101
Beaven, D., 26
Beck, J., 203
Beck, U., 14, 63, 78
Becker, R., 73
Beckett, A., 175
Bell, C., 103
Bell, E., 108
Bennett, B., 102, 105
Bennett, P., 115
Bennett, T., 16
Benson, R., 79
Best, G., 107
Beynon, H., 13
Bidinger, E., 97
Billig, M., 121

Biressi, A., 5, 59, 65, 84, 98, 141, 200, 202
Blain, N., 119, 123, 131, 205
Blair, T., 27, 60–2, 75, 81, 87, 119, 144–6, 175, 181, 203
Bloom, C., 50
Bonner, F., 136
Bonnett, A., 181
Boorstin, D., 97, 100–3
Bourdieu, P., 15–17, 85
Bourne, T. J., 134
Bourne, J. M., 124
Boyle, D., 192, 194
Boyle, S., 109–11, 114
Brake, M., 55–6
Bramall, R., 189–91, 195
Bridge, M., 185
Bridges, L., 44, 65
Brogan, B., 186
Bromley, R., 95, 112–13
Brooker, C., 71
Brunt, R., 7
Bryan, B., 6
Buckingham, A., 52
Burns, K., 135, 162
Bury, L., 108
Byrne, D., 61–2

Cahill, K., 126
Campbell, B., 5–7, 16, 59, 75, 174
Cannadine, D., 124, 129
Canoville, P., 108
Carvel, J., 145
Cassidy, M. F., 137
Charlesworth, D., 74
Charteris-Black, J., 146
Chester, L., 202
Church Gibson, P., 134–5
Clarke, J., 183
Clarke, P., 8
Clarke, S., 150, 160
Cockburn, C., 6

Cohen, S., 172
Collins, A., 156, 159
Collins, S., 204
Conley, D., 17
Conway, E., 60
Coombe, R., 203
Copsey, N., 144
Couldry, N., 12, 142, 157–8, 167
Coward, R., 134
Crawford, S., 108
Crewe, I., 25
Crosland, R., 71

Dahrendorf, R., 54
Davies, C., 39
Davies, H., 204
Davies, J., 123
Dayan, D., 205
De Groot, J., 111–13, 193
Deacon, M., 75
Dench, G., 88
Deuchar, R., 203
Devine, F., 15, 16, 83
Dodd, K., 97
Dodd, P., 97
Doepke, M., 124
Donald, J., 73
D'Onofrio, L., 149
Dorling, D., 19
Doyle, J., 213
Doyle, W., 124
Dubied, A., 204
Duffett, M., 110
Duffy, J., 152
Duncan, S., 59
Dunleavy, P., 144
Dyer, R., 204

Easton, M., 45
Eatwell, R., 144
Edgell, S., 52
Egawhari, E., 111, 204
Ehrenreich, B., 115
Eldridge, D., 200–1
Engel, M., 30, 40
Engelen, E., 11
Evans, B., 25, 32
Evans, E., 36
Evans, G., 29

Fairclough, N., 62
Fanon, F., 162
Fearnley-Whittingstall, J., 184
Feather, J., 106
Featherstone, M., 63
Ferguson, G., 84, 141, 200
Field, F., 202
Fletcher, R., 186
Foster, G., 102
Frost, B., 32
Fukuyama, F., 14
Fullerton, R., 202
Furlong, A., 77

Gallagher, V., 204
Gambles, R., 84
Gans, H., 54
Gardner, L., 207
Garner, R., 91
Garner, S., 150, 160
Garnett, M., 34, 176
Garratt, P., 202
Gascoigne, P., 108
Gaunt, J., 115–16
Gibson, S., 170, 206
Giddens, A., 5, 14, 63, 78, 129
Gidley, B., 49
Gilbert, J., 187
Giles, J., 126, 186
Gillies, V., 78–9
Gilmour, R., 150
Gilroy, P., 55, 167
Goddard, A., 201
Goldthorpe, J., 15, 203
Goodhart, D., 48
Gooley, D., 134
Gorin, V., 204
Granter, E., 98
Green, A., 147
Greer, G., 39, 41
Griffiths, S., 5
Groves, J., 203

Hale, C., 55–6
Hall, P., 23, 129
Hall, S., 7, 9, 13, 27–8, 49, 52, 54–5, 57, 127, 130, 200
Halpern, D., 85–6
Hanley, L., 8–9

Harrison, L., 77
Hartley, J., 205
Harvey, D., 1, 4–5, 11–12, 25, 63, 119
Hasan, R., 59
Hatherley, O., 186
Hay, C., 176
Hay, J., 72–3, 84, 176
Hayes, D., 23, 26, 28–9, 37
Hayward, K., 65
Heffer, S., 30–1, 186, 200
Hennessy, P., 183–4
Higgins, J., 17
Higham, W., 146
Higson, A., 125
Himmelfarb, G., 202
Hinton, E., 184, 188–9
Hobsbawm, E., 56–7, 63
Hodge, R., 93
Hoggart, R., 97, 108–9, 132, 164
Holland, P., 55
Hollows, J., 70–1
Holmes, S., 102, 110
Homans, M., 133
Hope, C., 79
Howker, E., 19
Hudson, A., 23, 26, 28–9, 37
Hunt, T., 129, 131, 133, 194
Hussain, Y., 202
Hutton, W., 10, 19

Ivens, S., 39–40

Jacobs, M., 55
Jefferson, T., 55
Jenkins, S., 36
Jones, C., 60, 62
Jones, O., 19, 104
Jones, S., 70–1
Joseph, K., 52
Joyce, P., 12–14, 29, 174–5

Kaplan, C., 74
Karl, I., 102, 135, 200
Katz, E., 204–5
Kay, P., 107
Kelly, P., 77
Kim, N.-K., 56
Kinnock, N., 36, 57, 181–2

Klein, N., 46
Klein, R., 161
Kleinman, M., 61
Kramer, A.-M., 113
Kurzman, C., 100, 112
Kynaston, D., 187

Laclau, E., 13, 190
Lahr, J., 134
Lansley, S., 122, 126
Lash, S., 63
Lawler, S., 16, 38, 132
Lawson, M., 106
Lea, J., 55
Leadbeater, C., 27–8, 85–6
Lee, Y., 193
Lehain, M., 90
Levitas, R., 62
Levy, A., 40
Lewis, L., 110
Lewis, O., 62
Lister, R., 54
Littler, J., 102–3, 125
Lockyer, S., 34
Lowenthal, D., 128
Lowenthal, L., 97–9
Lund, B., 62

MacDonald, K., 80
Macintyre, B., 187
Mahoney, P., 15
Malik, S., 19, 48
Mallory Wober, J., 205
Mann, K., 54, 57, 59–60
Mansell, W., 88
Marr, A., 130, 181
Marshall, P. D., 15, 52, 57, 98–9
Marshall, G., 15, 52, 57
Martin, N., 163
May, P., 31, 33
McAuley, R., 60, 62–4
McCabe, C., 13
McCarthy, A., 73
McClintock, A., 49
McCourt, F., 107
McDowell, L., 3, 5, 11
McGlone, F., 5
McGregor, J., 206
McGregor, P., 48

McGuigan, J., 125
McMurria, J., 73
McRobbie, A., 16, 135–6
Miles, A., 134
Milner, A., 122
Mooney, G., 64
Moore, A., 35
Moore, J., 35
Morley, D., 159
Morreale, J., 139
Morton, J., 130
Mouffe, C., 13, 190
Mulholland, H., 46
Mullard, M., 134
Munk, K., 149
Munt, S., 16–17
Murie, A., 62
Murray, C., 58, 60–1, 64, 202
Murray, D., 194
Murray, J., 71
Myrdal, G., 53

Naidoo, R., 121, 125
Naik, A., 70
Nairn, T., 129
Neilan, C., 204
Neill, G., 204
Newman, J., 183
Ngai, S., 16, 47
Nichol, M., 9
Nicolson, N., 130
Norris, C., 27
Novak, T., 60, 62
Nunn, H., 3, 5, 7, 56, 59, 65, 84, 98,
    123, 141, 159, 200, 202

Oakland, J., 122
O'Connor, A., 53
O'Donnell, H., 119, 123, 205
O'Flynn, P., 178
O'Grady, P., 19, 107, 111
O'Kane, J., 13
Olechnowicz, A., 129–30, 133
Oring, E., 39
Osborne, G., 170, 178, 183, 186, 195,
    197
O'Shea, A., 7
Ouellette, L., 72–3, 84

Pakulski, J., 13–15, 63
Palmer, G., 115, 200
Palmer, P., 115
Parkinson, M., 107
Parris, M., 49–50
Parsons, T., 26
Pascale, C.-M., 17
Paton, C., 175
Paton, G., 104
Pelzer, D., 107
Pemberton, H., 176
Philips, D., 138
Phillips, C., 115
Philo, G., 175
Pickett, K., 19
Pile, S., 140–1
Pimlott, B., 132
Pollard, S., 122
Porter, A., 45
Poulter, S., 185
Povinelli, E., 149
Prasad, Y., 162
Preston, J., 204
Price, K., 72
Prideux, S., 202
Prochaska, F., 131
Putnam, R., 85–6

Quinn, B., 48

Ramsaran, C., 6
Rayner, C., 114
Reay, D., 15, 81
Redclift, M., 184, 188, 189
Redmond, S., 5, 102
Rees, J., 107
Reitan, E., 5
Rhodes, C., 125
Rhodes, J., 207
Richie, S., 108–9
Ridell, M., 45
Roberts, K., 119, 122
Rojek, C., 33, 95, 101–2, 106
Rook, A., 49
Rosen, A., 118, 132
Roseneil, S., 59–60
Rosenthal, A., 132
Rowbotham, S., 13
Rowbottom, A., 129

Rowling, J. K., 193
Rutherford, J., 124

Salecl, R., 92–3, 99
Sanghera, S., 19
Särlvik, B., 25
Saunders, P., 15, 203
Savage, M., 8–9, 13, 15
Sayer, A., 16, 207
Scheiner, G., 137
Schumpeter, J., 28
Schwarz, B., 143
Shirley, J., 55, 57
Silverstone, R., 142, 159, 168–9
Skeggs, B., 15–16, 24, 37, 41, 200, 205
Slack, J., 147–8
Smith, A. M., 6, 13
Smith, L., 127
Smith, R., 35
Solomon, S., 105, 115
Solomos, J., 55
Spanier, G., 120
Spencer, Earl C., 126–7, 135
Standing, G., 11, 47, 67–8, 142
Steedman, C., 7, 16
Steel, D., 56, 112, 187
Steele, T., 112
Stephenson, D., 84
Stephenson, P., 107
Sternheimer, K., 94, 99–100
Stevenson, N., 74
Stewart, K., 159
Stewart, S., 127–8
Stewart-Liberty, O., 120
Sutherland, J., 106–7, 204

Taylor, B., 134
Taylor, C., 48
Taylor-Gooby, P., 5
Temple, M., 151
Thatcher, M., 5, 6–8, 9, 10, 25, 33, 35, 36, 39, 52, 55, 56, 57, 77, 175, 202, 207
Thomas, D., 102
Thomas, J., 175–6
Thompson, E. P., 172–4
Thomson, A., 75–6
Tomlinson, M., 63, 77–8
Tomlinson, S., 87, 203

Townsend, P., 53
Tucker, I., 70, 76
Turner, G., 95–6
Tyler, I., 24, 102, 105, 200, 206

Urry, J., 63, 127

Van Outen, D., 38, 40
Vasey, R., 19, 112, 116–17

Wacquant, L., 54, 67, 85
Walker, A., 61
Walker, C., 61
Walters, S., 107
Ward, P., 121
Waters, M., 13, 15, 63
Webber, R., 34
Welshman, J., 49, 53–4, 61
Wiggan, J., 64
Wilkes, D., 89
Wilkins, W., 203
Wilkinson, R., 19
Willetts, D., 9, 19, 133
Williams, R., 17, 54
Williams, S., 57, 71
Williams, Z., 47
Williamson, J., 131, 205
Willis, P., 204
Wilson, G., 46
Wood, H., 65, 67, 200, 205
Woodbridge, H., 106
Woodburn, K., 108
Woods, M., 128
Worsley, G., 126
Wright, P., 128, 187, 191, 193, 195
Wynne, D., 16

Yar, M., 65
York, P., 120
Young, A., 59
Young, H., 56
Young, J., 15, 55, 63–4, 202
Young, M., 86–8
Young, T., 90

Zaloom, C., 35
Zilibotti, F., 124
Zmroczek, C., 15

Subject Index

achieved celebrities, 106
affluence, 1, 2, 10, 57, 180
All in the Best Possible Taste, 18
All Roads Lead Home, 113
All White in Barking, 160–9
  home, theme of, 163
  hospitality in, 163, 166–7
  social realism in, 164–5
Althorp family, 127, 135
American Dream, 94, 99
American Idol, 92
Angela's Ashes, 107
Anti-Poverty Unit, 60
Any Dream Will Do, 100
Are You Thinking What We're Thinking?,
  145
aristocracy
  business of, 124–8
  of celebrity, 123, 134–5
  class-based deference for, 118
  decline of, 125
  land ownership and, 126
  national heritage and, 127, 198
  resurgence and refashioning of,
    120–1
  of talent, 134
  typecasting of, 124–5
  of wealth, 134
Aristocracy Business, The, 125–6
ascribed celebrities, 106
aspirations
  conservatism and new sociology of,
    25–9
  poverty of, 61–3
  Thatcherism and, 42
  see also working-class, aspirations of
At My Mother's Knee, 111–12
attributed celebrities, 106
austerity, 2, 170–96
  age of, 19, 148, 172, 182, 184, 188,
    195, 199
  within culture, 2, 12

  feminine ideal of, 184
  myth of 1970s, 172–82
  politics of past and present, 188–91
  of royal family, 132
  see also 'Keep Calm and Carry On'
Austerity Games, 187, 191–2
authoritarian populism, 27

Basildon, 23, 26, 27
Basildonians, 37–8
Basildon Man, 29
Being Gazza, 108
Bermondsey Boy, 112
Big Brother, 115
Big Society, 127
Billericay Dickie, 29, 32
Billy, 107
biographies of celebrities, *see* celebrity,
  biographies
Birds of a Feather, 40
Black and Blue, 108
black working-class, 38
Blair, Tony, 119, 175, 181
  immigration policy, 144, 145–6
  premiership of, 145
  Ruskin College speech by, 87
  social exclusion, problem of, 61–2
blended celebrities, 106
Blessed, 107
Blitz spirit, 182
border security, 145
Boyce, Frank Cottrell, 192
Boys from the Blackstuff, The, 5
Bragg, Billy, 161
Branson, Sir Richard, 119
Brideshead Revisited, 125
Britain Forward Not Back, 145
Britain's Got Talent, 109
British economic and social
  development, 192–3
British National Party (BNP), 144, 152,
  160, 162, 165

British Social Attitudes Survey, 144–5, 149
Broken Britain, 66, 127
Brookside, 6
Brown, Gordon, 155–8, 181, 192
Brown, Roy 'Chubby' (Royston Vasey), 112, 116–17
Bulger, James, 60
'bully-boy' socialism, 175, 182

cabbies' manifesto, 150–4
Cameron, David, 175, 183
Campaign for the Protection of Rural England, 128
capital, 7, 9, 17, 62, 84, 86–7
  choice-directive, 84–5
  meritocratic model of education, 87–8
  parent-citizen and, 84–8, 198
  see also cultural capital; social capital
capitalism
  celebrity culture and, 99
  in marginalised communities, 63
  production, 99
  social ideals under, 99
Cawston, Richard, 132–3
celebrity
  aristocracy of, 123, 134–5
  ascendancy, 100–1
  autobiography, 94–5, 106, 110–11, 115
  biographies, 97–102
  criticisms and defences of, 105
  idols of consumption, 98
  idols of production, 98
  origins of, 106–13
  politico-celebrity figures, 98–9
  talent of, 101, 104, 106
Celebrity Big Brother, 41, 71
celebrity life stories, 95–6
chav, 65
Chavs: the Demonization of the Working Class, 19
Child Support Act, 59
Child Support Agency, 59
choice
  educational, 21, 69, 80, 91
  lifestyle and, 63–4
  meritocracy and, 105

middle-class advocacy as, 80
  as negative, 83
  neoliberal framework of, 73
  parental, exercising, 80–1, 83, 88
  rhetoric of, 7, 12, 83
  underclass and, 54
  see also choice-directive
choice-directive, 84–5
  in education, 92–3
  in *Jamie's Dream School,* 91–2
  or choosing to choose, 80–3
  poor choices and, 91–2
  see also choice
Clarke, Charles, 146–7
class
  as concept, 13, 15
  persistence of, 17–19
  scholarly interrogations of, 15–17
  see also social class; *specific types of*
class-based authenticity, 139
class-based deference, 118
Class Ceiling, The, 18
Class Dismissed, 18
class distinctions, 120
class fractions as cultural capital, 16
class-making, social processes of, 105–6
class outsiders, 140
class politics, 50, 55
  English riots and, 50, 51
  in industrial strife, 56
  meritocracy and, 88
  meritocratic culture and, 87
  natural constituencies of, 6
  in Northern Irish conflicts, 56
  organised labour as, 171
  white working-class, 20
class power, 4, 12, 120, 173–4, 184, 189, 191
class stereotypes, 38, 42
class stratification, 2, 12, 15
class war, 6
Common as Muck!, 112
comprehensive schooling model, 88
Connolly, Billy, 107
Conservatism, 23–5, 32
Conservative Party, 25, 146
Conservative Party Conference, 36
conspicuous consumption, 4, 7, 33

Constantine, Susannah, 135–6
consumer lifestyle, 63
Consuming History, 193–4
*Cooler, Faster, More Expensive: The
    Return of the Sloane Ranger*, 120
Country House Rescue, 125
Countryside Alliance, 128
creative destruction, 28–9
credit crunch, 9, 173
Crisis at the Castle, 125
cultural capital, 85, 86–7, 135
    in *Jamie's Dream School*, 86
    social distinction through, 16, 75
    social mobility and, 93
    of taste, 123
    of tasteful consumption, 123
cultural critique, principle of, 13–14
cultural values, 38–9, 86, 90, 97
culture
    austerity within, 2, 12
    as expression of social change, 12
    importance of, 15–16
    of poverty, 62
    socio-economic analysis of, 2
    of white working-class, 163
    see also specific types of
culture wars, 194
Cutting Edge documentaries, 82, 91, 92
cycle of deprivation thesis, 53

Death of Class, The, 14
democracy, 8, 9, 73, 134
Department for Education, 89
Department of Health and Social
    Security (DHSS), 5, 6
dependency culture, 5
deprivation, 52–4, 108, 112, 114
deregulation of ('Big Bang') city, 3–4,
    11, 34
Destruction of the Country House
    exhibition, The, 125
Diary of a Wimpy Kid, 76
Dig for Britain, 182, 190–1
Dig for Victory era, 189–90
Dining with the Duchess, 140
Dispatches, 182
Distinction, 15
Duchess In Hull, The, 123, 140
Duffy, Gillian, 155–8

Duggan, Mark, 44
Duke and Duchess of Cambridge
    (William and Catherine), 129–30,
    132
Duke and Duchess of York, 118

EastEnders, 90, 108
Edgbaston speech of 1974, 52–3
education, 69–94
    choice-directive in, 80–3, 92–3
    dream schools, 88–91
    educational guidelines for
        parenting, 80–1
    middle class and competition for
        resources, 77–80
    parent-citizen and deployment of
        capital, 84–8
    state, and resourcefulness of
        middle-class, 79–80
educational achievement, 21
educational choice, 21, 69, 80, 91
educational milestones, 81
educational policies, 77, 78–9
educational reform, 91
educational values, in children, 84
Electrical Power Workers' strike,
    172–3, 177–9
Elizabeth R, 130
Enfield, Harry, 33–4
English Heritage, 127
English Heritage, 128
English riots, 50–2, 64–6, 182
    Anglo-Jamaican tragedy, attitudes
        following, 48–9
    antagonism, importance of, 47
    blaming of, responsible for, 45
    class politics and, 50, 51
    class struggle of, 45–6
    diversity of motivations for, 50–1
    Mark Duggan, death of, 44
    outcome of, 44–5
    underclass and, 44–52
    see also underclass
entitlement, 76
    dependency culture and, 5
    lazy, 47, 72
    moral judgments and, 17
    public debates about, 144, 173–4
    social distinctions and, 17

special exception and, 79
  welfare, 24, 150
entrepreneurialism, 7, 24, 42, 70, 73,
    80–1
Essex, 23–43
  aspirations, conservatism and new
      sociology of, 25–9
  authoritarian populism, 27
  Basildon, Thatcherite values in, 26
  conception of progress in, 27–8
  consumption and, 20
  creative destruction, 28–9
  'Loadsamoney,' 33–7
  New Labour Party, downfall of, 25
  stereotypes in, 26
  Thatcherism in, 20, 27–8
  Thatcherite dream in, 29–30
  see also Essex Girl; Essex Man
Essex Girl, 20, 24
  celebrity, 38
  concept of black, 38
  consumption and, 20, 24
  denigration of, 39, 42
  jokes about, 39
  Margaret Thatcher and, 39–40
  'Sharon and Tracey,' mythical
      figures, 40
  stereotyping of, 40–1
  whiteness of, 39
  working-class, 41–2
Essex Man, 20, 23–4, 26, 29–33
  Billericay Dickie, 29
  characteristics of, 30, 33
  consumption and, 20
  cultural phenomenon of, 31–2
  discovery of, 29–33
  Essex, Thatcherite dream in, 29–30
  'Loadsamoney,' 35–6
  as political animal, 30–1
  sketches of, 31, 33
Essex Wives, 40
Estates, 19
European Social Survey, 149
Extreme Makeover: Home Edition, 137
extremism, 152, 154

Fabian Society, 19
Faking It, 139–40
Falklands War, 3

Family Confidential: Basildon Boobs, 40
family responsibility, 46, 80–1
family values, 31, 114–15, 139
Famous, Rich and Homeless, 131
Fast Show, 125
female success, normalising, 7
feminisation, 11
finance capitalism, 24, 42–3
financial capital, 62, 84
financial crisis of 2007–8, 11–12, 18,
    195
financial deregulation, 10
Formations of Class and Gender, 15–16
Frankfurt School, 99
free market, 2, 30, 32, 36
Free Schools, 89–91
From Ladette to Lady, 92, 123, 137, 140
From Rags to Richie, 108
Frost, Jo, 84

General Election, 145–6, 151, 155
gentry
  Cotswold, 36
  landed, 118, 125–6, 134
  land ownership and, 126
  resurgence and refashioning of, 120
  typecasting of, 124–5
Geordie Finishing School For Girls, 140
Gillian Duffy media scandal, 155–7
Golden Jubilee in 2002, 130
Great British Class Survey, 18, 124–5
Grown Up Guide to the Politics of Class,
    19

Hague, William, 183
Harrow School, London, 82
Heath, Edward, 180–1
heritage debates of 1980s, 125, 128
*Heritage Industry: Britain in a climate of
    decline, The*, 125
Historic Houses Association, 127
Home Front, 182, 188–9
home-owning democracy, 9
Honey We're Killing the Kids, 84
Hope not Hate, 152
Horgan-Wallace, Aisleyne, 115
hospitality, 21, 140, 143, 145, 148,
    158–9, 160, 163, 166–7, 168–9,
    206

House I Grew Up In, The, 113
Housewife, 49, 185–6
housing market, 9–10, 12
Howard, Michael, 146, 148
human capital, 62, 86, 87
Hylton-Potts, Rodney, 151–4
hyper-consumption, 4–5

Identities and Social Action, 150
If You Don't Know Me by Now, 19
I'm A Celebrity: Get Me Out of Here, 105
immigration
  annual quota limitations on, 147–8
  British National Party, support for, 144
  New Labour plan on, 145–6, 148, 153
  public debates about, 144–50
  saloon bar racism and, 146–7
  white working-class and, 161
Imperial War Museum, 184, 189
industrial activism, 177–8
Information Centre about Asylum and Refugees (ICAR), 149
inheritance, 9, 85–6, 113, 122, 198
Injustice, 19
Institute for Public Policy Research, 129
'Isles of Wonder' ceremony, 191–6
see also London 2012 Olympic Games

Jamie's Dream School, 70–7
Jamie's Food Revolution, 70
Jamie's Kitchen, 70
Jamie's Ministry of Food, 70
Jamie's School Dinners, 70
Jarrow Hunger March of 1936, 193
Jenny From the Block, 103
Jilted Generation, 19
judgment
  classed hierarchies and, 16
  for class outsiders, 140
  dispensing, 18, 197
  process of, 16
  social, process of, 16, 18
  of whiteness, 149

Keating, Roly, 162
'Keep Calm and Carry On', 182–8
Keith, Penelope, 128

Kelly, Lorraine, 151
Kershaw, Liz, 156
Keynesianism, 176
King's Speech, The, 129
Kirsty's Hand Made Britain, 184

Labour Government of 1945–51, 194–5
Ladette to Lady, 138, 139
landed gentry, 118, 125–6, 134
land ownership, 126
Last, Nella, 185–6
Les Misérables, 109
Likes of Us: A Biography of the White Working Class, The, 19
Living Marxism, 192
'Loadsamoney,' 33–7
  Essex Man, 35–6
  Harry Enfield, 33–4
  Loadsamoney economy, 36–7
  property market, 33–4
  Thatcherism and, 34–6
London 2012 Olympic Games, 66, 121, 184, 187, 191–6
  Austerity Games, 191–2
  see also 'Isles of Wonder' ceremony
London Stock Exchange, 10
Lopez, Jennifer, 103
Lord Sugar, 119
Love on the Dole, 108

makeover shows, 136–41
Manufacture of News, The, 172
market capitalism, 32, 35
McElderry, Joe, 104
Melvin Bragg on Class and Culture, 18
meritocracy, 2, 21, 60, 62, 69, 88, 105, 122
meritocratic culture, 87
meritocratic model of education, 87–8
middle-class
  advocacy, 80–1
  choice, exercise of, 77–8
  class power and, 173–4
  competition for resources and, 77–80
  educational policies, 77, 78–9
  entrepreneurialism, 80–1

feminine ideal of austerity, 184
Royal Family as, 132–3
*Middle Class Handbook: An Illustrated
  Field Guide to the Changing
  Behaviour and Tastes of Britain's
  New Middle, The*, 79
Middleton, Catherine, 130
  marriage of, 130, 134
  royal family, incorporation of,
    133–4
  see also Duke and Duchess of
    Cambridge (William and
    Catherine)
Migrationwatch UK, 147
Miliband, David, 181
Miliband, Edward, 181
miners' strikes 1984–5, 6, 173, 182,
  195
Ministry of Food, 184
monarchy, 128–31
Monarchy: the Royal Family at Work, 130
monetarism, 176
Mukherjee, Sarah, 162–3
mumsnet.com, 81
My Fair Lady, 138
My Kind of People, 110

National Health Service, 193
neoliberalism, 2, 11–13, 15, 20, 62–3,
  73, 157
neoliberal settlement, 183–4
New Jerusalem, 194–5
New Labour Party, 8, 25, 26, 27, 29,
  57, 82
  asylum, five-year plan on, 145–6,
    148, 153
  border security by, 145
  downfall of, 25
  immigration, five-year plan on,
    145–6, 148, 153
  meritocracy, promotion of, 88
  as political aspirations, 25
  social exclusion, 61
  welfare agenda of, 78
'new money' classes, 24, 29, 33, 125
New Rabble, 58
Newsnight, 151
Northern Irish conflicts, 56
nouveau riche class, 4, 39

O Dreamland, 164
Official Sloane Ranger Handbook, The,
  3–4, 120
Only Way is Essex, The, 37, 40
Operation Withern, 65–6
Operatunity, 100
Opportunity Knocks, 110
Osborne, George, 178

Panorama, 182
parental advocacy, 88–9
Parental Choice, 82, 85
parents/parenting
  classed process of, 82
  educational guidelines for, 80–1
  financial capacity of, 81
  middle-class, 83
  parental responsibility and, 81–2
  pedagogic models for, 84
  political expectations of, 84
  poor choices of, 91
  responsibility and choice of, 81–2
  as teaching adjuncts, 81
Passion Play, 195–6
Patten, Marguerite, 184
Peckham Finishing School for Girls, 140
Pet Shop Boys, 4
Pinch, The, 19
Policing the Crisis, 55–6
political activism, 6–7, 103, 196
Pop Idol, 100
popular Conservatism, 25
popular culture, 4
populism, 27, 121
Portraying the Poor, 18
postmodernisation14
poverty
  of ambition, 45
  of aspirations, 61–3
  in Britain's consumer society, 60
  culture of, 62
  cycle of deprivation thesis and, 53
  declining standards of behaviour
    and, 51
  of deeply excluded, 61–2
  of discipline, 45
  of soul, 45
power workers' strikes of 1970, 177
precariat, 67–8

Precariat, The, 11, 67–8
Prescott: The Class System and Me, 18
Prince and Princess of Wales, 118
Prince of Wales, 130–3
   see also Prince and Princess of Wales
Prince of Wales, The, 130
Princess Anne, 131
Princess Diana, 121, 123, 133
   see also Prince and Princess of Wales
Prince William, 130–2
   see also Duke and Duchess of
      Cambridge (William and
      Catherine)
private education, 80–3
production, 97–102
property market, 33–4
property-owning democracy, 8
property values, 9, 133
Prospect, 48
Pygmalion, 138–9

Queen, The, 129
Queen for a Day, 136–7

race riots, 3, 55–6
racism, 13, 53, 142, 146–8,
      154, 162
radicalism, 181–2, 195
Ration Book Britain, 184
Reid, John, 147–8
Reinventing Yourself, 140
resentment, 47
Rich Kid, Poor Kid, 92–3
Rise of the Meritocracy 1870–2033, The,
      86
River Cottage, 191
Royal Family, 128–34
   austerity of, 132
   Catherine Middleton, incorporation
      of, 133–4
   commoners and, 131
   as ideal-typical model family, 133
   image modifications of, 133–4
   job of, 131–2
   media coverage of, 129–30
   as middle-class, presentation of,
      132–3
   social inequality, 129–30, 131
Royal Family, The, 132

Royal Jubilee, 121, 185
Royal Upstairs Downstairs, 128

Scargill, Arthur, 181–2
Secret Millionaire, 131
Serious Money, 4
service class, 11
70s, The, 182
'Sharon and Tracey,' mythical figures,
      40
Slumdog Millionaire, 192
Smith, Iain Duncan, 120
social capital, 17, 62, 75, 85–6, 88–9,
      122, 135
social class, 1–4, 11, 15, 17, 150
   celebrity culture and, 100, 105
   individualisation of, 78
   politics of, 10–11, 55
   scholarly interrogations of, 16–17
   white working-class and, 142
social contract, 8
social deprivation, 114
social differentiation, 63–4, 74
social disenfranchisement, 9
social distinction, 16, 17, 75
social exclusion, 11, 61–3, 116, 150
Social Exclusion Unit, 62
social inequality, 129–30, 131
socialism, 175, 182
Socialist Worker, 162
social judgments, process of, 16, 18
social mobility
   American Dream of, 99
   aspirations toward individual, 7, 96
   celebrity culture and, shift towards,
      99
   celebrity life stories of upward,
      94–117, 94–118; *see also*
      celebrity; celebrity life stories
   cultural capital and, 93
   individual aspiration towards, 7
   paradigms of, 94
   working-class, 20
social realism, 164–5
Spencer, Earl (Princess Diana's brother
      Charles), 126–7, 135
Spirit Level, The, 19
Spitting Image, 33, 38
State We're In, The, 10

stereotypes/stereotyping, 26, 38, 40–1, 42, 153
Stock Exchange, 3–4, 10, 30, 34
stock market, 10, 35
Strictly Come Dancing, 120
'structures of feeling', 17
sufficiency agenda, 188–9
summer riots of 1991, 10
Supernanny, 84
Superscrimpers, 184
Survival of The Fittest 1970–1997, 126

Teacher's Union, 103
Thatcher, Margaret, 6–8, 10, 25, 33, 36, 175
  as mother of all Essex Girl, 39–40
Thatcherism
  aspirations and, 42
  conception of progress under, 27–8
  economic liberalism during, 8
  economic order of, 10
  in Essex, 20, 27–8
  Essex Man, development mirroring, 32–3
  ideological drivers of, 11
  neoliberalism, significance of, 11, 20, 157
  neoliberalism during, role of, 11, 20
  social aspiration during, 9
  solution of, 175
  underclass during, 51–2, 55
  values of working-class constituencies during, 6
  working-class and, 23, 24, 28
Thatcherite economics, 36
Thatcherite free market capitalism, 32
Thatcherite values, 6, 24, 26, 34
Thatcher revolution, 34–5
Them and Us, 19
Third Way philosophy, 26
Too Poor for Posh School?, 82
To the Manor Born, 125
To the Manor Reborn, 128
Trainspotting, 192
Treasure Houses of Britain, 128
Tucker's Luck, 5–6

Unbeaten: The Story of My Brutal Childhood, 108
underclass, 44–69
  academic theorisation of, 52, 53–4
  'Anglo-Jamaican tragedy' and attitudes of, 48–9
  antagonism, 47
  choice and, 54
  class labeling of, 51, 57, 60, 64–5
  class struggle and, 45
  consumption of, 65
  crime, blame for, 51
  declining standards of behaviour of, 51
  emergence of, in 1980s, 52–7
  'get now, pay later' values, 46–7
  language of, 49–50
  lifestyle, consumerism, and precariousness of, 62–8
  as lifestyle category, 65
  reinvigoration of, 50–1
  social exclusion and, in 1990s, 57–62
  sociological concept of, 56
  stereotyping of, 153
  during Thatcherism, 51–2, 55
  Tony Blair, deployment of, 60
  welfare system and, 46
  working-class, attachment to, 52
  see also English Riots
underprivileged, 53–4
Unemployment Benefit Offices (UBOs), 5
UK Independence Party, 144
Up For Hire Live, 105
upper-class, 118–42
  aristocracy, 119, 122, 124–8, 134–5
  entertainment celebrities, 135
  Faking It, 139–40
  From Ladette to Lady, 140
  makeover shows, 136–41
  royal family, 128–34
  upper-class lifestyle gift, 140–1
  women, 135–8
upper-class values, 137

Victorian values, 56
voice, 142–3, 146–7, 157–8
Vote For Me, 151–4

waged work, patterns of, 5, 11
wealth, aristocracy of, 134
welfare agenda of New Labour Party, 78
welfare dependency, 62
welfare entitlement, 24, 150
welfare state reform, 10–11
welfare system, 5, 46, 148–9, 150
Welfare to Work, 62
West London Free School, 90
Whatever Happened to the Working Class, 18
What Not to Wear, 135, 137, 140
White Girl, 162
whiteness, 39, 149, 150
White Season (BBC), 18, 161–3, 167
white working-class, 142–3, 151–2, 160–2, 167, 174, 198–9
   cabbies, background of, 152
   class politics, 20
   culture of, 163
   debates about, 21, 163
   immigration and, 161
   Loadsamoney as, 34
   middle-class, concerns of, 163
   Roy 'Chubby' Brown, 112
   social class and assumptions about, 142
   see also working-class
Who Do You Think You Are?, 113
Wigan Pier Revisited, 5
Winter of Discontent, 174–8, 181–2
Woman I was Born to Be, The, 109
Woman Who Bought A School For Her Son, The, 89
Woodall, Trinny, 135–6
work, public debates about, 173–4
work-based political protests, 174–5
working-class, 3, 109
   aspirations of, 23, 52
   black, 38
   bully boy socialism, 182
   changing culture of, 25, 35

   Conservatism and, relationship between, 32
   cultural differences and economic competition between, 199
   greed of, 4
   laddish behaviour of, 24
   naturalness, 139
   self-identity as, 52
   social advancement, 109
   social mobility, 20
   taste of, 38
   Thatcherism and, 23, 24, 28
   Thatcherite, 38
   threat of exclusion of, 74
   underclass, attachment to, 52
   white, 142–3, 151–2, 160–2, 167, 174
   see also social class; white working-class
working-class aspirations, 23, 52, 104
working-class boys, 104
working-class 'bully boy' socialism, 182
working-class children, 103
working-class Conservatism, 23–5
working-class entertainers, 109
working-class Essex Girl, 41–2
working-class girls, 140
working-class identity, 143
working-class male identity, 30
working-class masculinity, 116, 184
working-class parents, 78
working-class politics, 180
working-class power, 184
working-class romanticism, 109
working-class taste and values, 38–9
working-class women, 24, 41, 138
world communism, collapse of, 14–15

X Factor', The, 71, 104, 110

zero tolerance, 62

Lightning Source UK Ltd.
Milton Keynes UK
UKOW06f1248010216

267528UK00007B/75/P